GENERAL ERICH HOEPNER

DIE WEHRMACHT IM KAMPF

GENERAL ERICH HOEPNER

A Military Biography

W. CHALES DE BEAULIEU

Translated by
LINDEN LYONS

Series editor
MATTHIAS STROHN

CASEMATE
Philadelphia & Oxford

AN AUSA BOOK
Association of the United States Army
2425 Wilson Boulevard, Arlington, Virginia, 22201, USA

Published in the United States of America and Great Britain in 2021 by
CASEMATE PUBLISHERS
1950 Lawrence Road, Havertown, PA 19083, USA
and
The Old Music Hall, 106–108 Cowley Road, Oxford OX4 1JE, UK

Originally published as Die Wehrmacht im Kampf 45: Walter Chales de Beaulieu, *Generaloberst Erich Hoepner: Militärisches Porträt eines Panzer-Führers* (Scharnhorst Buchkameradschaft GmbH, Neckargemünd, 1969)

Hardback Edition: ISBN 978-1-61200-976-6
Digital Edition: ISBN 978-1-61200-977-3

A CIP record for this book is available from the British Library

Printed and bound in the United States by Sheridan

Typeset by Versatile PreMedia Service (P) Ltd

For a complete list of Casemate titles, please contact:

CASEMATE PUBLISHERS (US)
Telephone (610) 853-9131
Fax (610) 853-9146
Email: casemate@casematepublishers.com
www.casematepublishers.com

CASEMATE PUBLISHERS (UK)
Telephone (01865) 241249
Email: casemate-uk@casematepublishers.co.uk
www.casematepublishers.co.uk

Front cover: Colonel-General Erich Hoepner, with General Georg-Hans Reinhardt behind.

Contents

Introduction

This book tells of the actions of General Erich Hoepner in World War II. Hoepner had joined a dragoon regiment in 1906 and his socialisation in this branch of the army not only earned him the nickname 'the old cavalryman', but also resulted in him becoming one of the early advocates of mechanisation and armoured warfare. He served as a corps commander at the outbreak of World War II, and by 1941, when Germany invaded the Soviet Union, he was commander of the 4th Panzer Group, consisting of two panzer corps. His troops took part in the advance on Leningrad and, subsequently, in Operation *Typhoon*, the failed German assault on Moscow. In January 1942, Hoepner ordered the withdrawal of his overextended forces. This gave Hitler the chance to make him one of the scapegoats for the failed attack, and he was dismissed from the Wehrmacht.

The author of this book, Walter Chales de Beaulieu, was born in Saalfeld in 1898. He joined the Prussian artillery as an ensign in 1915, fought on both the Eastern and Western Fronts and was awarded the Iron Crosses second and first class. After World War I, he remained in the army and was trained as a general staff officer. When the Germans invaded the Soviet Union in June 1941, Chales de Beaulieu, holding the rank of full colonel, served as chief of the general staff of the 4th Panzer Group under Hoepner. It was at this time that Chales de Beaulieu's respect, perhaps even admiration, for Hoepner was formed. This positive view of Hoepner is visible throughout the book that you, the reader, hold in your hands now.

The book ends with the dismissal of General Hoepner as a consequence of the failed offensive on Moscow. The rest of Hoepner's life is only very briefly touched upon in the very last paragraph: this is a book about Hoepner the military man. But Hoepner's story did not end in 1942. He had wholeheartedly supported the war against the Soviet Union, but he was also critical of the National Socialist regime. Hoepner was involved in the 20 July 1944 bomb plot to kill Hitler, and the conspirators had earmarked him for a senior military position in a post-Hitler Germany. After the failed coup, he was arrested by the Gestapo, tortured and faced trial at the infamous Volksgerichtshof (People's Court). The court sentenced him to death, and Hoepner was hanged at Plötzensee prison in Berlin on 8 August 1944. His family were arrested too, and his wife and children were sent to concentration camps. Chales de Beaulieu was also directly affected by this. As Hoepner's former chief of the general staff, he was now regarded as untrustworthy by the regime. He had been promoted to the rank of Generalleutnant in June 1944, but was dismissed from active service on 31 January 1945. He survived the war and died in Kressbronn at Lake Constance in the 1970s.

This book gives a vivid account of the deployment of German armoured formations in the early stages of the war. It shows the panache with which these formations were deployed and won their tactical and operational victories. Having said this, Chales de Beaulieu also clearly highlights some of the shortcomings of the German concepts of armoured warfare. The campaign against Poland, for instance, is often glossed over by people interested in World War II, because, apparently, everything went smoothly and the Polish Army was quickly and easily defeated. The chapter in this book shows that this was not entirely true and that the German Army went through a number of crises. The book is therefore not only of interest to those who would like to learn more about General Hoepner. Despite the fact that it was written a rather long time ago, the book provides insights into the enduring challenges of formation command. It also mentions the frictions between the German generals. The book is therefore more than a mere operational study or a glowing description of Hoepner as a military leader. The underlying constant truths of the nature of war make this book so readable even today.

Prof. Matthias Strohn, M.St., DPhil., FRHistS
Head of Historical Analysis,
Centre for Historical Analysis and Conflict Research, Camberley
Visiting Professor of Military Studies,
University of Buckingham

Foreword

This book is about a man and a soldier whose ups and downs in life are almost unparalleled. After achieving the greatest military successes, he was dismissed from his beloved profession, sentenced in the People's Court, and executed. The journey of Colonel-General Erich Hoepner very much reflects his character and personality. He would always raise objections against a course of action if it was inconsistent with his conscience and sense of responsibility, and this led to his eventual opposition to the regime in Germany. This was a natural development for someone with a personality as strong as his. His strength of character was shaped by his combat experience during World War I, his service on the general staff in the interwar period, and his confident leadership during World War II. It is his command of panzer formations between 1939 and 1941 that this book will endeavour to describe.

The only son of a successful doctor, Hoepner grew up in the ever-stimulating city of Berlin at the turn of the century and was the first in his family to pursue a military career. His urge to be free and to seize the initiative, paired with his love of horses, led him to become a cavalry officer in 1905. His post was in Metz, at that time near the western border of Germany, and he was soon the adjutant of his regiment. In 1913, he graduated from the staff college. During this time, there were a couple of characteristics he possessed which emerged and which shaped the course of his life to follow. He felt a strong sense of duty and responsibility, and, already as a young officer, he constantly strove for clarity of thought.

The experience of World War I created a lasting impression. He had become a first general staff officer of an infantry division by the end of that war, and it was around that time that he wrote to his wife: 'I believe I may have learnt how to command.' This was rather a modest statement, but it indicates that he had committed himself to a profession which demands one's full attention. Being a general staff officer was first and foremost; everything else, even one's family, took second place. 'The officer at war really ought not to be married,' he wrote to his beloved wife in October 1915. And she completely understood and supported her husband. In addition to such commitment, an officer had to be thoroughly aware of his own will. As Hoepner wrote to his son in the winter of 1942–43: 'The military commander requires an inner freedom and a high degree of self-confidence. He must trust his own abilities and be prepared to exercise his own will.' These words paint a clear portrait of the type of military leader Erich Hoepner was during World War II.

In writing this book, the author has had access to the documents produced by the headquarters of the formations commanded by Hoepner. The author himself, as a general staff officer, directly experienced the events described. He was Hoepner's first general staff officer during the campaign in Poland and his chief of staff during the campaigns in France and Russia. Hoepner's dismissal from the army brought our memorable and close-working relationship to an end.

The author would like to express his thanks to Colonel–General Franz Halder, the former chief of the general staff of the German Army, who willingly and attentively answered my many questions.

Walter Chales de Beaulieu
Hamburg-Volksdorf, autumn 1968

Translation of Place Names

German	English
Poland	
Borowa-Berg	Borowa Hills
Bromberg	Bydgoszcz
Nw. Brzeznica	Nowa Brzeźnica
Oberschlesien	Upper Silesia
Petrikau	Piotrków
Posen	Poznań
Puszcza Kampinoska	Kampinos Forest
Tschenstochau	Częstochowa
Warschau	Warsaw
Warthe	Warta River
Weichsel	Vistula River
France	
Argonnen	Forest of Argonne
Dixmuiden	Diksmuide
Lothringen	Lorraine
Löwen	Leuven
Lüttich	Liège
Maas	Meuse River
Nieuport	Nieuwpoort
St. Trond	Sint-Truiden
Tirlemont	Tienen

Russia (advance on Leningrad)

Düna	Western Dvina River
Finnischer Meerbusen	Gulf of Finland
Nowoßjelje	Novoselye
Pleskau	Pskov
Porietschje	Porechye
Rossienie	Raseiniai
Sapolje	Zapolye
Schaulen	Saule
Sholtzy	Soltsy
Tschudowo	Chudovo
Waldai-Höhen	Valdai Hills
Wolchow	Volkhov River

Russia (assault on Moscow)

Andrejany	Andriany
Jachroma	Yakhroma
Juchnow	Yukhnov
Spaß Djemjenskoje	Spas-Demensk
Swenigorod	Zvenigorod
Sytschewka	Sychevka
Uwarowk	Uvarovka
Weliki Luki	Velikiye Luki
Welish	Velizh
Wischni Wolotschek	Vyshny Volochyok
Wjasma	Vyazma
Wjerja	Vereya
Wyschogrod	Vyshegorod

CHAPTER I

The Campaign in Poland in 1939

(a) Introduction

The military leader Erich Hoepner became well-known on 8 September 1939 when the formation under his command, the XVI Panzer Corps, stood before Warsaw only eight days after the outbreak of war with Poland. The panzer corps had covered the 250-kilometre distance from German Upper Silesia in this short time, and had crushed any resistance that had been put up against it. Yet the surprisingly rapid military thrust represented only the beginning of the destruction of the bulk of the Polish Army to the west of the Vistula, the first operational objective that had been set by the High Command of the German Army (OKH). This objective now had good prospects of being able to be achieved, but it would still require time to be carried out. The swift advance on the enemy capital was also a great success from the point of view of foreign policy. It revealed to the world the military weakness of Poland and rendered impossible any active assistance from its allies, if any such assistance had ever truly been intended. Despite the declaration of war by the Western Powers, it now seemed as if the fighting could be restricted to the Polish zone, thereby preventing its expansion into a second world war.

The extent of the astonishment of the outside world at that time at the rapid appearance of German tanks before Warsaw is difficult to assess in detail. At the very least, the success of the German panzer arm received a great deal of attention in the press. The operational capabilities of a modern, independent panzer arm had been demonstrated most clearly for the first time.

Before World War II, there had been a lively and ongoing critical debate over the value of armour, its ability to be employed, the way in which it should be equipped and led, and even its right to exist at all, especially in the countries that had at first been so intensely interested in their development, England and France. However, there had been few practical results from which lessons could be drawn. France had created large armoured formations even before Germany had done so. Specifically, these were two motorised or mechanised divisions, but it was envisioned that their independent use would be limited. England also possessed small and well-trained armoured units. But only Germany had striven to create an independent panzer arm on a large scale, one that would have an impact on the realm of operations, and it was in October 1935 that the first three panzer divisions were united under a single command. They were outfitted and trained for long-range thrusts and for mobility on the battlefield. By the beginning of World War II, they were superior to their opponents in the East and West due to their ability to fight with greater manoeuvrability. Nevertheless, German tanks still exhibited a number of defects at the start of the war, so it would be inaccurate to speak of German matériel superiority. What compensated for this was the mobility of the panzer divisions and the concentration of those divisions against a point of main effort.

The reputation of the superiority of the German panzer arm that arose at that time was based on this rapid advance by the XVI Panzer Corps towards Warsaw, as well as on the simultaneous, albeit slightly less deep, thrust of the XIX Panzer Corps through the Polish Corridor towards East Prussia. Surprise successes like these would become the hallmark of the new and fast motorised combat arm. However, these panzer formations had fought through enemy forces that were mostly no match for them. It was the battle of encirclement near Radom that was conducted by the XIV and XV Panzer Corps, as well as the achievements of the motorised arm on the outer wings, in the south by Army Group South, and in the east (Brest-Litovsk) by Army Group North, that secured the everlasting reputation of the panzer arm. Despite the ups and downs in its development, the panzer arm had been tremendously successful during the campaign in Poland in 1939! Unfortunately, as the war progressed, there was a growing tendency on the German side to overestimate the abilities of the new arm and to place overwhelming demands upon it. Although decisive when employed correctly, the effectiveness of the panzer formations in combat was dependent on several preconditions.

This observation touches on a matter that was important at that time: knowledge and mastery of the panzer arm. The fact that this arm was brand new in the years leading up to World War II should be emphasised most strongly. The creation of the first three panzer divisions in the autumn of 1935 has already been mentioned. Light divisions and motorised infantry divisions were created shortly afterwards. At the outbreak of war, the oldest panzer divisions were barely four years old, and the others were much newer. This was one of the reasons why the military leadership was strongly opposed to any military conflict! All of the elements of the motorised divisions were at that time described as 'mobile troops', with the term 'panzer arm' only arising at a later stage. The latter term will nevertheless be used here, for it was quite distinct from the bulk of the forces of the army that marched on foot, i.e. the infantry. The principles of the conduct of battle of the infantry were considerably different to those of the panzer arm.

The details of the development of the panzer arm, of the manner in which it was led in combat, and of the way in which its tactics contrasted to the prevailing, and proven, tactics of the infantry cannot be examined here. Such details, whether theoretical or practical, will only be considered to the degree that they are relevant to the operations conducted by General Hoepner. As the Old Cavalryman, the desire for modern heavy cavalry was in his blood, be it through replacing or supplementing the horse with the motor.[1] The high ratio of cavalry allowed by the Treaty of Versailles in relation to the infantry (three cavalry divisions for every seven infantry divisions) compelled him to think about their modernisation, for they would otherwise possess too little value in combat. In the 1920s, when he was still a cavalry captain on the general staff, Hoepner paid close attention to the question of a modern panzer arm. He belonged to the unfortunately rather few of those in the interwar period who gave careful consideration as to how the small 100,000-man army that

---

[1]   Hoepner joined the 13th Dragoons Regiment as an officer cadet in Metz, in the former Imperial Territory of Alsace-Lorraine, on 10 March 1905.

had been imposed by the Treaty of Versailles could be turned into a modern, manoeuvrable defensive instrument that would be capable of resisting its superior neighbours in the east, west, and south. Hoepner's efforts to develop a German panzer arm are to be seen and understood from this point of view. The creation of independent panzer formations, from panzer divisions to panzer armies, was the centre of attention from the outset. General Hoepner was proud of the fact that he had been able to play a substantial role in the development of the panzer arm. It was under his command that a large panzer formation was utilised for the first time in March 1939. The result was the decisive occupation of Prague. It was therefore no coincidence that the panzer corps under the command of General Hoepner was assigned an important objective for the campaign in Poland.

(b) The task of the XVI Panzer Corps in the operational plan

1. *The objectives of the operational plan of the OKH*

According to the plan of the OKH, the outcome of the campaign in Poland was to be decided near Warsaw. The assumption was that the bulk of the Polish armed forces would conduct the defence of their country to the west of the Vistula. The OKH expected that the leadership of the Polish Army would not follow the recommendation that had been made by French General Maxime Weygand in the 1920s that the defence of the country be carried out behind the Narew and the Vistula.[2] Given the political situation, the Polish national character, and the personality of Marshal Edward Rydz-Śmigły, it was unlikely that so much Polish territory would be relinquished without a fight. Any Polish defensive forces placed too far to the west, in the area of the Warta, could therefore be enveloped by German attack forces from the geopolitically favourable flanks that were Upper Silesia and East Prussia. On top of its geographically disadvantageous position, Poland would have to deal with an enemy whose forces were superior to its own. It could not be assessed to what extent Poland had already factored the German panzer arm into its considerations. Germany

---

[2] In those days, Weygand was the military advisor to the Polish government.

was counting on the panzer arm for a successful outcome, even if the surprising rapidity of the advance had not been foreseen.

The OKH decided that the objective of the first phase of the operation would be Warsaw, so that the possibility of a pincer attack against any Polish forces to the west of the Vistula could be fully exploited. If Poland concentrated most of its forces west of the river, this part of the campaign might prove to be decisive. Not only would it be a military success; it would also be a political one with the seizure of the enemy capital.

Two army groups were earmarked by the OKH for the execution of the operation: Army Group North and Army Group South. The main thrust in the area of Army Group North would be launched by the Third Army from East Prussia in the direction of Warsaw. To take place before this, though, would be an advance through the Polish Corridor from the west so as to connect East Prussia with the rest of the Reich. There was a chance that this plan would change over time. Much would depend on the progress made by the XIX Panzer Corps in its advance through the corridor. While Army Group North would conduct its two-stage advance on the left flank with the possibility of subsequently extending it eastwards, perhaps even as far as Brest-Litovsk, Army Group South would carry out the main attack of the entire operation by driving directly towards Warsaw from Upper Silesia. This attack would run roughly along the major road that led from Częstochowa to the capital. If it succeeded, the bulk of the most quickly organised, and probably most combat-capable, Polish divisions would be encircled. The preliminary phase of the campaign could then quite possibly be the most decisive one.

For Army Group South, the right pincer, the point of main effort would clearly lie in the direction of Warsaw. The strongest panzer forces at the disposal of the OKH were to be concentrated under the command of the Tenth Army and applied against this objective. Two panzer divisions, three light divisions, and two motorised infantry divisions were to comprise the XIV, XV, and XVI Panzer Corps. This was effectively the first panzer army to have ever appeared in the history of military operations. For support and security, the Tenth Army would also be assigned two infantry corps. These were the IV and XI Army Corps, which made a total of six infantry divisions. The northern flank of the advancing panzer army would be protected by the Eighth Army, for it was there that the most sustained enemy resistance was anticipated. The Eighth Army had four infantry divisions under its command and another two in its rear area under the direct control of the army group. On the southern flank, opposite Polish Upper Silesia and Kraków, the Fourteenth Army assembled in the Carpathian Mountains. It was equipped with relatively strong forces (five infantry divisions, three mountain divisions, two panzer divisions, and one light division) due to the rather extensive border there. It was not assigned a specific task by the OKH at that stage. It could therefore choose the direction of its advance, provided that its northern neighbour could remain committed to the drive on Warsaw. In the event of an attempt by the Poles to fall back behind the Vistula, the role of the Fourteenth Army would become clearer. With a quick eastward advance through Galicia over the San, the Fourteenth Army could either prevent a retreat by the enemy to the south towards Romania or support the Tenth Army in crossing the large obstacle that was the Vistula. As will be seen, the army group, more so than the OKH, strongly favoured an early advance by the Fourteenth Army in this direction in any case. What was most important was the ability to recognise and evaluate the reaction of the enemy after the first few days of the campaign. The development of the situation would either confirm or disprove our assumptions about what he would do.

Further details will not be considered here. The focus will predominantly be on the actions of the XVI Panzer Corps, the spearhead of the Tenth Army.

2. The organisation of Polish forces

In hindsight, the way in which the Polish forces were organised is astonishing. Enemy formations seemed to stand along or just behind the entire length of the western and northern borders, a stretch of more than 1,300 kilometres. Armies Pomorze, Poznań, Łódź, Kraków, and Karpaty secured the western and southern frontiers, while Armies Pomorze and Modlin, as well as Independent Operational Group Narew, covered the border with East Prussia.[3] Behind these formations were a main reserve on

---

[3] These were the Polish designations. See Nikolaus von Vormann, *Der Feldzug in Polen im September 1939: Die Operationen des Heeres* (Weißenburg: Prinz-Eugen-Verlag, 1958), 45.

Colonel-General Erich Hoepner

Colonel-General Erich Hoepner, with General Georg-Hans Reinhardt behind.

either side of the Pilica, near Tomaszów, and a smaller one between the Narew and the Bug. The preparation of the border forces had generally made headway. The reserve forces were just being organised by the time the war began. If a line were to be drawn from the area south of Oppeln (in Upper Silesia) to Warsaw, and another from the area east of Allenstein (in East Prussia) to the Polish capital, the mass of the Polish Army would be found between these lines. The OKH could not be entirely sure of the disposition of the Polish forces at that time, but it was nevertheless well-informed. Yet the Poles also had a good idea of the way in which German forces were assembled.

As stated, a defensive position behind the Narew and the Vistula did not appear to be the intention of the Polish leadership. It seemed that the enemy planned to defend the country along a line that ran behind the lower Vistula downstream from Bydgoszcz, southwards through the area of marshes and lakes of the upper Noteć, and then from the vicinity of Koło along the upper Warta. Why, then, was the entirety of the powerful Army Poznań placed to the west of this line, roughly near the city of Poznań? The Polish leadership was aware that there were barely any German forces next to the border there. A similar picture is to be found along the rest of the frontier. He who defends everything defends nothing![4] This situation could only be an advantage to the OKH. There must have been many political considerations that Marshal Rydz-Śmigły was pinning his hopes on that informed the way in which the Polish forces were positioned. This is because, from a military perspective, the Polish deployment in the autumn of 1939 did not fulfil what was needed or possible for conducting a pure defence. Judging from some of his remarks and from his reliance on English guarantees, it can be assumed that Marshal Rydz-Śmigły had decided by early 1939 that a military conflict was inevitable and that the positioning of strong Polish forces far to the west would enable an advance into the German Reich in conjunction with an attack by the Western Powers from the other side. He had yet to recognise that he had misunderstood the military situation on both sides. Although the Polish Army was relatively strong at that stage, the geopolitical position

---

[4]   Translator's note: This was an axiom of the Prussian King Frederick the Great.

was disadvantageous for Poland. Moreover, the 100,000-man German Army of the Weimar period had in the meantime been reinforced significantly. The Polish national character was inclined towards the offensive rather than the defensive, and the Polish leadership had given in to this. If Poland were indeed to conduct an attack, then East Prussia would have been its best objective. This was something that had been feared in Germany in the 1920s! It would have been easy for the southern part of East Prussia to be taken in a pincer attack. In such an operation, the Poles would have had to adopt a defensive position everywhere else, with the Vistula ultimately being the main line of resistance. What needed to prevail in Poland if it were to have any chance of success at all was a clear political and military will in combination with self-restraint. Instead, the Poles at that time were filled with ambivalence, and that was demonstrated in thought and action, as well as in political and military events.

3. *The task of the XVI Panzer Corps*

The spearhead of the planned thrust towards the main operational objective, Warsaw, would be formed by both panzer divisions that were available to the Tenth Army. These were the 1st and 4th Panzer Divisions, directly under the command of the XVI Panzer Corps. Before the war, this panzer corps had been entrusted with overseeing the development of the panzer divisions. General of Cavalry Hoepner had been its commander since November 1938. The task that he was assigned was one whose theory he had committed himself to for a very long time: employing the panzer arm as a large and independent formation to conduct a deep operational envelopment. In this case, the distant objective was the capital city of Poland.

The penetration of the first line of the enemy defence was the prerequisite for the deep thrust envisioned by the OKH. It could not be predicted whether this penetration would take place swiftly or whether it would be delayed by enemy resistance. We had no prior experience with the use of armour. However, the OKH was counting on a rapid success. According to the war diary of the chief of the general staff of the German Army, General of Artillery Franz Halder, in August 1939: 'It must be clear to the world in 8 to 14 days that Poland is in danger of collapsing.' These words were written down with the possible reaction of England in mind. He was of the view that a rapid military success would discourage Poland's indecisive allies from intervening and that, as a result, it would be possible to prevent the expansion of the conflict into a global conflagration. A quick victory in Poland would be a political shock for England. 'The operations themselves can of course take longer,' concluded Halder. 'Up to eight weeks.'

After the infantry had broken through the front, the panzer corps of Hoepner was to drive directly towards Warsaw. To ensure that its full striking power could be committed to overcoming the 250-kilometre stretch, its rear flanks were to be protected by the other two panzer corps against any counter-attack that might be carried out by the retreating Polish forces. The intended line of attack of the XVI Panzer Corps would be along the Częstochowa–Piotrków–Tomaszów–Rawa–Warsaw road. This would also be the main supply road of the panzer corps. It should be noted in this regard that panzer units are far more dependent on lines of supply than are infantry units! The panzer corps would enter this road after it had advanced eastwards from its assembly area near Rosenberg, in Upper Silesia, and crossed the Warta. On the right would be the XV Panzer Corps, with two light divisions; on the left the XIV Panzer Corps, with a light division and two motorised infantry divisions. The Tenth Army decided that one of these motorised infantry divisions would be kept in reserve to begin with: this was the 29th Motorised Infantry Division. For the defence of the deep flanks of the advancing Tenth Army, the IV Army Corps would be placed on the right and the XI Army Corps on the left.

The panzer thrust from the south-west towards Warsaw would therefore resemble a sharp and ever-widening wedge formation. For this thrust to succeed in the manner envisioned by the operational plan, the spearhead would need to maintain its penetrative power for as long as possible. There would need to be sufficient reserves to the rear that could be used for decisive effect in any eventuality. The infantry units would follow at a distance, provided that the panzer troops did indeed manage to achieve the operational rapidity desired by the OKH. The panzer arm would thus be on its own to begin with in the fight on the outskirts of Warsaw.

For carrying out the plan of the OKH, Army Group South issued its Order No. 1 on 30 August 1939. Paragraph 3 was as follows:

> In conjunction with Army Group North, the task of Army Group South is to annihilate the Polish forces to the west of the Vistula. This will be achieved with a thrust by the Tenth Army towards Warsaw and the Vistula upstream from the city. While the Fourteenth Army will eliminate Polish forces in West Galicia, the Eighth Army is to cover the advance of the Tenth Army against enemy forces in the Kalisz-Łódź area and against any counter-attack that might come from Poznań.

Paragraph 5 of the same order elaborated on the way in which the advance of the Tenth Army was to unfold:

> It is imperative that the Tenth Army cross the Warta and then secure freedom of movement in the vicinity of the Vistula and to the north of the Pilica as quickly as possible. This will be achieved by sending mobile units towards Radom, Grójec, and Tomaszów.

The intelligence on the distribution of the Polish forces shortly before the commencement of the campaign seemed to indicate that everything would go according to the plan of the OKH. The information received from the OKH on the morning of 25 August stated: 'The bulk of the Polish divisions are placed along the frontier, but, as a result, they are distributed rather thinly. It seems to be the intention of the enemy to be in a position to go into battle as soon as possible.' The preconditions for a potential success were in place.

Based on this intelligence, the commander of the XVI Panzer Corps formed the opinion that the forces of the enemy were not properly assembled. They might have been deployed in a manner suitable for fighting along the border, but they could easily be taken by surprise if panzer formations were to punch through their positions. There seemed to be no defence in depth whatsoever before the front of the panzer corps.

The two panzer divisions of the XVI Panzer Corps only gathered in the assembly area shortly before the attack was to begin, so as to keep the Poles in the dark regarding German intentions for as long as possible and thereby increase the likelihood that they would be taken by surprise. The panzer corps also had the 14th and 31st Infantry Divisions under its command. Their role would be to tackle the enemy on a wide front and then break through the point at which the enemy was weakest. The front of the panzer corps was approximately 30 kilometres in width. On the right, the 14th Infantry Division would advance into wooded terrain. Its point of main effort would be on its northern wing, and it would be responsible for the seizure of the city of Częstochowa. Even so, most of its forces were to bypass the city to the north. Only the rear formations of the division were tasked with the capture of the city itself. This is because the infantry would be needed to the north-east of Częstochowa in the area of the large bend in the Warta so as to cover the southern flank of the panzer forces.[5] To the north of the 14th Infantry Division, the 1st Panzer Division was to advance eastwards through the town of Kłobuck towards the bridge over the Warta, which stood over the eastern end of the large bend in the river. This bridge was the first important objective of the panzer corps. Further to the north was the 4th Panzer Division, which was also given the task of advancing into the territory surrounded by the large river bend. It was to cross the river to the south-west of Radomsko and then push towards the north. The 31st Infantry Division, initially in panzer corps reserve, was to follow the panzer divisions and mop up any Polish forces that remained on the battlefield. It would eventually be responsible for the security of the left flank of the panzer corps and would probably cross the Warta near the village of Nowa Brzeźnica. To the north of the XVI Panzer Corps would be the XI Army Corps, with the 18th and 19th Infantry Divisions, both of which were to attack towards the north-east. The southern neighbour was the IV Army Corps, which was to remain to the south of Częstochowa in an advance towards the east. Its role was to protect the right flank of the panzer corps, especially after the latter had crossed the Warta and had pivoted to the north-east. After the crossing of the river, the 14th Infantry Division would be handed over to the IV Army Corps. This was because infantry on the outer wing of a pivoting manoeuvre by armour would simply be too slow. It therefore seemed as if everything had been prepared to ensure the success of the operation.

---

[5] The Warta bends to the east as it flows through Częstochowa and then turns to the north after about 25 kilometres. After that, it circles further towards the west.

(c) The breakthrough of the XVI Panzer Corps towards Warsaw

1. *The creation of a point of penetration*

On 1 September, having assembled under cover of darkness, the XVI Panzer Corps set off at 0445 hours. It was a beautiful, and still somewhat misty, autumn morning. There was initially no resistance, but difficulties were immediately encountered in the form of sand and mud. There was a build-up of traffic everywhere on the German side of the border. This was especially the case in the sector of the 1st Panzer Division, where the severely marshy border river, the Liswarta, needed to be crossed.[6] Hoepner was at the command post of the panzer corps to the south-east of Grunsruh, on the Rosenberg–Kłobuck road. He wanted to obtain for himself a first impression of how the fighting would unfold near the border. There was barely any noise of battle to be heard that morning as both panzer divisions set off. Before long, there was no noise at all. Our units must have been moving forward! Only on the Liswarta did the traffic jam become worse. More auxiliary forces were therefore committed to the bridge site. The muddy ground in the vicinity of the stream placed great demands on the abilities of the pioneer troops. Only in the course of the afternoon was the accumulated traffic able to move. The commander of the panzer corps had been boxed in between several motor vehicles, but he was finally able to make it to the bridge site in the late afternoon so that he could visit the troops who had already advanced into Polish territory. From the bridge site, there was an approximately 3-kilometre stretch of gradually rising and sandy ground that led to the small market town of Przystajń. Many motor vehicles got bogged down again and had to be towed out. The troops had to accustom themselves to the conditions of these roads. It would become apparent in the next few days that their supply, especially of fuel, would suffer. There were even times when elements of the combat forces were compelled to stay put, for they had been rendered temporarily immobile. A few days of combat experience helped us come to grips with these initial difficulties. Strangely enough, it was

---

[6] The Liswarta is a left tributary of the Warta.

the slightly uncontrolled desire to send everything into battle that resulted in the concentration of so many forces and detained the fuel supply vehicles that were ever more urgently required by the troops fighting at the front. With such a chaotic mass of vehicles striving to push forward, those to the rear more or less came to a standstill. This reduced the opportunities for refuelling. What was worse, even the motorcycle messengers were unable to get through. Radio traffic was not yet possible, and the telephone lines that had been assiduously built along the roads were damaged. The most secure means of communication on that first day was the messenger on foot, although that was only if he managed to reach his destination.

It is not surprising, then, that the command post of the panzer corps, which was in Przystajń in the evening, did not have a particularly clear picture of how the situation at the front was unfolding. The 1st Panzer Division had fought its way into Kłobuck before nightfall, but the panzer corps only learnt of this on the morning of 2 September. The 4th Panzer Division, in light fighting, had made similarly good progress in its eastward advance. The 14th Infantry Division had combed through the forests it had faced on a wide front, and had covered approximately half the distance to Częstochowa.

On the second day of the campaign, it would be necessary to penetrate an organised defensive line on the west bank of the large bend in the Warta if we wanted to continue exploiting the element of surprise.[7] Was this line occupied? We knew that there had been some excavation work there before the beginning of the war. In fact, this line was neither fully occupied nor fully constructed. The 1st Panzer Division resumed its advance at 0600 hours, overcame weak resistance at the defensive line, pushed eastwards to the Warta, and took possession of two intact bridges over the river. The 14th Infantry Division still stood a few kilometres to the north-west of Częstochowa by the end of the day. The 4th Panzer Division was involved in heavy fighting with enemy infantry throughout the day of 2 September, but it was the Wołyńska Cavalry Brigade that seriously delayed its advance. The panzer division had come to a stop

---

[7] This organised defensive line ran northwards from Częstochowa and connected with the Warta roughly to the south of Nowa Brzeźnica.

that evening. Nonetheless, the initial objective of securing crossings over the Warta had been achieved. This would enable the situation to develop in our favour.

The commander of the panzer corps therefore ordered that the panzer formations regroup to the north-east on 3 September so that they could exploit our success and head in the direction of Radomsko. The 4th Panzer Division could not allow itself to be tied down in fighting the Polish infantry and cavalry. If necessary, it could lunge to the south and then push to the east, with the intention of crossing the Warta south-west of Radomsko. The 31st Infantry Division would cut through what had been the battlefield of the 4th Panzer Division and, on the left wing, would attempt to reach the bridge over the river south of Nowa Brzeźnica. The so very successful 1st Panzer Division had to be held back for a short time due to a shortage of fuel. Combat elements of this division committed further in the direction of Radomsko had to be topped up with fuel from other units so that they could at least regain mobility. The panzer corps intended to remedy the dreadful state of our fuel supply on 3 September by dropping goods from the air in the vicinity of the bridges that had been taken.

If Hoepner's plans for 3 September, namely the creation of a solid foundation for a subsequent thrust in depth, sound cautious, then what was actually achieved that day is all the more surprising. The initially rather weak leading elements of the 1st Panzer Division occupied Radomsko towards noon, and Kamieńsk was taken by 1600 hours. Reconnaissance units pushed even further to the east and captured the bridge over the Pilica in the vicinity of Przedbórz. The 4th Panzer Division also made good progress: it had reached the Warta and had built a bridge there. Crossing the river over the bridge and on ferries, the forces of the division bypassed Radomsko to the west and reached the area south-west of Kamieńsk. The 31st Infantry Division had fought its way to the Warta, built a bridge, and, by the evening, had established a bridgehead that extended as far as Nowa Brzeźnica. On the southern wing, Częstochowa was occupied by elements of the 14th Infantry Division. The bulk of the division continued to the north and north-east of this city in an advance towards the east. It would remain on this eastward trajectory and come under the command of the IV Army Corps early on 4 September.

How is the sudden decline in Polish resistance in this area to be explained? At the outset, the southern and central sectors of the panzer corps had faced the Polish 7th Division, while the northern sector had confronted some infantry and the Wołyńska Cavalry Brigade. Once we had crossed the Warta, though, there was very little enemy resistance. Reconnaissance units that were sent further to the east encountered no enemy troops whatsoever. The Polish formation on the southern side had belonged to Army Kraków; that on the northern side to Army Łódź. The panzer thrust had therefore struck the boundary between these two armies. The forces on the wings of these armies had been hurled back to the south and to the north-east. An open path into the interior of Poland had thereby been created. The enemy had no reserves at his disposal. The initial stage of the campaign in Poland had turned out well, and the drive towards Warsaw could begin.

2. *The breakthrough succeeds*

In the area of the panzer corps, it was clear by the evening of 3 September that the penetration of the Polish defence along the border had been a success. The southern part of the main defensive front behind the Warta had simultaneously been swept aside. Even the leading elements of the XI Army Corps, the northern neighbour of the panzer corps, had been able to cross the Warta near Dialoczyn that same evening. The spearhead of the panzer corps reached the Widawka in the vicinity of Kamieńsk. The enemy, having been pushed back from the Warta, might very well have established a new position behind the Widawka. It could not yet be assessed how far to the east this defensive line led. It might have extended as far as the Pilica, or it might have only gone as far as Rozprza or perhaps even no further than Kamieńsk. The task of the panzer corps would be to carry out an attack between the Pilica and the Widawka. It would ascertain precisely the nature of the situation there and would lunge towards Piotrków. This would cut off the eastward route of retreat of Polish forces situated behind the Widawka. The 1st Panzer Division would seek to envelop this enemy from the east, possibly even with an advance through Sulejów (on the Pilica) and then swinging back against the encircled enemy. The 4th Panzer Division would partake in this fight by driving along the main road from the west. On the left wing, the 31st Infantry Division was to approach the upper Widawka near Lenkawa, 10 kilometres north-west of Kamieńsk, so as to attack the eastern wing of the enemy position that was presumed to be there. It was an enormous task to have to cover a distance of 35 kilometres on foot and then go into combat, but it was something that had to be done. Throughout the day of 4 September, the infantry carried out this task brilliantly.

Aside from the performance of the infantry, the distances covered on 4 September did not quite match those of the previous day. This did not have anything to do with renewed enemy resistance. Rather, it was because the German combat units became ever further away from one another the deeper they advanced into enemy territory. And, unfortunately, the difficulties with the supply of fuel continued to have an effect. What was also increasingly problematic was the fact that both panzer divisions lacked motorised or mechanised infantry. In the course of the day, the Tenth Army promised that the 33rd Motorised Infantry Regiment (from the 13th Motorised Infantry Division) would be sent to help the XVI Panzer Corps. Elements of the regiment would be committed to mopping-up operations, while the rest would be placed at the disposal of the 1st Panzer Division. The number of prisoners of war had been increasing, but this was rather a burden for the panzer divisions, as these prisoners somehow had to be taken to the rear areas. Nevertheless, the panzer corps was able to re-establish a united attack front on 4 September. The task for the next day would be to obtain a decisive outcome in the vicinity of Piotrków.

The commanders of the front-line units felt confident with the way in which the situation was unfolding. The advance continued to make progress and the enemy was falling back. Every effort had to be made to tackle and destroy his forces. The army group had already expressed its fear on 3 September that the Polish leadership might conclude that it no longer wanted a decisive battle to the west of the Vistula. The army group also emphasised that the advance to the east must proceed as quickly as possible, primarily with the motorised forces, so that the Vistula could be reached at the earliest possible moment. It was expected that crossing this river from the south would be extremely difficult, so it would be necessary to get there swiftly and to choose the point at which the river could be overcome most easily.[8] This meant a fundamental change in the operational plan that was directed specifically towards Warsaw. The OKH nevertheless remained committed to its old objective, for the current development of the situation did not offer any reason for a change in plan. The fighting had only just begun, and our assumptions regarding the deployment of the enemy forces had been confirmed. We will come back to these differences in opinion later.

The Tenth Army found that its front was being ever more extended on the right, i.e. towards the east! This mostly affected the XV Panzer Corps to begin with. With its advance to the east of the Pilica in the direction of Radom, its right wing was now committed towards Kielce, which was far to the east. This must have given the commander of the XVI Panzer Corps some cause for concern. From the area of the town of Pilica, the XV Panzer Corps would be unable to bring its influence to bear on the Pilica River. Hoepner had hoped that it would be within reach of the right bank of the river so that it would be able to cover the right flank of his own panzer corps in the push towards Warsaw. In a conversation with Major-General Friedrich Paulus, the chief of staff of the Tenth Army, on the morning of 4 September, Hoepner expressed his concerns regarding the flank of his formation and received the following response:[9]

> The commander of the Tenth Army (Colonel-General Walther von Reichenau) orders that the farthest objective of the XVI Panzer Corps will be Tomaszów for the time being. Once the panzer corps has reached this town, it is to wait there until further forces arrive on the right and left. The left wing of the XV Panzer Corps shall advance through Kloszow towards Opoczno.

General Hoepner could agree to such a course of action. Opoczno lay only 25 kilometres to the south-east of Tomaszów. Kielce was more

---

[8] Paragraph 1b of Army Group South Order No. 2 of 3 September, 1900 hours, stated: 'The danger that the enemy will attempt to evade a decision to the west of the San–Vistula line altogether has become all the more likely due to the fact that an intervention by the Western Powers might take place.'

[9] This meeting took place on 4 September at 0915 hours. It was also when the allocation of the 33rd Motorised Infantry Regiment to the XVI Panzer Corps was discussed.

than another 60 kilometres further south, and it would turn out that the XV Panzer Corps would find itself ever more committed in this direction, going around the forested and mountainous region of Łysa Góra and missing out on the battle of Warsaw. This demonstrates how the new operational orientation of Army Group South was impacting the Tenth Army. On 4 September, the leadership of the Tenth Army had still been focused on the old operational objective (Warsaw). On 5 September, it had begun to think more along the same lines as those of the army group. By 6 September, it was clear from Tenth Army Order No. 7 that it was in full agreement with the operational view of the army group. Warsaw might have no longer been the point of main effort in the manner envisioned by the OKH.

The XVI Panzer Corps was increasingly losing its flank protection on the right the further it pushed in the direction of Warsaw. This was exacerbated by the fact that Polish reserves seemed to be gathering on either side of the Pilica, roughly around Tomaszów and Opoczno. The commander of the panzer corps could expect that this enemy would put up resistance, but he still thought on 4 and 5 September that the XV Panzer Corps would be able to intervene if need be. He also thought that assistance from the left might be possible in the form of the XIV Panzer Corps, which had in the meantime crossed the Warta downstream from Osjaków and reached the area north-west of Piotrków. But this possibility might also be taken away! General Hoepner was still counting on support in the drive towards Warsaw. However, given that German forces had thrust far into enemy territory, the strongest and therefore greatest threat was probably to their west. Enemy forces to the east did not seem to be as dangerous, so it was likely that the XVI Panzer Corps would have to deal with the Polish troops assembling in the vicinity of the Pilica on its own.

On the evening of 5 September, the panzer corps reported to the Tenth Army what it had achieved that day:

> Despite significant difficulties with traffic and supply, the XVI Panzer Corps was able to maintain momentum against increasing resistance. The 1st Panzer Division took Piotrków in the late afternoon, where much matériel has fallen into our hands. The 4th Panzer Division has reached Gomulin, and the 31st Infantry Division is still advancing towards the Borowa Hills in the face of strong enemy

resistance.[10] The panzer corps will summon all of its strength on 6 September in order to seize Tomaszów and Ujazd.

The Borowa Hills, the cornerstone of the Polish position behind the Widawka, were taken on the evening of 5 September by the 31st Infantry Division.[11] The fighting was fierce, and casualties were heavy. The 4th Panzer Division went past the western outskirts of Piotrków and reached a point roughly 10 kilometres to its north. Enemy units were to be found everywhere on the left flank, but they usually retreated to the north-west after a short fight. Aerial reconnaissance spotted concentrations of enemy troops in the large forested terrain to the south-east, east, and north-east of Piotrków. The 1st Panzer Division was particularly concerned about enemy activity in Łęczno Forest south-east of Piotrków. Our reconnaissance units encountered Polish security forces standing behind the Lucionza stream. Perhaps this was the reserve group we had anticipated would be in this area, and it was now on the move. The commander of the panzer corps had no motorised reserves at his disposal to intercept them. He did not want to deprive the panzer brigade of the 4th Panzer Division, currently standing to the north of Piotrków, of its motorised forces. He would bear such a measure in mind as a stopgap solution, but what he really wanted to achieve on 6 September was the capture of Tomaszów.

On the night of 5/6 September, the telephone connection with the 1st Panzer Division was suddenly lost. The panzer division had reported shortly beforehand that it suspected an enemy attack was going to be launched from the south-east. It was not clear whether the divisional headquarters itself had been attacked. Our radio messages remained unanswered. There was still no news by daybreak. Finally, towards 0900 hours, the situation was clarified. Under cover of darkness, an advance by the Polish 29th Division from the south-east (from Sulejów) had struck the elements of the 1st Panzer Division that were resting to the south of Piotrków. This had come as a surprise even for the Poles themselves. A firefight broke out. The superior training and greater firepower of our troops meant that we gradually gained the upper hand.

---

[10] Gomulin is 9 kilometres to the west of Piotrków, on the road to Bełchatów.
[11] The Borowa Hills are 12 kilometres to the west of Rozprza.

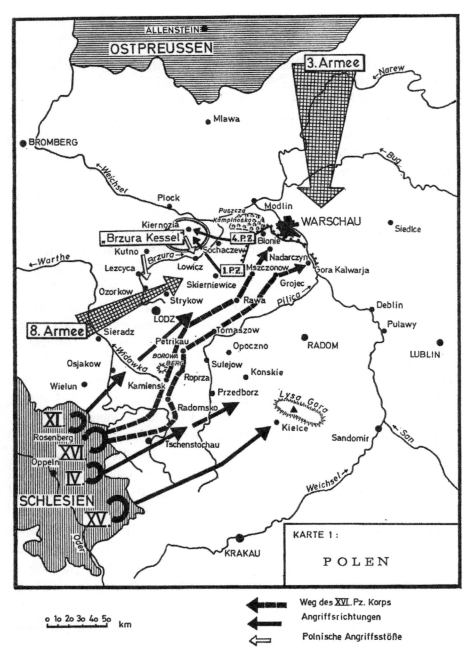

Map 1: Poland

It certainly helped that the enemy forces had still been moving forward in their march columns, not yet spread out for combat. They suffered heavy losses as a result. But another attack was carried out by the Polish 19th Division from the north-east, and Polish cavalry were approaching Piotrków simultaneously from the south-west. In fact, what was taking place there was a coordinated attack by the two Polish divisions, both of which belonged to the reserve group, with the intention of retaking Piotrków. The cavalry to the south-west did not seem to be a part of this plan, as they were retreating elements of Army Łódź. Towards 1000 hours, the commander of the panzer corps was able to report to the commander of the Tenth Army over the telephone that the situation of the 1st Panzer Division had been clarified and that some of the tanks of the 4th Panzer Division had been diverted to the south-east so that they could exert their influence on the battlefield. When the commander of the Tenth Army asked if the 3rd Light Division should also be diverted, General Hoepner responded that this would be unnecessary. By the time the commander of the Tenth Army had arrived at the command post of the panzer corps towards 1030 hours, the enemy counter-attack from the south-east had been repelled and elements of the 1st Panzer Division had already resumed the advance on Tomaszów. The Polish counter-attack had come as a surprise, but it had resulted in a significant victory for us. The enemy had suffered heavy losses. General Hoepner believed that this enemy reserve group had been deprived of its striking power and that it would be incapable of carrying out a pincer attack from the east and west against his Warsaw-bound panzer corps. But the Tenth Army had to secure the area to the south of the Pilica! Only reluctantly did Hoepner agree to the idea of the commander of the Tenth Army to create an opening for the XIV Panzer Corps, the purpose of which would be to allow this formation to head directly eastwards so that it could occupy the gap between the XV and XVI Panzer Corps. Hoepner would have been happy enough to have just been given the 13th Motorised Infantry Division from the XIV Panzer Corps.[12] He even would have been satisfied

---

[12] Aside from the 33rd Motorised Infantry Regiment, the XVI Panzer Corps had also received the I Battalion of the 66th Motorised Infantry Regiment from the 13th Motorised Infantry Division and had placed it at the disposal of the 4th Panzer Division.

if this division had simply been placed in army reserve and positioned in the Przedbórz–Radomsko area. He gained the impression that the commander of the Tenth Army, in contrast to his previous attitude, was no longer insisting on Warsaw as the objective. Instead, Colonel-General Walther von Reichenau seemed to think that the best chances lay in a rapid advance to the east so as to reach the Vistula as soon as possible. Yet the situation in the combat zone of the XVI Panzer Corps was still not entirely clear, and that to the north-west certainly was not clear at all! General Hoepner remained unaware at that time that there had been a change of view at the headquarters of Army Group South, i.e. that the advance should now proceed directly towards the east and that the point of main effort should therefore be placed on the southern wing.

By the evening of 6 September, both panzer divisions had fought their way through stiff resistance to positions that were very close to Tomaszów and Ujazd. The 31st Infantry Division had reached the Piotrków–Łódź road at a point roughly 12 kilometres to the north of Piotrków and had set up a good line of security against any threat from the north-west. The XI Army Corps was slightly further back, its leading elements to the north of Bełchatów.

For 7 September, the panzer corps ordered that Tomaszów and Ujazd were to be captured and that the advance was to continue further to the north-east as far as the eastern side of the large forested region that lay to the north-east of Tomaszów. From there, the thrust in the direction of Warsaw would be able to proceed through much friendlier terrain. Despite the fact that the other panzer corps were always increasingly further away, General Hoepner was determined that the Polish capital would remain the objective of his XVI Panzer Corps. It seemed as if the last defensive front that had been established by the enemy, that from which the counter-attack against Piotrków had been launched, had been destroyed. What was left of those defensive forces were now in the vicinity of Tomaszów, but there was little more they could do after our victory against them. Enemy forces to the south of the Pilica were now to be eliminated by the XIV Panzer Corps. Our reconnaissance units reported that there were no other enemy units in the area. It was quite possibly the case that nothing whatsoever stood between the XVI Panzer Corps and Warsaw. A final thrust straight to the enemy capital would be risky, but it was a risk that Hoepner believed could, and should, be taken.

However, a new and detailed written order from the Tenth Army arrived early on the morning of 7 September. The first two paragraphs made it clear that the objective had been changed:

1. The enemy is in full retreat to the Vistula south of Warsaw. The capital has been evacuated.
2. The Tenth Army is to be diverted from its advance on Warsaw and will instead pursue the retreating enemy with an attack towards the sector of the Vistula between Puławy and Góra Kalwaria. From there, it will stop the enemy from escaping across the river. This can only be achieved with the utmost effort of all the forces of the Tenth Army.

According to this order, Warsaw would no longer be the objective of the XVI Panzer Corps. It was instead to strike towards the Vistula at a point to the south of the city. Were the bridges over the Vistula in Warsaw to be left in the hands of the enemy? A pursuit of the retreating enemy forces made sense, but Warsaw had to remain the primary objective! We immediately telephoned the headquarters of the Tenth Army and emphasised the importance of Warsaw as the objective of the panzer corps. It was then agreed that the panzer corps would advance towards the sector of the Vistula between Góra Kalwaria and Warsaw.[13] In the order issued by the Tenth Army on the evening of 7 September, both Warsaw and Góra Kalwaria were stipulated as objectives for the panzer corps. Even so, Hoepner had gained the impression from his telephone call that the attention of the leadership of the Tenth Army was now directed towards the east, particularly on the battle that would take place between Radom and mountainous region of Łysa Góra.

The panzer corps took Tomaszów and Ujazd on 7 September against mostly weak enemy resistance, and the 4th Panzer Division managed to push even further, occupying Rawa and sending reconnaissance units as far as Babsk. Warsaw was only another 60 kilometres away from there!

---

[13] Hoepner, speaking to Paulus on the telephone, said: 'You can do what you want, but I'm heading towards Warsaw.' Major-General Paulus had been the chief of staff of the XVI Panzer Corps under Hoepner before the outbreak of the war. There was a strong bond of trust between these two soldiers.

Hoepner therefore issued a special order on 8 September at 0530 hours which supplemented the order issued by the panzer corps the previous evening and extended the objectives for the day for both panzer divisions to Góra Kalwaria and Warsaw. Hoepner himself set off early for the 4th Panzer Division so that he would be able to closely follow the development of the situation. As the first general staff officer of the panzer corps, I asked Hoepner whether our command post ought to be shifted forward to Rawa.[14] His response was that he would make a decision once he was at the front and that he would convey this decision by radio. It was his hope to reach Warsaw on this very day and perhaps even, if it were insufficiently defended, to capture it.

So that the 31st Infantry Division could approach Warsaw as quickly as possible, it was given authorisation on 8 September to make use of the main road leading to the city. The commander of the panzer corps had given this long and careful thought. The supplies of the panzer divisions were transported along this road, and there was a chance that they would be delayed if the infantry were marching on it. Hoepner regarded the swift advance of the infantry as being of the utmost importance at that time. Any disadvantage that might consequently arise had to be accepted. It was thus that the leading elements of the 4th Panzer Division reached Rawa in the course of the day, while the infantry of the XI Army Corps arrived there on 9 September. The XIV Panzer Corps would no longer be partaking in the advance on Warsaw. This was particularly unfortunate given that the bulk of the retreating Polish forces would soon make themselves felt. Where precisely would these Polish forces go? The panzer corps was faster than the Polish infantry, but what if some of them managed to retreat by rail? Would the XVI Panzer Corps run into these Polish forces before it reached Warsaw?

3. *Arrival at Warsaw*

A strange mixture of tension and confidence prevailed on 8 September in the sector of the XVI Panzer Corps. Since the early hours of the morning,

---

[14] The new location of the command post of the panzer corps would need to be made known to the divisions and other units as soon as possible so that its telephone lines could be laid in time.

all the men and their commanders had been filled with anticipation. Did each man know, or sense, that Warsaw would be reached on this day? Was it even possible? The level of confidence was high thanks to the stunning progress that had been made thus far. Even those who had been sceptical were beginning to change their minds. Everything had gone well up to this point. Even the critical situation near Piotrków had been resolved in our favour. Although our forces may have seemed small in relation to the large land and the enormous distances, the enemy was already completely demoralised. The belief in the panzer arm and what it could achieve had grown immensely. Even smaller armoured units in the German Army felt that they were masters of the situation, and they were indeed. Could the panzer corps be so bold as to commit everything it had to the advance on Warsaw? Its western flank would soon be exposed, covered only by aerial surveillance. It had been reported on 7 September that there existed strong enemy forces in the vicinity of Skierniewice and in the forests to its east. The enemy was also gathering his motor vehicles in several locations. It was clear that he was heading towards Warsaw or somewhere along the Vistula. The panzer corps would be far ahead of the rest of the Tenth Army and deep in enemy territory. It would be the advance guard, a description that had already been applied to it in an order that had been issued by the Tenth Army back on 3 September. The distance between the panzer divisions and the infantry had in the meantime become ever greater. The Eighth Army was still approaching Łódź, and it was possible that it might get there in the course of the day of 8 September. The panzer corps would initially be on its own when it reached Warsaw. It would be unable to depend on anything else and would have no mobile reserve at its disposal. It was for this reason that the 31st Infantry Division as well as the XI Army Corps had to make as much progress as possible. Despite the risks, the commander of the panzer corps was convinced that Warsaw had to be reached that day. While it is true that the city was his objective and that its capture was a military necessity, there was also a lot more at stake. If Poland could be defeated quickly, there was a chance that the expansion of the conflict into a world war could be avoided.

While the 4th Panzer Division was to proceed along the Mszczonów– Warsaw road, the 1st Panzer Division would advance through Nowe

Miasto, away from the Pilica Valley towards Grójec, and then towards
Góra Kalwaria, where it would subsequently establish a bridgehead over
the Vistula. However, the 1st Panzer Division was told to prepare for
the possibility that some of its units might be needed for the drive on
Warsaw. If so, these units would split up from the bulk of the panzer
division in Grójec and head towards the southern part of Warsaw via
Piaseczno. Enemy resistance before both panzer divisions was weaker
than it had been on the preceding days. No longer did our forces come
across any systematic defence. The number of prisoners taken by the 4th
Panzer Division along the main road increased considerably. It seemed as
if the Polish will to fight had been broken by the surprising penetrative
power of the German tanks.

From the early morning, we followed the progress of the advance
as best we could by radio at the command post of the panzer corps,
which at that time was still to the north of Piotrków. From what we
could gather from the few pieces of information that came through, the
progress that was being made was good. Hours passed, but we did not
hear any news from the commander of the panzer corps himself. It was
noon by the time we finally received the radio message: 'New panzer
corps command post in Nadarzyn.' Where was this place? We looked
for it on the map and eventually found it. It lay only 18 kilometres from
the centre of Warsaw. It certainly looked as if today would be the day
on which we would reach the objective we had been striving for over
the last seven days. The corps signals commander made preparations
for the extension of the telephone lines, we sent radio messages to the
headquarters of the Tenth Army regarding the relocation of the corps
command post, and then the chief of staff of the panzer corps, Colonel
Ferdinand Heim, and I set off for Warsaw. Innumerable prisoners of
war were to be seen as we drove through the large marketplace in
Rawa. Ever more columns of prisoners were marching southwards as
we approached Mszczonów. There were so many of them, and it barely
seemed as if they were guarded. All of this was under the glorious blue
skies and amidst the lush green of the surrounding countryside. It was
uplifting and depressing at the same time! There was still shooting to
be heard in Mszczonów, and it would turn out to be the trouble spot
on the following day. We nevertheless had to go through there and

meet the commander of the panzer corps in Nadarzyn. The units of the 4th Panzer Division had become rather spread out, with those to the rear still in the process of catching up. The attack on Warsaw would therefore be conducted with two battle groups. There had thus far been little enemy resistance.

At 1730 hours, both battle groups infiltrated the south-western suburbs of Warsaw, but they came to a standstill before reaching the city centre. The suburban land was rather flat, so the large stone houses of the city centre stood out quite clearly. But we were unable to reach them. The enemy had set up makeshift roadblocks with trams and other vehicles, and his firepower there was overwhelming. The divisional commander recommended that we withdraw from action. Hoepner, who had again visited the spearhead of the panzer division, was compelled to agree. The situation was hopeless with the forces that were currently available. The attack would have to be resumed on the following day.

The new attack commenced on 9 September at 0700 hours. Three groups of the 4th Panzer Division approached the city centre from the south-west and west. Committing as many tanks as we could to the battle, our forces infiltrated the streets of Ochota and pushed through heavy enemy resistance almost as far as the main railway station in Warsaw by noon.[15] The enemy then managed to hold our assault in check. He had set up barricades, laid mines, and positioned strong anti-tank artillery there. The narrow roads severely hindered movement and visibility for the German tanks. If we had possessed motorised or mechanised infantry, they would have been able to go through the houses from which enemy fire came in addition to clearing the side streets of any Polish troops.[16] Due to the increasing number of losses, especially in tanks, the commander of the panzer corps ordered towards noon that the attack be ceased. It had become clear that what we were dealing with was a highly systematic defence of a numerically superior opponent.

---

[15] Ochota is the south-western district of the city centre of Warsaw.

[16] The deficiency of the panzer divisions in motorised or mechanised infantry had already become quite apparent in the campaign in Poland, and would lead to the multiplication of such battalions later in the war.

The need to put up some sort of defence against the retreating Polish forces from the west played a role in Hoepner's decision to stop the advance into Warsaw. Aerial reconnaissance had reported that these forces had retreated over the lower Bzura and that they were on their way to the Polish capital. Most of them were at that stage moving along the Sochaczew–Błonie road. The 4th Panzer Division had only one reconnaissance battalion securing its western flank. This battalion did its utmost from the early morning to try to resist the increasing enemy pressure at a point halfway between Warsaw and Błonie, but it was eventually pushed back to the east and south-east. Something had to be done there. We did not want the rear of our forces in Warsaw to be under threat. The panzer corps had reached its operational objective, and it had done so more quickly than what we had thought was possible. We now had to hold on to what we had gained; otherwise, everything we had achieved thus far would have been for naught.

(d) The XVI Panzer Corps as the defensive line before Warsaw

1. *Going over to the defence*

Warsaw, the operational objective of the OKH, had been reached, but the XVI Panzer Corps now had to establish a reversed defensive front. The retreating enemy forces had overwhelmed our flank protection. They would need to be brought to a halt and, with the help of the approaching Eighth Army, annihilated. The situation was now developing so rapidly that any plans we made had no guarantee of being carried out. They might have been, but they could just as easily have been changed or abandoned altogether. The operational plan had begun to unravel. Indeed, the XIV and XV Panzer Corps had already been diverted elsewhere. This new phase of the campaign in Poland would be of a defensive nature. At its outset, the XVI Panzer Corps was already suffering from two handicaps. The first was the lack of forces; the second the unsuitability of the terrain for defence. A defensive line would ideally make use of a feature of the terrain that would be difficult for an enemy to overcome. This would enable even a numerically inferior defender to hold out given that 'the defensive is the stronger form of conducting war'.[17] The only terrain feature to the west of Warsaw that we could exploit for defence was the lower Bzura. German forces would need to establish a defensive line there at the earliest possible moment, with the XI Army Corps between Sochaczew and Łowicz and the XVI Panzer Corps between the mouth of the river and Sochaczew.[18] The army group had not thought of this solution at first, yet it was a task to which the XI Army Corps could easily commit all its forces. The XVI Panzer Corps, on the other hand, would have to draw upon some of its forces in Warsaw. As will be seen, the appraisal of the entire situation by the army group at that time was different to ours and corresponded to the objectives that it wanted to achieve. The panzer corps was in a predicament!

As a result of the way in which the fighting unfolded on 9 September, the commander of the panzer corps decided that it was necessary to set up a westward-facing front against the Polish forces that had crossed the Bzura. The most dangerous point was the road that led through Błonie, for we had nothing positioned there after the reconnaissance battalion had been thrown back. It was fortunate that an advance party of SS Motorised Infantry Regiment Leibstandarte Adolf Hitler (from the Eighth Army) arrived towards noon in response to the request made by the panzer corps the previous day for reinforcements.[19] This SS regiment was immediately placed under the command of the 4th

---

[17] Translator's note: This is the theory of Carl von Clausewitz in book 6, chapter 1, of *On War*. Clausewitz emphasises that although the defensive is stronger than the offensive, the defensive has only a negative objective, 'that of preserving', while the offensive has a positive objective, 'that of conquering'. He states that 'the latter increases our own means of carrying on war, but the preserving does not', and concludes that '[i]f the defensive is the stronger form of conducting war, but has a negative object, it follows of itself that we must only make use of it so long as our weakness compels us to do so, and that we must give up that form as soon as we feel strong enough to aim at the positive object' (quotes from the 1873 translation of *On War* by J. J. Graham).

[18] Given the speed of its advance thus far, the XI Army Corps would probably reach the Bzura on 11 September. The XVI Panzer Corps could be there earlier.

[19] SS Motorised Infantry Regiment Leibstandarte Adolf Hitler was a reinforced motorised infantry regiment of four battalions.

Panzer Division and allocated to the defence of the westward-facing front. It was specifically given the task of regaining the ground that had been lost by the reconnaissance battalion. So as to further reinforce the 4th Panzer Division, which was at that time the only formation responsible for the isolation of Warsaw as well as for the security of the westward-facing front, the 33rd Motorised Infantry Regiment was detached from the 1st Panzer Division and sent to take over the sector on the southern and south-western outskirts of the Polish capital. In return, the 4th Panzer Division had to hand over the I Battalion of the 66th Motorised Infantry Regiment to the 1st Panzer Division. It was hoped that this reinforcement of the 4th Panzer Division would enable it to push further to the north and completely cut off that part of Warsaw which lay to the west of the Vistula. At the very least, it would have to try to seize the road that ran along the riverbank. Such a limited thrust seemed to be necessary and was within the realm of possibility, even though most of the panzer corps had been forced to go over to the defensive.

2. *Wavering between offence and defence*

There had been a great feeling of elation on 8 September, for the XVI Panzer Corps had reached the operational objective that had been set by the OKH. However, the course of events on 9 September had highlighted that there was still a great danger from the west that had to be confronted. The panzer corps therefore ordered at 1600 hours that the 31st Infantry Division and 4th Panzer Division were to establish a defensive line against the retreating enemy forces. Nonetheless, the panzer corps remained under orders to use all the means at its disposal to establish bridgeheads on the east bank of the Vistula. Both the Tenth Army and the army group placed the greatest value on the establishment of such bridgeheads. It was their view that the enemy forces to the west of the river no longer possessed any strength or desire to fight. These superior headquarters were committed to an advance over the Vistula, and they expected the XVI Panzer Corps to be involved in this effort. The Tenth Army had already decided on 6 September that it would veer away from Warsaw. At about noon on 9 September, even Hoepner was contemplating whether the attack on Warsaw could be resumed and whether the city would indeed be best left aside for now. It seemed that the Tenth Army would no longer be responsible for the seizure of the city. Rather, it looked as if this task would be tackled by the approaching Eighth Army, which had reached Łowicz, on the northern wing of the panzer corps, on the morning of 9 September and had sent reconnaissance units as far as Sochaczew. With that, the most important locations for the defensive line against the retreating Polish forces were in our hands. If the Tenth Army had not allowed itself to become distracted by the idea of proceeding directly eastwards, there would now be sufficient forces in the vicinity of Warsaw and the Bzura, and there would consequently be no need for the panzer corps to hastily set up a reversed defensive front. Now, on 9 September, the enemy forces attacking from Błonie were so strong that the emergency units that had been sent there were pushed back further. It was there that SS Motorised Infantry Regiment Leibstandarte Adolf Hitler was to intervene early on 10 September. Its task was to retake the ground that had been lost and thereby create a sufficiently deep defensive zone. But would that be enough? The Polish forces were still moving. The Tenth Army and Army Group South could not sense the danger to the degree that the XVI Panzer Corps could!

The 31st Infantry Division was as yet unable to take up its position along the defensive line on 10 September. Despite its courageous march, its leading elements had only managed to reach Mszczonów on 9 September. The length of the column meant that it would have been able to protect the western flank of the panzer corps, but was it to be used for this purpose or for an advance through Warsaw and over the Vistula? Discussions on this matter continued with the headquarters of the Tenth Army on 10 September. It was decided that the bulk of the division would move into the line of security, and this took place on 10 and 11 September. Only one of its infantry regiments was sent to Warsaw. This was on the request of the 4th Panzer Division, and they were transported on trucks so that they could take over the sector to the south and south-west of the city. This allowed the 33rd Motorised Infantry Regiment to be released on 11 September. It went into panzer corps reserve for a short time before it was again needed by the 4th Panzer Division.

The wait for the 31st Infantry Division on 10 September had put a strain on the leadership of the panzer corps. The planned attacks of the 4th Panzer Division towards the north and west had been partially successful and had thereby relieved some of the pressure. However, there could be no thought at this stage of blocking the road along the bank of the Vistula. Some of the forces committed in that direction had to be withdrawn in the afternoon and committed further west, for the front there needed to be expanded towards the north. The enemy was attempting to envelop our northern wing, forcing us to extend our front ever more. The front of the 4th Panzer Division was already 40 kilometres in width, and it had to deal with Polish counter-attacks not only from the west but also from Warsaw. Neither the panzer division nor the panzer corps had any reserves available. Even the corps pioneer battalion had been handed over to the panzer division for use in combat. If still more was needed to stabilise the situation, Hoepner knew that he would have to draw upon the forces of the 1st Panzer Division. This formation had reached Góra Kalwaria and, with an eastward–facing front, was on the point of expanding its bridgehead there. Some of its forces also stood on its southern flank along the Pilica. But it was the plan of the Tenth Army and Army Group South that the 1st Panzer Division remain committed to its eastward advance so that it could make contact with Army Group North on the other side of the Vistula. General Hoepner emphasised to the headquarters of the Tenth Army that he could not do without the 1st Panzer Division under any circumstances. It would mean that he would have no reserves to draw on whatsoever. If the enemy managed to break through from the west or from Warsaw, the ring of encirclement that was being formed around the city would have to be abandoned immediately. The 1st Panzer Division was given the order to assemble the strongest forces it could manage in Grójec, including its panzer brigade. The bridgehead at Góra Kalwaria was to be held, but another in the vicinity of Otwock was to be given up. When it became apparent that enemy attacks near Góra Kalwaria were abating, the panzer corps issued a new order to the effect that the bridgehead there was to be held by just the I Battalion of the 66th Motorised Infantry Regiment. The rest of the 1st Panzer Division would be concentrated in Grójec and would then be sent rapidly towards Warsaw, Błonie, or Mszczonów.

The commander of the panzer corps felt justified in taking these measures. He could see from the written order of the Tenth Army from the evening of 9 September, which the panzer corps had received on the morning of 10 September, that the XI Army Corps had reached the Rawa–Brzeziny road, with both of its divisions alongside one another, on 9 September and that they were going to make a right turn early on 10 September with the intention of advancing, one division behind the other, eastwards via Biała towards Grójec and Góra Kalwaria. As a result of an error on the part of the Tenth Army, a gap came into being to the west of the panzer corps between Rawa and Mszczonów. This was just opposite Skierniewice, where strong enemy forces were to be found! In addition to that, the army corps would be crossing the major road roughly in the vicinity of Rawa. This would inevitably lead to the disruption of the supply of the panzer corps. We could not put up with this in such a critical situation! I immediately flew to the command post of the army corps in a Fieseler Storch in order to gain a picture of the situation in its area and convey to its leadership Hoepner's request that it not traverse the rear area of the panzer corps. I also pointed out that there was a dangerous enemy approaching from the west and that the army corps was ideally placed to bring it to a halt. Unfortunately, the leadership of the army corps remained of the view that the march to the Vistula was the more important task to be carried out.[20] It did, however, promise that it would put measures in place in Rawa that would ensure no delays to the supply traffic of the panzer corps. Our interpretation of the order of the Tenth Army on 10 September was that the battle against the main Polish forces was what was most important then! Such problems of interpretation had arisen from the fact that the Tenth Army, no doubt influenced by the line of thought of Army Group South, had been increasingly referring to the advance on the Vistula as an operational objective.

---

[20] Astonishingly, according to an order from the Tenth Army on 9 September, the XI Army Corps had two tasks to carry out. It had to march to the Vistula, *and* it had to block any breakout attempt by the enemy forces to its north. It was then to coordinate its efforts with those of the XVI Panzer Corps and the right wing of the Eighth Army in the annihilation of these enemy forces.

An unpleasant situation was in the offing for the XVI Panzer Corps. To the west, between Rawa and Mszczonów, there would be no German forces whatsoever. What was worse, the supplies of the panzer corps had to flow through this sector. If the enemy poured into this gap, the supply of the panzer corps would be cut off. The obstacle line to the west whose creation had been ordered by the OKH did not in fact exist any longer. Two more pieces of news reached the headquarters of the panzer corps on the afternoon of 10 September that caused Hoepner further concern. First, the Eighth Army had been attacked by Polish forces that had advanced from the north over the Bzura.[21] The situation remained unclear. Second, the 1st Panzer Division was to be placed under the command of the XI Army Corps from 11 September, an indication of the shift of focus of the Tenth Army.[22] It has been described earlier how the panzer corps would be unable to do without this panzer division in the fight for Warsaw.

After my return to the command post of the panzer corps, Hoepner immediately sought to clarify the situation with the headquarters of the Tenth Army. However, the signal strength of the telephone connection had been poor since the early afternoon, and it remained so the following morning. Our urgent radio messages remained unanswered due to atmospheric disturbances.[23] Since clarification of the situation was absolutely necessary, a staff officer would have to be sent to the headquarters of the Tenth Army in Końskie. Yet the only remaining Storch of the three that had previously been available was not ready for take-off, and the air support officer was not around to lend a hand. I therefore set off towards 1700 hours in an armoured car.

---

[21] The attack against the 30th Infantry Division near and to the east of Łęczyca had already commenced on the afternoon of 8 September and had compelled the Eighth Army to pivot to the north.

[22] The order of the Tenth Army on the evening of 10 September stated that the 1st Panzer Division was to be handed over to the XI Army Corps in return for the 18th Infantry Division. This exchange of divisions would take effect from 11 September at noon.

[23] The connection between the Eighth Army and Army Group South also suffered at this time due to the same atmospheric disturbances. According to the war diary of the Eighth Army, its commander had to make the decision on his own, under difficult circumstances, to pivot his forces to the north.

As none of the bridges over the Pilica had been rebuilt, I had to make the 250-kilometre journey around the river via Piotrków, Radomsko, and Przedbórz. It was already dark by about 1800 hours. So as not to attract the attention of enemy aircraft, only dimmed headlights were permitted in darkness. This dramatically reduced the speed at which I could drive. It seemed to be an utterly hopeless undertaking! That it had to be done underlines the urgency with which Hoepner's concerns had to be addressed. Only then would he be able to make informed decisions on how best to employ the forces of the panzer corps. The following message was what I had to deliver:

> The bulk of the enemy forces are approaching from the west. From what we have experienced thus far, these forces still possess striking power. The XVI Panzer Corps, standing before Warsaw, has had to go over to the defensive. We fear that the Tenth Army has misjudged how serious this situation is.
>
> Under the current circumstances, the 1st Panzer Division cannot be removed from the fighting near Warsaw. It is the only reserve force available to the panzer corps, and its role has already been taken into consideration in our defensive plans.
>
> A gap in the obstacle line to the west has come into being as a result of the decision to turn the XI Army Corps in the direction of Góra Kalwaria. This gap must be closed at once. We request that this army corps be turned back to the north-west in the direction of the lower Bzura, where it could then occupy the ground between the panzer corps and the Eighth Army. The supply of the panzer corps would be severely disrupted if the army corps were to cross its rear area. This must be prevented. Despite the current concentration of the forces of the panzer corps before Warsaw, the defensive line there and to the west is by no means strong enough. It is because of the lack of forces that the panzer corps is defending rather than attacking right now. The panzer corps must be reinforced so that it can conduct an active defence, be it in the vicinity of Warsaw or along the Bzura in conjunction with the army corps and the Eighth Army.
>
> The panzer corps regards an advance directly towards the east and over the Vistula to be impossible for now, but if it is to be carried out, please provide clarification on what precisely the objective is to the east of the river.

I arrived at the headquarters of the Tenth Army in Końskie towards 2330 hours and presented our view of the situation to the chief of staff, Major-General Paulus. He understood our concerns and, over the telephone, conveyed the details of the situation to the first general staff officer of Army Group South. The headquarters of the army group was aware of the setback suffered by the Eighth Army, but it did not consider it serious enough for any change in plan. The army group was of the view that the Eighth Army would be able to regain control of the situation on its own. This would not be comforting for the XVI Panzer Corps. I therefore requested permission to speak with the commander of the Tenth Army personally. It was not until well after midnight that Colonel-General von Reichenau arrived in his command car and listened to the concerns that we at the panzer corps harboured. Reichenau turned to his chief of staff at the end of the conversation and said:

> Well, Paulus, I don't share the optimism of the army group either. Hoepner doesn't cry out if it's not urgent. We'll have to help somehow. What he says about the XI Army Corps seems practical to me. Talk to Manstein about it.[24]

He then departed in his command car. The telephone conversation between Paulus and Manstein was short and did not go well. The army group saw no reason to alter its plans.

It was with this unsatisfactory result that I prepared to leave. The panzer corps would at least receive the 18th Infantry Division in return for the loss of the 1st Panzer Division. In addition, the Tenth Army promised that it would not insist on a directly eastward advance by the 1st Panzer Division. My overall impression from my visit to the headquarters of the Tenth Army was that the focus was primarily on the fighting in the vicinity of Radom and the mountainous region of Łysa Góra.

The need to refuel meant that my departure was delayed by roughly half an hour.[25] It was approaching 0100 hours, and I wanted to report to the commander of the panzer corps as soon as I could. It was then that Paulus called out and asked me to wait a moment. He had just been on the phone to the army group. He told me that the XI Army Corps would turn to the north-west after all and that it would attack in the direction of Łowicz. The order to hand over the 1st Panzer Division to the army corps was cancelled, although the army group was keen that

---

[24] Lieutenant-General Erich von Manstein was the chief of staff of Army Group South.
[25] The headquarters of the Tenth Army had only just been set up in Końskie. A refuelling point had not yet been established there. I had to take the fuel from other motor vehicles, waking up their drivers in the early hours of the morning in the process.

this panzer division continue to head directly towards the east for the time being. The headquarters of the Tenth Army emphasised that it was in full agreement with General Hoepner's appraisal of the situation. Major-General Paulus finally requested of me that, to be on the safe side, I return to the panzer corps via the command post of the army corps so that I could deliver the new orders in person. There was no radio connection to the army corps at that time.[26]

It had eventually been realised that Hoepner's assessment of the situation was correct. Unfortunately, the XI Army Corps had lost two days, the first in the futile march to the east and the second in the return march to the north-west. This return march was difficult, for Polish forces had started to push through the gap near Mszczonów on the night of 10/11 September. Mszczonów was lost that very night. The rear infantry regiment of the 31st Infantry Division (the 12th Infantry Regiment) had to be committed there early on 11 September. The town was too important to be left in enemy hands, as it was through there that supply traffic needed to flow. If only the army corps had already been in the correct position! Now it had to fight its way through to the Bzura. It would only arrive there on 13 September, but the Polish assaults along the river were to begin on 12 September.[27] Two extra days would have enabled the army corps to reach the river more easily and defend the stretch between Sochaczew and Łowicz more effectively. The severity of the Polish assaults on 13 and 14 September compelled the army corps to concentrate its forces more on the left, but the result was the loss of Sochaczew. The ineffectiveness of the obstacle line would increase the difficulty of the fighting for the XVI Panzer Corps, and especially for the 4th Panzer Division. The development of the situation on 9 and 10 September had confirmed Hoepner's view that it was into the area of the panzer corps that the bulk of the enemy forces were headed. These forces were dangerous and had to be eliminated. No matter what the leadership of Army Group South might have believed, an advance over the Vistula was by no means a possibility at that moment. General Hoepner was sure of this, and further developments would prove him to be correct.

---

[26] It turned out that a radio message with the new orders did get through in the end.
[27] Łowicz would be lost on 12 September.

3. *Defensive fighting to the east and west*

As already mentioned, Polish forces had broken through the obstacle line early on the morning of 11 September and had captured Mszczonów. We suffered heavy losses in supply troops and supply equipment. The supply traffic had come to a stop and did not get moving again until the late afternoon. This was a serious handicap for the troops fighting at the front. The Polish assault in this region could only be brought to a standstill in the course of 12 September thanks to the employment of strong elements of the 1st Panzer Division under the command of the leader of the 1st Panzer Brigade. Mszczonów was retaken and secured with the motorcycle battalion of this panzer division. The fierce defensive fighting to the east of Błonie on 11 September needed to be resolved in our favour. The commander of the panzer corps therefore decided that the 31st Infantry Division (except for one infantry regiment in Warsaw) would conduct a northward attack towards the town on 12 September so as to relieve the struggling forces of the 4th Panzer Division.[28] The infantry division pushed forward and reached a point approximately 4 kilometres to the south of Błonie. Its task for 13 September was to take the town, whilst the 4th Panzer Division would attack from the east in the direction of Leszno, which lay 7 kilometres to the north of Błonie. Such an attack by the 4th Panzer Division would likely aid the northward advance by the 31st Infantry Division. The commanders of the panzer division and the panzer corps were both convinced that an attack there would have better prospects than pure defence. It would probably favour the numerically superior enemy if we only defended. And it was indeed the case that the attack was carried out successfully on 13 September. We took Błonie and Leszno, as well as many prisoners.

It had been a difficult day of fighting on 12 September for the elements of the 4th Panzer Division to the east of Błonie. The relief attack by the 31st Infantry Division had been executed in a timely manner. But

---

[28] With the advance of the XI Army Corps towards the north-west (Żyrardów), the 31st Infantry Division was relieved from its previous task of defending the western flank of the panzer corps.

the fighting before Warsaw had also been difficult. Strongly supported by tanks, the enemy attacked the lines of the 82nd Infantry Regiment (of the 31st Infantry Division) early in the morning. The Polish tanks broke through and drove past the regimental command post, but the situation was brought under control with a counter-attack by those elements of the 33rd Motorised Infantry Regiment, which had been relieved by the 82nd Infantry Regiment the previous day, that were still in the area. Even the bridgehead at Góra Kalwaria was hit hard throughout the day by a Polish division.[29] We managed to hold on to the bridgehead with a counter-attack supported by tanks, capturing a number of prisoners and a large quantity of matériel. However, this had necessitated the employment of strong elements of the 1st Panzer Division, something that the commander of the panzer corps would have preferred to avoid given his desire to maintain a powerful mobile reserve. The heavy fighting in the vicinity of the Eighth Army was shifting ever further eastwards and was bound to encroach upon the area of the panzer corps before Warsaw. Our forces had been successful near Błonie, but this was partly because the enemy that had been stopped there had been able to withdraw northwards into the large area of the Kampinos Forest. This impenetrable region possessed sandy rather than developed roads and covered the terrain between the lower Bzura, the Vistula, and Warsaw. Enemy forces could conceal themselves in this forest and easily flee to Warsaw if need be. The forest extended right up to the northern side of the Warsaw–Leszno–Sochaczew road. We found it necessary to station security forces along this road, for the enemy was increasingly launching raids against it from the forest. For as long as there were no forces available to clear out the large forest and secure the road along the bank of the Vistula, which was the final route of retreat to Warsaw for enemy forces from the Bzura or from Modlin, the northern wing of the obstacle line would be vulnerable and could quite possibly collapse at any moment. The connection between the western enemy and Warsaw was far from being cut. The commander of the panzer corps had repeatedly pointed out the dangers in this regard. Unfortunately, no further forces

---

[29] We identified all three infantry regiments of the Polish 10th Division attacking this bridgehead.

were available. The fighting in the vicinity of Radom, the mountainous region of Łysa Góra, and the Vistula had been increasing in intensity, demanding the full commitment of the XIV and XV Panzer Corps. But the Kampinos Forest continued to be more and more populated with enemy forces. By the time both divisions of the XV Panzer Corps were eventually assigned to mop up these forces, it looked as if it would be an almost impossible and most unpleasant task. The situation was resolved in the end when the enemy units along the Bzura surrendered, for it was with that that the Polish will to resist was extinguished.

But that stage had yet to come to pass! Even though the coordinated attack of the 4th Panzer Division and the 31st Infantry Division on 13 September had led to success at Błonie and Leszno, it would be difficult, in that area, to resist the concerted effort of a strong and combat-capable enemy for long under the prevailing circumstances. We were certainly missing the presence of the 1st Panzer Division where it was most needed. It could very well have been used to attack towards the Bzura, the ideal location for our obstacle line. If the 4th Panzer Division were to be employed for such an attack, the 31st Infantry Division would have to be on its own in holding a line of security, 60 kilometres in width, that faced Warsaw and the north. However, General Hoepner wanted to obtain freedom of movement for his panzer forces for this attack towards the west. He therefore decided that the 4th Panzer Division and the 31st Infantry Division were to swap roles on 14 September, all the more so because we were suddenly told that the 1st Panzer Division would be reallocated to the XIV Panzer Corps, which at that time was fighting to the south of the Pilica. This reallocation was to take effect from the early hours of 13 September. We immediately made our objections known to the headquarters of the Tenth Army, but, regardless of what the outcome of this objection might have been, we had to try to master the situation before Warsaw with the forces that were still under our command at that time. We at the panzer corps were unable to comprehend the measures that the army group had taken, especially at such a crucial moment! The order for the reallocation would later be cancelled, but this does not negate the fact that the panzer corps had been severely hampered in what it could do, particularly during the decisive period between 10 and 13

September. No one was more aware of this than the man responsible for holding the line before Warsaw, the commander of the XVI Panzer Corps: General Erich Hoepner.

(e) The result on the Bzura

1. *The concentration of forces for an attack*

Although the enemy forces in the vicinity of the Bzura had almost been encircled, there had been no coordinated effort up to 12 September to see to their annihilation. It was certainly good that Army Group South had decided on the night of 10/11 September that the XI Army Corps would provide support in the area of the Eighth Army, and the army corps arrived just in time to intercept the enemy forces near Łowicz. However, the enemy assaults continued to increase in intensity, and it soon became apparent that further help would be needed if the situation were to be resolved in our favour. After a visit by the commander of the army group and his chief of staff to the headquarters of the Eighth Army on 12 September, it was decided that the 9th Rifle Regiment (of the 3rd Light Division) and the 16th Air Landing Infantry Regiment would be sent on 13 September to reinforce the defensive line in the vicinity of Łowicz. The 7th Air Division was also given the task of providing support from 13 September. The army group then gave the order on 13 September that the Bzura pocket was to be sealed and the XVI Panzer Corps was to launch an attack towards the lower Bzura, downstream from Sochaczew. The panzer corps, which was still fighting in the vicinity of Błonie, received a radio message from the Tenth Army on 14 September at 0650 hours to the effect that it was to be temporarily placed under the command of the Eighth Army. This was to last for the duration of the planned attack towards the lower Bzura. The radio message also emphasised that, in the meantime, the panzer corps was to hold the ground it had taken near Góra Kalwaria, near Warsaw, and on the northern flank. The only formation that General Hoepner could foreseeably use for the attack towards the lower Bzura was the 4th Panzer Division, but it was at that stage still in the process of being relieved by the 31st Infantry Division before Warsaw and on the northern flank. It would have been pointless for him to explicitly order the 4th Panzer

Division to carry out an attack, for it was not yet ready to do so. All he could reasonably do at that moment was to request of the commander of the panzer division that any forces that could be spared be sent towards the Bzura as soon as possible. Demanding the impossible of your troops never inspires confidence. Elements of the 4th Panzer Division arrived at a point roughly 4 kilometres away from the Bzura throughout the course of 14 September. By 15 September, they were to the north of Sochaczew. The fighting near the city was fierce that day. Although it remained in German hands, it would not be safe for as long as it continued to be the point of main effort of Polish attempts to break through.

General Hoepner deeply regretted the fact that far too much was being expected of the troops under his command. The army group had ordered that the panzer corps launch an attack, while the Tenth Army had ordered that the panzer corps hold on to the ground it had taken. The 4th Panzer Division was confronted with the overwhelmingly difficult task of attacking towards the west, but it would receive no help whatsoever from the 1st Panzer Division. Even though the bulk of the latter had been on standby in the vicinity of Grójec since 13 September, the army group wanted it to push eastwards. How could it be that one of the panzer divisions of the panzer corps was to be withheld from the most important battle? Was it not absolutely clear that the eastern side of the Bzura pocket needed to be sealed and that it was therefore towards this point, near the lower Bzura, that our greatest efforts had to be directed? The assessment of the situation by the army group was quite different to that by the panzer corps.

The OKH was responsible for the conduct of the entire campaign in Poland and had been following the development of the situation on the Bzura with concern. It now decided that the time had come to intervene. It stated that the operation to the west of Warsaw took precedence over any other objectives. We had to deprive the enemy of the initiative and bring this operation to a swift conclusion. The chief of staff of the German Army, General Franz Halder, telephoned the commander of Army Group South, Colonel-General Gerd von Rundstedt, and said that further panzer forces had to be sent to the Bzura at once. There needed to be sufficient reinforcements by 14 September to deliver a final and decisive blow against the enemy pocket.

The result of this telephone conversation was a new order issued by Army Group South at 0500 hours on 14 September to the Eighth Army and the Tenth Army. The army group itself would assume direct control of the conduct of the Bzura operation:

> Army Group South will use the Eighth Army and elements of the Tenth Army to attack the enemy forces to the south of the Vistula from the east, south, south-west, and north-west. The escape of these enemy forces is to be prevented. The Eighth Army shall send the III Army Corps towards and to the north of Kutno, the 3rd Infantry Division from Płock towards and to the east of Żychlin, and the X Army Corps also in the direction of Kutno. The 3rd Light Division is to be handed over from the Tenth Army to the Eighth Army and, by the evening of 15 September, is to be in the area of Łask.[30] The western wing of the Eighth Army will push forward and firmly seal the western rim of the Bzura pocket. The Tenth Army will conduct the attack against the eastern rim of the pocket from 15 September at noon. It shall do so with the XVI Panzer Corps, the XI Army Corps, and the approaching units of the XV Panzer Corps (the 1st Light Division, the 2nd Light Division, and the 29th Motorised Infantry Division).

The groundwork had been laid for decisive action on the Bzura. Its execution was now up to the Tenth Army.

2. The decisive panzer thrust

It was the plan of the commander of the Tenth Army, Colonel-General von Reichenau, that an attack on the Bzura be carried out and a victory be attained there rapidly. The Poles had launched multiple assaults against the Eighth Army, but Reichenau was of the view that their will to fight had dropped somewhat and that a united panzer attack against them could and should be ventured. It was obviously the commander of the XVI Panzer Corps that would be given the task of carrying out such an attack. General Hoepner fully agreed that this was the best course of action, especially if something were to be done straightaway. The only other possibility that might bring about a decisive outcome was to extend the obstacle line all the way up to the mouth of the Bzura, but Hoepner, based on his assessment of the enemy and his

---

[30] One of the units under the command of the 3rd Light Division was the 9th Rifle Regiment, which at that time was already in the combat zone of the Eighth Army.

knowledge of the local conditions, was doubtful whether this could be achieved quickly enough. The bulk of the enemy forces seemed to be approaching the lower Bzura at that moment with the idea of carrying out a final breakthrough in the direction of Warsaw.[31] This required of us an immediate attack despite the fact that many of the panzer forces that had been ordered to the area had yet to arrive. Quick action was essential! The Tenth Army therefore ordered that both panzer divisions of the XVI Panzer Corps commence the attack over the Bzura on either side of Sochaczew on the morning of 16 September. So as to maximise the effectiveness of the panzer attack from the outset, an attempt was to be made to establish bridgeheads over the river beforehand. The 19th Infantry Division would create one for the 1st Panzer Division to the south-west of Sochaczew on 15 September, while the 4th Panzer Division would have to create its own to the north of the city. The line of attack of the 4th Panzer Division would be towards the west, in the direction of Kiernozia, and that of the 1st Panzer Division towards the north-west, also in the direction of Kiernozia. Our aerial reconnaissance had revealed that most of the enemy forces would be in that area. This indicated that the Poles intended either to continue with the attack near Łowicz or break through over the Bzura downstream from Sochaczew. The XV Panzer Corps was on its way from Radom and would only reach the area to the west of Warsaw on 17 September. Once it did arrive there, it was to push northwards towards the Vistula. It would then advance along the south bank of the river in the direction of Modlin, mop up enemy forces in Kampinos Forest, and support our final efforts in the battle of the Bzura. So that it could oversee this decisive attack, the Tenth Army would establish its command post in Guzów, 12 kilometres to the south-east of Sochaczew, on 15 September. The XVI Panzer Corps also placed its command post there in order to coordinate its efforts closely with the Tenth Army.

The panzer corps made preparations on 15 September. The 1st Panzer Division moved forward from Grójec into a position closer to

---

[31] The Polish forces in the Bzura pocket were those of Armies Poznań and Pomorze, as well as elements of Armies Modlin and Łódź. There were eight to 12 divisions and many cavalry units.

the front. Reconnaissance troops went right up to the Bzura to identify the best locations for crossing the river. In the meantime, the 19th Infantry Division (of the XI Army Corps) succeeded in establishing a bridgehead across the river. It came across enemy forces that were preparing to attack, but it fought hard and extended the bridgehead so that it was 3–6 kilometres in depth. The division on the left of the XI Army Corps, the 18th Infantry Division, had to deal with a number of Polish assaults in the vicinity of Łowicz. The commander of the panzer corps and his chief of staff, separately from one another, spent the entire day on the Bzura and in the bridgehead, assessing where best the troops, especially the panzer and artillery troops, could be committed. The most ideal points for crossing the river had to be found. As many forces as possible needed to make the crossing without exceeding the load-bearing capacity of our bridges. There were not many locations along the river that seemed to be suitable. Nevertheless, all the combat troops of the 1st Panzer Division, including the large quantity of artillery that had been allocated to it, were brought safely across the river in time for the planned attack of 16 September.

The attack of the 4th Panzer Division over the Bzura to the north of Sochaczew commenced on 16 September at 0700 hours; that of the 1st Panzer Division from the bridgehead only gained momentum later that morning.[32] Against non-stop enemy resistance, both divisions pushed forward approximately 6 kilometres, their inner wings coming to within 3 kilometres of one another. The force of the attack then began to wane. Our tanks were in the middle of enemy territory, and it was clear that the Polish forces there had been preparing to strike over the Bzura in the direction of Warsaw on 17 September. Enemy troops were everywhere. They shot at us from all around: from every village, from every farmstead, from the edges of woods, and from the bushes. The Polish resistance was perhaps unsystematic, but it still had to be overpowered! There was flanking fire that had to be eliminated, and the mass of enemy forces before the panzer divisions meant that our advance became ever slower.

---

[32] The 4th Panzer Division had been unable to set foot on the west bank of the river on 15 September, for it had been involved in heavy fighting on the east bank that day.

The progress of the 19th Infantry Division was even less. One battle group of the division had moved forward with the left wing of the 1st Panzer Division, whilst another had been assigned the task of crushing enemy resistance between both panzer divisions, i.e. primarily to the west of Sochaczew. Despite the best efforts of the infantry division, enemy resistance remained strong.

As intended, the panzer corps had advanced against the enemy and had inflicted heavy losses on him. However, by the evening, the thrust had not gone as far as needed and had not compelled the enemy to capitulate. In any case, our attack had to continue the following day. After nightfall, though, the commanders of the panzer divisions were increasingly concerned about the way in which the attack was unfolding. There had been no news from the 1st Panzer Regiment of the 1st Panzer Division. It had been driving towards Kiernozia, but its presence after dark remained unknown. The divisional commanders thought that a further advance, if it were at all possible, would only increase the vulnerability of their flanks. The commander of the 4th Panzer Division had found it necessary to withdraw his spearhead to deal with the enemy threat on his flank and establish a line of security there for the night.

The commander of the panzer corps was faced with the question of whether to continue with the attack or whether, at least temporarily, to go over to the defensive. The latter had been urgently requested overnight by the three divisions on the other side of the river. The precise nature of the situation certainly needed to be ascertained before any continuation was ordered. If the advance was to proceed, the barely covered flanks would become deeper and thus more vulnerable to attack. Yet pure defence, even if only temporarily, would mean the cessation of movement just a short time after the operation had begun. After all, we had successfully attacked across the river and had delayed the Polish plan of breaking out towards the east. We were inclined to think that it would be best to continue to attack, but, given the experiences that day and the realities of the situation, it seemed practical to rotate the main direction of the attack from the north-west to the north. Our forces would now head towards the mouth of the Bzura rather than towards Kiernozia. The entire area to the west of the river was filled with enemy forces, and there were probably more even further west. These forces, against whom it had been difficult to advance, still had a chance of escaping to the east. If we advanced to the mouth of the river, the enemy would be forced into battle or capitulation. There would be no danger on our eastern flank, for the advance would be following the course of the river. Should perhaps the 4th Panzer Division cross to the east bank, push to the north, and seal the ring of encirclement? An advance along the east bank could well be faster than one on the west bank. The only question was whether the 4th Panzer Division could safely pursue this course of action. It needed the 19th Infantry Division to arrive and to hold on to the bridgehead it had established before it could set off. The 19th Infantry Division and the 1st Panzer Division were therefore to strike northwards on 17 September with all the energy they could muster. Only a few forces would provide cover to the west. Despite sporadic enemy attacks overnight, the commander of the panzer corps believed that the Poles were shaken and in a state of confusion. The attack over the Bzura had resulted in some success and had now to be exploited. The 1st Panzer Division could feel the pressure on its western flank, and its headquarters was concerned that the enemy might launch further attacks against it on 17 September. General Hoepner regarded this as unlikely.

New orders were issued to the attacking divisions that specified the new directions of advance and new objectives. General Hoepner conveyed to the 4th Panzer Division that it was to be committed on the east bank of the river once its bridgehead was safely held by the 19th Infantry Division. He then made his way to the command post of the 1st Panzer Division on the morning of 17 September. Given that this panzer division was not only the western cornerstone against any Polish attack but also the main striking force for the planned advance along the west bank of the Bzura, he wanted to see for himself the combat situation there and to assess the possibilities. After that, he wanted to visit both the 19th Infantry Division and the 4th Panzer Division.

The situation on the morning of 17 September proved to be far more favourable than had been expected. Enemy assaults from the west had largely come to a stop. All the Poles could manage were a few small attacks. The missing 1st Panzer Regiment had returned with barely any losses and had taken many prisoners. It had pushed as far as Kiernozia, but it had then had to take up a position of all-round defence in the darkness. The enemy was in retreat and had suffered heavy losses. His will to fight was low. It is no surprise that, in the pleasant autumn weather, the commander of the panzer corps greeted the commander of the 1st Panzer Division with a warm smile once the latter had returned from the front in his command car. Both men felt confident. The attack to the north had begun and had charged into Polish infantry and vehicle columns. The enemy suffered heavy casualties, and many more of his men were taken prisoner. Indeed, the number of prisoners continued to increase constantly. General Hoepner could leave the area of the 1st Panzer Division in the knowledge that the final victory was not far off. What mattered now was that the last phase of the operation be executed as swiftly as possible. This would involve a rapid advance by the 4th Panzer Division along the east bank of the river to its mouth. It could be assumed that there would be a large quantity of Polish troops moving through there, although it was probable that they would be unwilling to put up resistance.

Less confidence was radiating from the command post of the 19th Infantry Division. Perhaps the mood was dampened by the primitive, albeit spacious, farmhouse with its wooden beam ceiling and small window. Although their troops were fighting hard, progress was slow. Polish forces had infiltrated Sochaczew during the night, causing the infantry division great concern.[33] Nevertheless, the infantry division was regrouping for the new attack, which it expected to be able to carry out without too much difficulty. After all, the 1st Panzer Division already stood near the village of Ruszki, in the vicinity of the bridgehead of the 4th Panzer Division.[34] General Hoepner made it clear that enemy morale had dropped considerably and that his visit to the area of the 1st Panzer Division had confirmed this assessment to be true. He emphasised that now was the time for the troops to put in the greatest possible effort. The faster the infantry division could push forward and relieve

---

[33] It was not long before the Poles were once more thrown out of Sochaczew.
[34] Ruszki had been the objective of the 4th Panzer Division the day before! The village, which lies 7 kilometres to the north-west of Sochaczew, had been taken and then relinquished due to powerful enemy counter-attacks.

the 4th Panzer Division, the sooner the battle would come to an end. He concluded by expressing his thanks to the infantry division for its perseverance in such a difficult situation.

The command post of the 4th Panzer Division was on the east bank of the Bzura, approximately 6 kilometres to the north of Sochaczew. General Hoepner arrived there towards noon, and was pleased to see that the panzer division had been reinforced and had commenced its attack towards the Vistula. It was withdrawing any forces no longer needed in the bridgehead and sending them to support the attack to the north. This withdrawal from the bridgehead was able to be carried out in full throughout the course of the day of 17 September, and it turned out that the panzer division could be given extra artillery to provide further impetus to its northward advance. Aside from this artillery, the panzer division would be on its own in extending the line of encirclement along the east bank of the Bzura. On 18 September at 1300 hours, elements of the 36th Panzer Regiment reached the Vistula on the eastern side of the mouth of the Bzura. With that, the Bzura pocket was sealed, although the battle was not over yet. The 4th Panzer Division was now spread rather thinly and was unable to effectively cover every spot in its sector, especially in those areas with trees and bushes. With so many Polish troops seeking to escape, it was inevitable that some would slip through. The bulk of the enemy forces started to cross the Bzura from about 1500 hours. Our artillery fire inflicted heavy losses on them as they assembled and crossed the river, but there were nonetheless so many of them that there were still several, especially after nightfall, who made it to the east bank and into Kampinos Forest. On the night of 18/19 September, a Polish storm tide surged forward at several points and swept eastwards.[35] Despite this, the enemy's will to fight had been broken, and it was not long until the remaining forces in the Bzura pocket surrendered. The battle of the Bzura had determined the outcome of the campaign in Poland, and the Polish leadership was fully aware of this.

---

[35] Georg-Hans Reinhardt, who was the commander of the 4th Panzer Division during the campaign in Poland, provides a detailed description of this situation in *Wehrkunde*, vol. 7, no. 5 (May 1958).

(f) Reflections on the German conduct of operations in Poland

1.   The success of the breakthrough of the XVI Panzer Corps

The battle of the Bzura ended on 20 September. The following day, the XVI Panzer Corps and both of its panzer divisions were withdrawn and placed to the south of the field of combat for a short and well-earned rest. The fighting was over for the panzer corps and the 4th Panzer Division. The 1st Panzer Division was soon employed to help the XV Panzer Corps remove the enemy forces scattered throughout the impenetrable Kampinos Forest. This action was quickly brought to a satisfactory conclusion. After achieving a decisive victory on the Bzura, General Hoepner would take no further part in the campaign in Poland.

Before turning our attention to the events that followed, it is worth recognising and evaluating the way in which the military commander Erich Hoepner carried out the task that he had been assigned. The objective that had been given to the XVI Panzer Corps was Warsaw. It was therefore the panzer corps that had the most important role in the operational plan and had the greatest chance of ensuring victory. After some minor successes at the outset of the campaign, General Hoepner fully exploited the mobility of the panzer corps with a powerful thrust from Piotrków and Tomaszów. This was a difficult decision to make at the time. The thrust would be conducted between two groups of numerically superior enemy forces, Army Łódź to the west and the main reserve on either side of the Pilica to the east. It was a risky venture because the two other panzer corps that were supposed to have been on the right and left in accordance with the operational plan of the OKH were in fact not there. The XVI Panzer Corps also lacked its own reserve forces, even though reserves were much more important for the panzer arm than for the slower infantry due to the ever-changing situations it faced. Yet we could not afford to await intelligence on precisely what the enemy was up to; otherwise, we probably would have lost our chance to achieve a breakthrough. The Polish divisions near Piotrków and Tomaszów had been annihilated, but if they had been allowed one more day to establish a proper defensive front, the deep penetration by the panzer corps might never have taken place. General Hoepner was by no means thinking of a pointless rush into the unknown. He had a remarkable ability to be able to assess the strength and potential of his opponent. He also knew that the panzer troops, as a last resort, had the option of fighting their way back to wherever the rest of the German forces were, especially if the enemy was slower. This was something he once explained to me when we faced a similar situation during the campaign in Russia. It was of course always necessary to keep in mind what we could achieve and to recognise at the right time when decisive action could and should be taken. It was his belief that maintaining self-control was what was most important if one did not want to miss the boat. And that was what was most difficult! An opportunity had arisen for the panzer forces to drive all the way to Warsaw. Although these panzer forces were weak and would be leaving the infantry far behind, General Hoepner decided that the opportunity had to be seized. The panzer divisions ended up more than 100 kilometres in front of the infantry. There were many things that could have happened on the way to the Polish capital, but the commander of the panzer corps was lucky! No Polish forces were to be found at that time in the entire region between Warsaw, the Pilica, and Skierniewice (in the west). The enemy had nothing with which to bar the way to Warsaw. Polish forces in the west had been overtaken by the panzer corps, an achievement nobody had thought possible. Only from 9 September did those Polish forces begin to arrive, although the mass of them, as we have seen, would not appear until much later.

2.   Differences of opinion and the reasons therefore

The operational plan of the OKH had stipulated Warsaw as the objective, and it was the will of the commander of the XVI Panzer Corps to carry out the task he had been given as quickly as possible that brought him and the formation under his command all the way to that objective. General Hoepner was utterly convinced of the necessity of a rapid advance on Warsaw. He could not be swayed when the order was given by the Tenth Army on 6 September to pivot away from Warsaw and pursue a fruitless advance to the east. He committed the 4th Panzer Division to the drive on Warsaw on 7 September, and it arrived there on 8 September. Was this disobedient? His discussion with Major-General Paulus about this matter has been described. Hoepner, immediately before Warsaw, simply could not understand why the operational objective would be altered so suddenly, especially as he, at the spearhead of the German advance, was more aware than anyone else of the precise nature of the situation. Warsaw was a location where the Vistula could be crossed easily and was an important centre of traffic and communications. It did not make sense to leave it in enemy hands. On top of that, it had to be borne in mind that the capture of Warsaw would have boosted German morale and been a tremendous political victory on the world stage. General Hoepner carefully considered at all times the way in which the operation was unfolding and remained of the view that the objective set by the OKH had to be adhered to. Bypassing Warsaw to the south would have achieved little.

The fighting in which the panzer corps was involved before Warsaw in the period between 8 and 14 September was extremely challenging. The panzer corps had to struggle with insufficient forces whilst carefully balancing the need for defence with the demands of superior headquarters for multidirectional attacks. The troops of the panzer corps were tied down in several locations, and it was not always clear where the greatest effort should be applied. General Hoepner knew that dealing with the Polish forces in the west took priority, and, from about 10 September, he did his best to persuade his superiors of the correctness of his assessment. However, they remained fixated at that time on the idea of advancing directly to the east.

One example of this fixation was the intention of Army Group South to send at least one panzer division over the Vistula. The result of this was that the commander of the panzer corps did not always have the power to use the forces of the 1st Panzer Division for the crisis before Warsaw. The 1st Panzer Division continued to be withheld by the army group on 13 September and was even placed under the command of the XIV Panzer Corps, which at that moment was still fighting far to the south of the Pilica. It was also a moment when the situation on the Bzura was threatening to become overwhelming and needed to be brought under control. General Hoepner did not want the 1st Panzer Division to be tied down near Góra Kalwaria; he needed it as a reserve force that could be sent to deal with any emergency that might materialise near Warsaw, Błonie, Sochaczew, or Mszczonów. As he explained to the headquarters of the Tenth Army, committing the panzer division over the Vistula would deprive him of any means of reinforcing the defence before Warsaw or that in the vicinity of the Bzura. The Tenth Army tacitly agreed to the postponement of an advance by the panzer division over the Vistula.

An example of an order that was unable to be carried out by the XVI Panzer Corps was that of the army group on the evening of 12 September which stated that the 4th Panzer Division and the 31st Infantry Division, without the 1st Panzer Division, were to attack towards the Bzura in the area of Sochaczew on 13 September.[36] Both the 4th Panzer Division and the 31st Infantry Division were at that time defending against a strong Polish attack near and to the north-east of Błonie. What was being demanded of the panzer corps was impossible. It was an order that failed to take into account the time required for its execution, the nature of the prevailing combat conditions, and the lack of troops that were available. Who was supposed to cover the rear against Warsaw, not to mention the forgotten northern flank? We have seen how the commander of the panzer corps sought to fulfil the multitude of demands that were being made of him. Even so, the panzer corps could not do without the 1st Panzer Division! General Hoepner had to do the utmost to ensure he could hold on to it.

While the Tenth Army and Army Group South pushed for an advance over the Vistula, Hoepner, based on his observation of the behaviour of the enemy, knew that the decisive battle would have to be fought in the vicinity of Warsaw. It had been relatively easy to reach the city. Barely any Polish forces were to be encountered there to begin with. In the eight days it took to reach Warsaw, there did not seem to be any

---

[36] According to the war diary of the Eighth Army, the order issued by Army Group South on 12 September at 2000 hours was as follows: 'The XVI Panzer Corps, without the 1st Panzer Division, will advance early on 13 September with the 4th Panzer Division and the 31st Infantry Division in the direction of Sochaczew, Kutno, and the area to the north of there. It can then help the Eighth Army in its fight. In carrying out this advance, the panzer corps will ensure that its rear against Warsaw is sufficiently covered.'

Polish forces arriving from the west, nor did any defence to the east of the Vistula appear to have come into being. Yet it was inevitable that the forces in the west would arrive eventually. With Warsaw as their destination, the city or the area to its west would become the main battleground. Hoepner's certainty in this regard highlights a couple of memorable qualities of his character. First, he possessed a strong sense of responsibility. Second, he selflessly committed himself to the cause. This could be seen in everything he said, be it to those under his command or to those who commanded him, and in all the measures he took. He was not prepared to act in a manner that was contrary with what he believed was right. He would not hide the fact that his view of the situation often ran counter to that of the army group, be it in relation to the assessment of the enemy, the direction of advance, or the utilisation of the 1st Panzer Division.

Hoepner managed to convince his superiors that the 1st Panzer Division ought to remain in the area of the panzer corps, but he found it difficult to make them agree with his appraisal of the strength of the enemy in the west. It has of course been seen how the headquarters of the Tenth Army increasingly showed its understanding of the point of view of the panzer corps. However, from 8 September, the time at which the panzer corps reached Warsaw, the Tenth Army had become more interested in the region between Łysa Góra and the Vistula than the ground before the Polish capital. As mentioned, the change in the operational objectives of the Tenth Army was probably a result of the influence of the army group. The focus of the latter on an advance directly towards the east was bound to lead to a lack of emphasis on Warsaw.

How did these different perspectives on the conduct of the enemy come about? What was it that led to the shift in the operational plans of the army group? The reasons are to be found at the highest levels, between the OKH and the army group, and the way in which they interpreted the unfolding of events.[37] We at the panzer corps could perceive that the objective was changing, and, to the degree that the terrain and the situation allowed, we even made an effort for a time to send some forces

---

[37] This is to be seen in the records of the OKH, Army Group South, the Eighth Army, the Tenth Army, and the XVI Panzer Corps.

directly eastwards. Yet, after the advance on Warsaw, the panzer corps was compelled to turn ever more to the west to stop and then destroy the enemy forces there, rather in the manner that had originally been foreseen in the operational plan of the OKH.

It was due to the easy advance of the panzer corps that the army group had become doubtful whether the Polish leadership wanted a decisive battle to take place to the west of the Vistula. As early as the evening of 3 September, the headquarters of the army group, in its appraisal of the situation, expressed the view that it was no longer certain that Polish forces could be contained and annihilated to the west of the river. It would therefore be best, said the army group, to advance on a wide front towards the river as quickly as possible.[38] The army group feared that too many divisions would be concentrated in the region between the Pilica and the upper Warta if the entire Tenth Army were to continue towards Warsaw. This would limit the freedom of movement of the divisions. The army group therefore emphasised that the focus needed to be shifted to the southern wing, which could advance swiftly over the San and then make the crossing of the Vistula for the bulk of the army group much easier. Army Group South Order No. 2, issued on 3 September at 1900 hours, specified how the forces were to be regrouped. The most significant result of this was that the XIV and XV Panzer Corps were to be diverted directly towards the east. Warsaw had been given up as the point of main effort of the offensive. Even the concentration of forces before the capital was now regarded as a disadvantage. The army group remained committed to this new point of view even when the Eighth Army was increasingly under attack from Polish forces. Any request by the XVI Panzer Corps for more panzer forces was rejected. Instead, the 1st Panzer Division was constantly being drawn away to the east and south-east.

In contrast to Army Group South, the OKH stuck to its original point of view. This is demonstrated by the response of General Halder on the afternoon of 4 September to the appraisal of the situation by the army

---

[38] This appraisal of the situation was signed by the chief of staff of Army Group South, Lieutenant-General Erich von Manstein, and was sent to the operations department of the army general staff of the OKH.

group: 'I consider the basis of the operational plan to be the same.'[39] This is clear evidence of the different perspectives of the OKH and Army Group South. It came to a head on 13 September when General Halder telephoned Colonel-General von Rundstedt and said that panzer forces were to be diverted immediately to partake in the battle of the Bzura. After that, the army group submitted to the original operational plan. This enabled the XVI Panzer Corps, which had been suffering in the vicinity of Warsaw, to be reinforced.

In this connection, there is a characteristic of German military leadership which can help with an understanding of how the situation unfolded but which has been forgotten or obscured by post-war propaganda. Superior commanders gave subordinate commanders tasks rather than orders. A subordinate commander was given an objective and the forces that were needed, or available, to reach that objective. The way the task was carried out and the way the available forces were employed was up to the subordinate commander. This enabled the personality of a commander to come to the fore. He could seize opportunities much more easily than he would be able to if required to adhere strictly to orders. Agility was favoured over rigidity. It permitted a commander to adapt to changing situations. This liberal and practical approach meant that higher levels of command remained of central importance without needing to interfere with operational and tactical details. The opposite approach, pure execution of orders, was practised in its most crass form by Stalin during the early stages of the war in Russia. He issued orders to every front-line division, and those divisions would not dare deviate from what they had been told to do. It was for this reason the Russians suffered heavy defeats to begin with. Even if a potentially favourable situation arose, they felt unable to exploit it. As the war progressed, Russian units were gradually permitted to act on their own initiative, although the Russian leadership remained prone to following detailed schemes. The English, French, and Americans established a middle ground between these two approaches. They developed detailed plans that were always firmly

---

[39] This response by Halder is recorded in the war diary of Army Group South, 4 September 1939.

based on the prevailing situation, but they did not insist on adherence to orders.

The approach of the German military leadership, which tended to emphasise the effect of individual subordinate commanders, could occasionally be disadvantageous. As is often the case in large corporations, only rarely could a superior intervene with the task being carried out by a subordinate. Such intervention can erode the basis of trust between superior and subordinate commanders. Corporate intervention is justified, and necessary, if a loss in value is anticipated. In the military, the potential loss of men or matériel demands intervention. When the OKH intervened on 13 September, it was because it was necessary. Army Group South had distributed its forces too widely. The resulting lack of forces in the vicinity of Warsaw could mean the loss of the decisive battle with the enemy. The army group had announced in its Order No. 7 on the evening of 11 September that 'the operation to the west of the Vistula is nearing its conclusion while that to the east of the river, involving the annihilation of the approaching enemy forces there, is about to begin'. In accordance with this announcement, the army group had started to reinforce its southern wing (the Fourteenth Army) with the panzer forces of the XIV Panzer Corps. This made it difficult to pursue the operational objective that had been set by the OKH.

The OKH had been watching the operations of both army groups and had even prevented Army Group North from reinforcing its outer wing too early on, even though this was something that its commander, Colonel-General Fedor von Bock, had strongly recommended.[40] While the OKH approved this reinforcement of the outer wing of Army Group North at a later stage, it could not do the same for Army Group South. This was because the panzer forces of Army Group South were urgently needed near Warsaw. If a superior headquarters begins to have doubts about the conduct of a subordinate headquarters, it takes time for these doubts to be examined carefully before they can mature into conviction.

---

[40] Bock wanted to reinforce the outer wing of Army Group North even before the encirclement of Warsaw from the east was complete (see Halder's war diary, 9 September 1939).

The superior headquarters depends on the depiction of the situation of the subordinate headquarters, in this case of Army Group South, in forming its own opinion. Army Group South had underestimated the strength of the enemy and had misjudged his intentions.[41] Given the actual strength and conduct of the enemy, the OKH justifiably intervened and was able to ensure that the necessary panzer forces were available just in time to determine the outcome of the battle of the Bzura in our favour. The attack of the XVI Panzer Corps on 16 and 17 September struck the enemy, who had thus far been successful against the Eighth Army, at the most favourable moment. The enemy had just conducted a couple of assaults near Łęczyca and Łowicz, and he was now preparing to make a final decisive attack over the lower Bzura in the direction of Warsaw. The demoralising impact that the tanks of the 1st and 4th Panzer Divisions had against the unsuspecting mass of Poles was what ultimately brought about the final victory in Poland.

An operational lesson can be drawn from the way the situation unfolded in the area of Army Group South. The underestimation of the enemy can lead to the omission of necessary measures. The danger to the Eighth Army might never have taken place if the XIV Panzer Corps had remained to the left of the XVI Panzer Corps and continued its advance on Warsaw. With both panzer corps working in conjunction with one another, Warsaw could have been encircled completely and the Bzura pocket sealed properly. Neither of these tasks would have been needlessly delayed. The fighting in the vicinity of Radom and the mountainous region of Łysa Góra should have been a secondary operation for Army Group South until the situation near Warsaw had been resolved satisfactorily.

One question remains to be touched on that caused General Hoepner quite a headache after he arrived before Warsaw: how many Polish forces would be coming from the west? After Hoepner had gained the impression that these forces were probably significant and nowhere near as small as had been assumed, he urgently requested aerial reconnaissance

---

[41] Army Group South initially assumed that the Eighth Army was facing two or three Polish divisions and two cavalry brigades. It later revised this estimate to three or five divisions and three cavalry brigades. The real strength of the enemy was far greater.

so that a more accurate picture could be obtained. However, the Luftwaffe was unable to ascertain the exact strength of the enemy. We know in retrospect that the Polish leadership, in recognition of their aerial inferiority, only carried out troop movements after nightfall, and they were able to do so with precision and success. Yet the German leadership was soon forced to acknowledge that all the Polish forces in the west were heading towards Warsaw and that these forces were numerically overwhelming! The pressure was small to begin with, but it gradually increased. Initially, there were just supply columns and vehicles; after that, there were smaller groups of troops that sought to break through to the east; finally, there were larger groups that carried out powerful attacks. The assaults of the Polish 1st Division in the vicinity of Błonie proved to be of great concern. In contrast to the leadership of the Eighth Army, which had been taken by surprise by the systematic attack of the enemy, General Hoepner could foresee that large numbers of enemy troops were approaching. But he could also perceive that the Tenth Army and Army Group South did not regard the urgency of the situation to be great enough to justify the diversion of forces from the area south of the Pilica.

The Polish assaults against the Eighth Army may have contributed to the erroneous assessment by the army group. The Poles carried out two limited attacks on the Eighth Army with the goal of obtaining more room for the thrust over the lower Bzura. However, the army group assumed that the Eighth Army had achieved a tremendous defensive success. This was not the case! The Eighth Army had been reacting to the enemy since 10 September and had been compelled to place most of its forces in its central sector to prevent a threatened breakthrough there.[42] This weakened Sochaczew and Łowicz, even though holding on to these points was so important for the encirclement of the enemy. The western wing of the Eighth Army was also in danger. Its 30th Infantry Division was in bad shape, as was the formation sent to relieve it in Ozorków on the evening of 11 September, the 17th Infantry Division. If the first Polish attack had continued near and to the east of Łęczyca,

---

[42] The central sector of the Eighth Army was to the north-east of Łódź, between Głowno and Stryków.

it might not have been possible to hold on to Łódź. The Eighth Army shifted its focus to ensure the defence of the city. But then something else happened! The Polish commander, Major-General Tadeusz Kutrzeba, did not possess freedom of action.[43] He was under orders to avoid a serious fight and to bring his forces to Warsaw. It was for this reason he conducted limited attacks, creating room for the main thrust to the east whilst also frustrating the efforts of the German forces. But, fortunately, these limited attacks meant that the Eighth Army was not overrun and that there was still time for the German leadership to act. Although it had been delayed, the Bzura pocket was eventually sealed. The enemy may have lost the battle, but the fighting spirit of his leadership and of his troops is deserving of recognition. Despite the hopelessness of his position, he fought bravely and achieved some successes. The threat of a Polish breakthrough in the vicinity of Łódź had been very real. However, by the time he was fully encircled, the enemy had lost. His troops were no match for our tanks.

Erich Hoepner is closely associated to this day with the swift victory achieved in the campaign in Poland. His panzer corps played a decisive role in the fighting near Warsaw. It is worthy of study for the new panzer arm in the post-war era. The panzer corps had conducted an effective, long-range operation and had rapidly reached the objective it had been given. The study of the campaign in Poland offers the opportunity to learn about movement and combat, about planning and decision-making, and about responding to complications that might arise, in a theatre of war that, in comparison to later operations, is reasonably restricted in terms of the period of time it took and the amount of ground it covered. It is with this in mind that we examine the achievements of Erich Hoepner. Warsaw was his greatest military success, but it was not yet the height of his military career.

---

[43] Major-General Tadeusz Kutrzeba was the commander of Army Poznań and, by this point, all the Polish forces to the west of the Vistula.

CHAPTER 2

The Campaign in France in 1940

(a) The preparatory period

1. *The plans of the leadership*

The Western Front at the start of the war was the German border with France and the Benelux countries. This front had played a considerable role in the considerations of the German leadership from the outset. Our strongest military opponent, France, stood to the west, and its conduct, whether active or passive, would have a decisive influence on our prospects of success. However, we could only leave the weakest of forces in the west whilst in pursuit of a rapid victory in Poland. The lack of German troops in the west at the outbreak of World War II was risky. There were no panzer forces there, even though they would have been the best means of defence on such a wide and weakly occupied front. It would be necessary to reinforce the Western Front as soon as possible and to whatever degree allowed by the situation in Poland.

The OKH occupied itself quite early on with the question of reinforcing the west. On 10 September 1939, a discussion took place on shifting the focus from the east to the west.[44] The transfer of the first troops was contemplated so as to compensate for our weakness at that time in relation to France. The idea of an offensive in the west surfaced for the first time in a conference on 29 September. Although victory in Poland was by then a foregone conclusion, the OKH displayed a fair

---

[44] See Halder's war diary, 10 September 1939. This discussion formed the basis for further considerations by the OKH with regard to sending troops westwards.

amount of reserve. It recommended that German forces should stand ready behind the Dutch and Belgian frontiers so that they could meet any advance by the enemy. The OKH was of the view that it was too late in the year to launch a decisive operation. The days were too short and the weather too unpredictable. There would be no certainty that the Luftwaffe could be employed effectively. We would be unable to fully exploit the men and matériel at our disposal, something that was necessary given the strength of the enemy. The panzer arm had been somewhat weakened during the campaign in Poland. Its units needed to be reorganised and brought to full strength.

Hitler's attitude on this question was quite different! Primarily for political reasons, he thought the offensive in the west ought to be carried out at the earliest possible moment. It was his opinion that, despite the difficulties, we could force a favourable outcome in the west if only we decided to fully commit ourselves. We only needed to get everything going, and with the greatest urgency! But this was precisely the difficulty that needed to be overcome. The military leadership could see this, but not Hitler. If we wanted to be able to attack decisively with all our might, it would require time and preparation. The debate between Hitler and the commander in chief of the army, Colonel-General Walther von Brauchitsch, went back and forth throughout October. Hitler was not to be convinced by informed or objective explanations. He persisted with his own personal view of the matter, one that he had advocated since the beginning of October despite all objections: 'We must pre-empt the enemy with a decisive operation. Even if the objective is not reached, we can establish a line that protects the Ruhr region.'[45] Hitler was not worried that we would come up against a prepared enemy and could not be persuaded 'that our method of attack in Poland is no recipe for taking on the well-organised army in the west'.[46] It was not clear to Hitler that an unsuccessful operation in the west, one in which the objective was not reached, would be unnecessarily costly in terms of men, matériel, and morale. The two most senior military leaders in the OKH, Colonel-General von Brauchitsch and General

---

[45] According to Halder's war diary, this remark was made by Hitler on 7 October 1939.
[46] Halder's war diary, 29 September 1939.

Halder, continued to advise caution. This is perhaps most clear from an entry in Halder's war diary which was written down shortly after the first wave of troops was concentrated in the west: 'There are three possibilities. We can attack, we can wait, or we can make fundamental changes. None of these offer resounding prospects, particularly the last one. Regardless of that, we must perform our duty, we must be level-headed in examining military opportunities, and we must pursue any chance of peace.'[47] This last statement reflects the political attitude of both military commanders. They were aware that another offensive in 1939 would be impossible. They considered it best, after the success in Poland and Hitler's pronouncement that he was ready for a settlement with the West, to exercise restraint with any measures aimed at launching a new attack. We should not spoil any chance of peace for as long as such a chance existed. It was under these circumstances that the first deployment orders for the attack in the west came about. These initial measures were hasty and temporary in nature, so they would need to be improved over time. For the time being, though, Hitler remained firm in his desire for an attack to be carried out soon.

2.   *The question regarding the date of the attack*

What was the earliest point at which an attack could be carried out? The factor that would cause the greatest delay was the preparedness of the panzer formations. These had been weakened during the campaign in Poland, so they would need to be regrouped and re-equipped. In addition, the light divisions would need to be converted into full panzer divisions. The tanks themselves would need to be upgraded, for those that the French possessed were much stronger than ours.[48] It all depended on how quickly new tanks could be delivered and how much time should be granted the panzer arm for learning how to use them.

Hitler pressed for faster preparations and showed a great deal of mistrust. During a conference that took place on 10 October,

---

[47]   Halder's war diary, 14 October 1939.

[48]   The German Panzer I was the tank that was most widely used by the panzer divisions during the campaign in Poland. It had to be replaced with a stronger model, but it could still be used as an armoured communications vehicle on the battlefield.

Hitler stated that 'we can never be strong enough for an attack' anyway and suggested that we 'plunder' some divisions so that those earmarked for the attack would be ready more quickly.[49] On 19 October, the OKH officer responsible for the panzer arm, Colonel on the General Staff Adolf von Schell, reported that the earliest the first two mobile divisions could be ready would be 10 November. These were the 8th Panzer Division and the 3rd Motorised Infantry Division.[50] Hitler therefore wanted the attack to begin on 12 November, but he failed to take into account that these divisions would still need to be transported to the front and deployed. More importantly, the troops would require time for training with the new equipment. This was an obvious precondition for the use of new tanks in combat! Yet Hitler interpreted the request for more time for training as a delaying tactic on the part of the army leadership. He dismissed the concerns expressed by Brauchitsch on 5 November with the remark: 'Your arguments for training will be the same in four weeks!'[51] And when, at the same meeting, Brauchitsch objected that we would run into bad weather if we attacked too early, Hitler responded that it would be no better in spring. Given that this claim was incorrect, we had to draw the conclusion that Hitler would simply respond without any objectivity if something we said did not suit him. As Halder noted down in his diary on 5 November: 'Discussing these things with Hitler is impossible. He thinks that the army does not want to fight and that the rate of rearmament is slow and sluggish.' Cooperation with Hitler was difficult under such conditions! Nevertheless, the OKH did not give in. Objectivity had to prevail in this situation.

It went back and forth, and the earliest date for an attack kept changing. On 17 October, the plan was that the attack would commence between 15 and 20 November, for which there would be an advance warning of seven days.[52] On 22 October, Hitler suddenly threw 12

---

[49] See Halder's war diary, 10 October 1939. The divisions that Hitler suggested should be plundered were the 4th Light Division and the 29th Motorised Infantry Division.

[50] There was no plundering when it came to making these two divisions ready.

[51] Halder's war diary, 5 November 1939.

[52] An advance warning was needed so that the troops, especially the panzer troops, would have time to be transported and deployed.

November into the discussion. The commander in chief of the army seriously objected to this. Halder noted down in his diary on 1 November: 'The attack that has been ordered by the OKW cannot yet be carried out successfully by any of the field units. We cannot expect a decisive victory at this stage.'[53] The discussion that took place on 5 November has been described. On 7 November, the OKW ordered that the movement of motorised units to the west was to come to a stop. Major-General Alfred Jodl, the chief of the operations staff of the OKW, elaborated on this order in the afternoon, stating that the movement to the west would resume no earlier than the evening of 9 November. The date for this resumed westward movement was then set for 15 November. Shortly afterwards, it was postponed to 19 November. December arrived! On 6 December, it was decided that the movement of units to the west would resume on 12 December, meaning that the earliest date for the offensive would be 17 December. Hitler gradually realised that the weather was indeed not good and that it could impact negatively on any chance of military success. There were of course several other difficulties that had yet to be overcome. It would have hardly dawned on Hitler that all this toing and froing must have made the troops feel constantly on edge. At the turn of the year, he had to accept that the offensive in the west would have to take place in spring.

3. The plans for the XVI Panzer Corps

The XVI Panzer Corps was the first of the panzer units to be transferred to the west. It arrived in Düsseldorf at the beginning of November 1939. Already there, under the command of Colonel-General von Reichenau, was the headquarters of the Sixth Army (formerly the Tenth Army). It was with the Sixth Army that the point of main effort of the upcoming operation was supposed to lie. The Sixth Army was subordinate to Army Group B, whose commander was Colonel-General von Bock. The headquarters of the army group was also in Düsseldorf. The XVI Panzer Corps would be allocated the 1st and 3rd Panzer Divisions. In the middle of November, the XIX Panzer Corps, under

---

[53] The OKW was the High Command of the Wehrmacht, Hitler's military headquarters.

the command of General Heinz Guderian, arrived in Düsseldorf. It was initially intended that it too would be employed in the sector of the Sixth Army. However, the XIX Panzer Corps was soon transferred to Koblenz, which was in the area of the army group on the southern wing, Army Group A (Colonel-General von Rundstedt).[54] This transfer was the first indication of the changes to the operational plan that would occur over the coming months.

Case Yellow, the operational plan for the campaign in France, was subjected to so many different influences whilst it came into being. Even a short description of the frequent changes that were made until the plan reached its final form would go far beyond the realm of what needs to be considered here.[55] These developments will only be examined to the extent that they had an impact on the plans for the use of the XVI Panzer Corps, which would in any case end up remaining where it had originally been allocated.

There were essentially two phases in the development of the operational plan for the campaign in the west, each associated with different people. The first phase ranges from the time such a campaign was first considered until February 1940, and it includes the ideas of carrying out an attack in autumn or winter. This was the phase during which Hitler and the OKH had opposing views on what was possible, what preconditions were necessary for the operation to be carried out, and what date the operation should commence. Colonel-General von Brauchitsch and General Halder believed that it was too early to launch a campaign against the stronger and well-prepared enemy in the west. The days were too short at this time of year, the weather was unpredictable, the level of training was insufficient, the reorganisation of forces was still underway, and the re-equipping of units was incomplete. These factors were just the most important reasons why it was too early. If we were to send our army into difficult terrain, we would not want anything else contributing to unfavourable combat conditions. These perfectly reasonable arguments failed to convince Hitler, but it would

---

[54] See Heinz Guderian, *Erinnerungen eines Soldaten* (Heidelberg: Vowinckel, 1951), 75.

[55] An overview of the constant changes that took place is provided in Erich von Manstein, *Verlorene Siege* (Bonn: Athenäum, 1955), 94ff.

have been irresponsible if Brauchitsch and Halder had just changed their lines of thought to match those of the Führer. The two military leaders nevertheless issued the first deployment orders for Hitler's attack plan, but they did not realistically anticipate that these orders would be carried out before the spring. Once the weather did indeed deteriorate, Hitler finally agreed to postpone the offensive.

Hitler's abandonment of the idea of an offensive in the autumn or winter represents the end of the first phase. The second phase began in February 1940, and it brought about the final deployment orders and the mobilisation of everything that was available. The preparedness of the panzer arm in this second phase was far greater than it had been in the first. It would be possible to commit 17 mobile divisions and two mobile brigades to the offensive, and the bulk of them would be employed against the point of main effort. It had originally been planned that the point of main effort would be applied in the area of the northern army group, but it was eventually shifted to the area of the southern army group. The main strike would go over the Meuse between Dinant and Sedan and would arrive at the coast of the English Channel to the north of the mouth of the Somme with the objective of isolating and destroying the enemy forces in Belgium, Holland, and northern France.

How did these developments influence the plans for the use of the XVI Panzer Corps? As mentioned, it was initially envisioned that the main panzer thrust would take place in the sector of the Sixth Army. This thrust was to go past the northern outskirts of Brussels in the direction of Ghent. The panzer forces were to penetrate as far as possible and crush any enemy forces they encountered. The enemy was bound to be taken by surprise, for Belgium and Holland, in our estimation, would barely be defended. The assembly zone of the Sixth Army lay on the left bank of the Rhine between Krefeld and Aachen, and it was there that the two panzer divisions of the XVI Panzer Corps would begin. Any advance on Ghent would at first have to go through the Dutch municipality of Maastricht, crossing the Meuse and proceeding into Belgian territory. Circling around the southern tip of Holland would be prevented by the complex of fortifications in the Belgian municipality of Liège. These fortifications had been built after

World War I and were the most modern of their kind in the world. We would not want to get stuck there at all. The zone to the south of Liège was the attack sector of the Fourth Army, which was only to be allocated weak panzer forces. It was expected that an advance into Belgium would meet stiff resistance, whilst one into Holland would make progress more easily.

It was anticipated that the panzer corps would need to be reinforced if it were to be the main strike force of the offensive. The first obstacle it would need to overcome was the Meuse. The river would have to be crossed in the vicinity of Roermond, where the Rur flows into the Meuse, and in the vicinity of Maastricht. The plan was that one panzer division would advance through Roermond and the other through Maastricht. However, if the river could not be crossed in one of those cities, then both panzer divisions would have to advance through the second city. In November 1939, neither crossing looked promising. There would be five canals or watercourses to overcome in Roermond, after which the panzer corps would need to arrive to the south of the Albert Canal before the operation could really get underway. An advance through Maastricht might not necessarily be any easier. The Albert Canal flowed around the western side of the city and would probably be impossible to cross if the two bridges that led over it were blown up. We will revisit this problem later.

It may have been because of these difficulties that the desire arose to equip the Fourth Army with a powerful panzer group. The idea was to leave the Liège region alone and to send two powerful groups forward on either side, thereby bringing about a 'catastrophe for the enemy on the Meuse in a manner similar to what had taken place on the Vistula'.[56] The Sixth Army would advance on Ghent and the Fourth Army on Charleroi. Yet would it not just be best to allocate most of the panzer forces to the Fourth Army, thereby creating just one point of main effort which would be on the southern wing? After so many changes, the decision was made that the main attack would indeed be carried out on the southern wing and that it would proceed through the Ardennes. One factor that certainly contributed to the abandonment of the plan

---

[56] Halder's war diary, 25 October 1939.

for a main attack in the north was the fact that a Luftwaffe officer, with maps of the northern plan in his possession, inadvertently landed his aircraft in north-east Belgium.

The constant changes to the operational plan meant that adjustments had to be made to how the XVI Panzer Corps would be used. The main problem was whether the panzer corps would advance through Roermond or Maastricht. It had been discussed whether the panzer corps could avoid this area altogether, but this was unfeasible. It would have involved the abandonment of taking the enemy by surprise in Belgium and Holland. On top of that, the absence of German tanks in the north would have quickly revealed to the enemy that our point of main effort was in the south. The panzer corps therefore remained in the sector of the Sixth Army for an advance through Belgium.

The discussion about whether the panzer troops could avoid the municipality of Maastricht had been sparked off by concerns about the major obstacle that had to be overcome there. This obstacle was the Albert Canal. On Belgian ground, it flowed to the west of the Meuse from Liège to the north and then, just to the north-west of the city of Maastricht, it turned to head in the direction of Antwerp. It was no ordinary canal. Although it had been constructed for economic reasons after World War I, it also served as a defensive line for the north-east region of Belgium. It had been carved deep into the rocky terrain with such steeply sloping embankments that no tank would be able to surmount them. The canal spanned the western and south-western outskirts of the city of Maastricht, and there were only two road bridges that led over it. One was in Vroenhoven and the other in Veldwezelt. If these bridges were blown up, it would take at least four weeks to rebuild them. It would make no difference how hard the pioneer troops worked or how much they prepared the necessary building material beforehand. The German military leadership therefore concentrated at quite an early stage on how to deal with this potential operational difficulty. The problem was raised with Hitler on 28 October 1939, and, on 17 November, Colonel Jodl was beginning to doubt that the bridges over the Albert Canal could be taken by surprise.[57] The planned employment

---

[57] Halder's war diary, 28 October 1939 and 17 November 1939.

of troop-carrying gliders against both bridge sites was assessed as having little chance of success.[58] On 21 November, the question was raised as to whether the XVI Panzer Corps would best be held back at the beginning of the offensive.[59] The idea was rejected at that time, but it was eventually what was done. There can certainly be no doubt that the headaches caused by the Albert Canal are an indication of how good a defensive line it was.

When the offensive began in May 1940, the panzer corps was held in reserve by the Sixth Army. Under the command of the panzer corps were the 3rd Panzer Division and the 20th Motorised Infantry Division. The 1st Panzer Division had been taken away from the panzer corps and was committed elsewhere. The 4th Panzer Division was at the front and was initially subordinate to the IV Army Corps. The task of the 4th Panzer Division would be to relieve the special assault squads that had been sent ahead to seize Maastricht and the two bridges over the canal. Should the bridges be taken intact, the panzer corps would roll forward through Maastricht and drive in the direction of Nivelles (30 kilometres south of Brussels). Should the bridges *not* be taken, the panzer corps would be detached from the Sixth Army and transferred to the south, in the zone of Army Group A, to partake in the main attack.

The ever-changing operational plans and the slippery date of the offensive did not help to inspire the confidence of the troops. The men became anxious due to the frequency with which their training was interrupted. They were almost paralysed by the constant need to be ready for action. Periods of leave could hardly be granted, even though the troops were very much in need of time off. Furthermore, the Rhineland was very wet in the autumn of 1939, with rain and mist prevailing in November and December. Many of the roads and paths that the troops would use to approach the front were covered with pools of water. One of the main roads to be used by the 3rd Panzer Division ran along the Rur Valley. It was flooded for a long time and

---

[58] The gliders were supposed to drop off troops without noise at the bridge sites at dawn.
[59] Halder's war diary, 21 November 1939.

could not be circumvented. The river that flowed through the assembly area of the panzer corps always carried high water. Constant surveillance near the border was necessary under such circumstances. With such muddy ground, vehicles could barely move through the terrain. The use of the panzer troops in battle would be severely limited, if not impossible.[60] The few hours of brightness during the winter days would reduce the prospects of a successful campaign to a minimum. While there were only six hours of daylight in December, there was three times that amount in May and June! He who wants to bring about a decisive battle and has even just a rudimentary understanding of what it would entail would know that only in the rarest of cases could six hours offer chances of victory. Even if the enemy suffers a defeat, it is usually only after a period of six hours of battle that the situation can be properly exploited, be it the pursuit of the fleeing enemy or the destruction of remaining groups of resistance. The more time that is available for such exploitation, the greater the magnitude of the victory. It is daylight that provides this time. An advance into darkness, even with well-trained troops, is risky and can only have a chance of success against a demoralised enemy. General Hoepner, while in Düsseldorf, had clearly articulated the hopelessness and impossibility of the winter offensive operation proposed by Hitler. We would, on the one hand, be giving the enemy all the advantages. He would be fighting on his own territory, and the weather would help him with his defence. All we would be giving our troops, on the other hand, was a multitude of difficulties.

(b) The advance into Belgium

1. The initial fighting

On the morning of 10 May 1940, the day on which the offensive in the west began, the XVI Panzer Corps was on standby rather than in action, for the manner in which it would be employed would depend on the development of the situation around the Albert Canal. The headquarters

---

[60] There were similar problems caused by the weather in the area of Army Group A (Manstein, *Verlorene Siege*, 63).

of the panzer corps was on that day shifted from Düsseldorf to Rheydt, which was also where the headquarters of the Sixth Army was located. The operation carried out by the paratroopers and troop-carrying gliders against the two bridges over the canal ran smoothly. Both bridges fell into our hands. In contrast, the seizure of the bridges over the Meuse in Maastricht was a failure. The assault squads that had been sent ahead of the panzer corps saw these bridges blown sky-high right before their eyes. There was only passive resistance in the Dutch municipality of Maastricht, but it was well-prepared. On the Belgian side of the border, though, there was active resistance. Uncertainty reigned on the morning of 10 May as to whether the 4th Panzer Division, the only unit of the panzer corps that was in action, would manage to relieve the troops that had landed and established bridgeheads over the Albert Canal before they were struck by Belgian counter-attacks. The panzer division arrived in time. In the course of the day, both bridgeheads were expanded and united. On the night of 10/11 May, a military bridge was built over the Meuse in the city of Maastricht. From 0530 hours, enough reinforcements flowed into the expanded bridgehead so that any Belgian counter-attacks could be repelled. By 1600 hours, German troops had thrust further and had captured the city of Tongeren. The panzer brigade of the panzer division pushed beyond the road that connected Sint-Truiden and Liège, thereby denying the enemy the ability to use this road.

The promising developments of the day led to the decision to employ the XVI Panzer Corps as originally intended. It assumed responsibility for the bridgehead to the west of Maastricht and was to send the 3rd Panzer Division, the 4th Panzer Division, and the 20th Motorised Infantry Division against the deep flank of the enemy. The general direction of advance would be towards Gembloux and Nivelles, with the first objective to be aimed for being the high ground where the Tienen–Huy road was situated. It became increasingly clear on 11 May that Belgian resistance was broken. Both France and England had promised to support Belgium, and their motorised columns were on the way from the south-west. We could expect that these forces would man the Dyle Position, a prepared defensive front which ran along the west bank of the Dyle southwards from Leuven to Wavre and from there along the Wavre–Gembloux–Namur road. Approximately 10 kilometres to the east of this well-built line of fortifications was a parallel line of anti-tank obstacles. However, when hostilities broke out, there were still a number of gaps in this parallel line. Our aerial reconnaissance spotted the enemy motorised columns occupying the Dyle Position on 11 May, as expected, but there were some units that continued to the north-east to try and plug the gaps.

This was the situation faced by the commander of the panzer corps on the evening of 11 May. He was by then at the command post of the panzer corps, which had been set up at the barracks of the Royal Netherlands Marechaussee in Maastricht. It was his view that the French and English forces proceeding to the north-east of the Dyle Position were planning to absorb the remaining Belgian forces and slow down the German advance. The approaching enemy probably included the French Cavalry Corps. It consisted of two motorised or mechanised divisions, and it was roughly an equal match for the panzer corps in terms of training and equipment. It was an elite unit of the French Army. How would the encounter between the panzer corps and the cavalry corps go? The main line of attack of the panzer corps was in the direction of Gembloux, towards the south-west, and the halfway point was the city of Hannut. The junction there was the first objective of the panzer corps, and it also lay halfway between Tienen and Huy. Hoepner assigned the 4th Panzer Division the task of reaching Hannut on 12 May, but it was not to involve itself in combat with the enemy until the 3rd Panzer Division had caught up. We needed both panzer divisions to coordinate their efforts in any attack against the enemy! Hoepner wanted the 3rd Panzer Division to be ready on the morning of 12 May, but there were a number of delays which meant that it would not be prepared to attack until the early hours of 13 May. It was of the utmost importance that the 4th Panzer Division avoid combat with the entire cavalry corps on its own. It was permitted to conduct reconnaissance, but it could do nothing else other than secure the line of advance of the 3rd Panzer Division to Hannut.

The suspected conduct of the enemy played an important role in General Hoepner's decision to choose Hannut as an objective. If the enemy were to risk a meeting engagement, he could not easily arrange his forces to the north-east of the city. He would already be aware of the German advance through Tongeren, but we had less knowledge of precisely from which direction he would come. If he wanted to await our advance from a forward line of security, this security line would have to be at least as far in front of the anti-tank line as the anti-tank line was in front of the Dyle Position in order to be effective. Either way, we could anticipate that any security line would be near or just a little to the west of Hannut. Contact with the enemy was likely to occur on 12 May, but he was still better prepared than we were on that day. It was for that reason that the 4th Panzer Division had been warned to avoid combat to begin with. General Hoepner accompanied the panzer division so that he could form an impression of the situation and intervene if need be. The plan for the 3rd Panzer Division was to place it to the north of the 4th Panzer Division, for it would be able to arrive there more quickly and would have more room to manoeuvre.

2. *The tank battle of Hannut*

It was clear on the morning of 12 May that the 3rd Panzer Division was going to be delayed and that the 4th Panzer Division would be on its own for the time being. The 4th Panzer Division would have to restrict its activities to reconnaissance, determining the best location where the entire panzer corps could attack the following day. The fact that there were at that moment no enemy forces in the immediate vicinity had to be exploited, but it would still be necessary to await the 3rd Panzer Division before a full-scale advance could get underway.

The panzer brigade of the 4th Panzer Division rolled forward and reached Hannut at 0730 hours. The weak enemy forces in and to the south-east of the city retreated immediately. From the north-west, hostile tanks attacked throughout the morning. German tanks clashed with the enemy, with the fighting gradually increasing in intensity. By noon, the enemy had been hurled back and had disappeared somewhere to the north-west. The panzer brigade seemed to be victorious, but its consumption of fuel and ammunition had been considerable. Its readiness to be used again was therefore limited. It was vulnerable at that moment and urgently needed to be resupplied. Aerial deliveries of fuel helped somewhat, but ammunition was still lacking. In Hannut, General Hoepner agreed with the decision of the panzer brigade not to pursue the enemy to the north-west, especially as it was not the direction in which the 4th Panzer Division was supposed to advance. The area to the north-west would instead be the attack sector of the 3rd Panzer Division. It was more important for the 4th Panzer Division to conduct combat reconnaissance in its own attack sector, which would be towards the south-west. The enemy's combat outposts had been driven out of Hannut, but it was probable that they had retreated to positions not too far to the south-west. Reconnaissance units set off in that direction in the late afternoon. Encountering artillery and anti-tank fire on the outskirts of the next village, they soon returned to Hannut. Yet the reconnaissance mission had achieved its objective. The location of the enemy's line of resistance had been found. We had also ascertained that this line was manned by the French 3rd Light Mechanised Division, a unit of the cavalry corps.

The enemy had chosen defence over offence. He had additional forces positioned on the south bank of the Mehaigne, a left tributary of the Meuse. The security line extended from there far to the east, on the flank of our line of advance. These additional forces probably belonged to another division of the cavalry corps. Aside from carrying out a few minor assaults over the river, their conduct was passive. Nevertheless, enemy tanks had been spotted moving into position behind the river.

The fighting that had taken place that day strengthened Hoepner's belief that a rapid thrust with both panzer divisions in the direction of Gembloux was the correct course of action. The terrain on either side of Hannut seemed suitable for tanks. An attack against the enemy forces to the south would be pointless. Given the strength and preparedness of the enemy, a concentrated attack by both panzer divisions would offer the best chances of success. The commander of the 4th Panzer Division was concerned about what effect an attack by the enemy tanks from the south might have, but General Hoepner did not share this concern. The southern flank of the panzer corps would have to manage with the available anti-tank defences. If the enemy forces further north, to the west of Hannut, could be destroyed in one powerful panzer strike, a French attack from the south, even if it achieved some initial success, would barely be threatening. It was not certain at that stage whether the southern enemy would even launch an attack. The point of main effort of the attack of the panzer corps would lie in the sector of the 3rd Panzer Division. This attack was to be carried out as early in the morning as possible. The 4th Panzer Division would time the commencement of its advance to coincide with that of the approaching 3rd Panzer Division.

Both panzer divisions attacked with all their might on 13 May. Four panzer regiments with a total of approximately 560 tanks penetrated the security line of the 3rd Light Mechanised Division to the west of Hannut at noon. They shattered one counter-attack after another in the enemy's main defensive area and, in conjunction with the motorised infantry, reached the Tienen–Namur railway line before nightfall.[61] It seemed as if enemy resistance had been crushed. The counter-attacks by French tanks had diminished almost entirely. The 3rd Light Mechanised Division had lost approximately 80 tanks, and several of its men had been taken prisoner. More prisoners were taken in the vicinity of the Mehaigne by the 4th Panzer Division. This was where another light mechanised division had been spotted, but it had not, as feared, taken part in the fighting that day.

Encouraged by the progress that had been made on 13 May, the commander of the panzer corps ordered that both panzer divisions would continue their attack to the south-west on 14 May. The 20th Motorised Infantry Division would follow behind the left wing so as to meet any assault by the enemy forces to the south. The Belgian anti-tank line on either side of Perwez would be used to further slow our advance, and it was bound to be reinforced by those French forces that had managed to retreat. Nevertheless, General Hoepner hoped that both panzer divisions would be able to near the Dyle Position in the course of 14 May.

The battle of Hannut on 12 and 13 May was the first major clash that took place during the offensive in the west in 1940. It was also the

---

[61] The details of this battle are contained in an article written by the author in *Wehrkunde*, vol. 9, no. 5 (May 1960), 'Die Panzerschlacht bei Hannut am 12./13. Mai 1940'.

only time in the whole campaign that two evenly matched opponents came up against one another: the French Cavalry Corps under General René Prioux and the German XVI Panzer Corps under General Erich Hoepner. It ended with a German victory, which raises the question as to how, if 'the defensive is the stronger form of conducting war', the cavalry corps was defeated in its seemingly well-prepared security line.[62] The cavalry corps had been in position before our attack had begun. The terrain ought to have been favourable for the enemy. The ground he occupied was at a slightly higher altitude and should have afforded him a good view of our approach. The French were also able to make use of a couple of watercourses for their defence, with the Mehaigne in the south and the Jette in the north, and this was something that had certainly posed quite a challenge for the 3rd Panzer Division in the first phase of its attack. However, the enemy lacked any natural obstacles to the west and south-west of Hannut. This was the attack sector of the 4th Panzer Division. The French tanks had often been able to conceal themselves prior to launching their counter-attacks, but, once they revealed themselves, the German tanks always stopped them with fire before outflanking and destroying them. Although the enemy was courageous in carrying out these counter-attacks, it was an approach that failed miserably. The concentration of both panzer brigades against a single point was what proved decisive. They established local superiority against the 3rd Light Mechanised Division, the one formation that the French had in action. The 2nd Light Mechanised Division had largely remained in its initial position to the south of the Mehaigne. It had taken no part whatsoever in the fighting of 13 May. The reason for this is that the leadership of the cavalry corps felt that its freedom of movement was limited. General Prioux had been explicitly instructed not to endanger the cavalry corps in serious combat to the east of the Dyle Position. He had therefore intended to withdraw from the security line on the evening of 13 May and had not taken advantage of the opportunity to strike the southern flank of the panzer corps.

---

[62] The quote is from Clausewitz, *On War*, book 6, chapter 1.

In addition to the restricted utilisation of the cavalry corps, a particular tactical disadvantage for the French was the wide dispersal of the forces of the 3rd Light Mechanised Division along the security line. Even the individual tanks themselves were widely spread out. This meant that they could easily counter-attack anywhere, but any attempt to concentrate them, if at all possible, would take too much time. It was too late by the time the 3rd Light Mechanised Division, the bravery of whose leadership ought to be recognised, sought to gather together its forces. It fell back on its hindquarters and was helpless against the united German panzer attack. Our decision at the outset to concentrate our forces proved to be decisive. The battle of Hannut was therefore one of the greatest victories of the panzer arm. We had employed our tanks swiftly and skilfully and at the right moment.

3.   *The attack against the Dyle Position*

In contrast to the events before and during the battle of Hannut, the advance against the Dyle Position would be a far greater challenge for the troops of the panzer corps. They would be conducting an attack against a truly solid defensive position. We were aware that this position had been expanded recently and that it would be occupied by the enemy. The attack against it would need to be highly systematic. We would have to prepare carefully and would need to determine beforehand how we were going to neutralise or eliminate the enemy's means of dampening our attack. His defensive means would include artillery, emplacements, obstacles, mines, reserves, and much more. Our attack front would have to be of such strength and of such combat preparedness that it would be not just a match for but rather superior to the enemy. This would demand that reconnaissance be carried out, that the enemy be observed, that our troops move into position, and that all our units be topped up with ammunition. All these measures would require time! After the troops reached their positions, it was expected that they would need approximately 24 hours to be fully prepared for storming the Dyle Position.

The commander of the panzer corps could be satisfied with the result of the fighting of 13 May. Many tanks had been captured, and several men were taken prisoner. There was no longer any threat to the south. The 2nd Light Mechanised Division had abandoned its positions overnight and was retreating towards the Dyle. It was important that we pursue this fleeing enemy. This was our task for 14 May. We would have to punch through the anti-tank line and destroy the new line of resistance that we suspected the cavalry corps was creating behind it. And we did so with tremendous success! Although the enemy delayed our advance and caused difficulties with our flow of supplies, our ability to overcome the anti-tank line reinforced the confidence of the troops. It was clear that the enemy had been significantly weakened by the force of our attack. We would want to maintain the momentum we had built up when storming the Dyle Position. General Hoepner initially thought that, while the troops would be able to approach the Dyle Position, there would be too few hours of daylight remaining for reconnaissance to be conducted and attack preparations to be made. These activities, he thought, would have to be carried out on 15 May, meaning that the attack on the enemy position would be earmarked for 16 May. Yet the divisional commanders did not want to wait that long. The 4th Panzer Division in particular pushed for the immediate continuation of the attack. It had already reached the Dyle Position to the north of Gembloux and had forced enemy tanks and outpost troops to retreat. The commander of the panzer division therefore wanted the assault against the enemy position to commence on the morning of 15 May. Elements of the divisional artillery had arrived throughout the afternoon, and the rest were not far off. General Hoepner was increasingly convinced that delaying the attack by 24 hours would be unnecessary, especially as the troops themselves were eager to press on. The Sixth Army was also optimistic about our prospects and urged for the continuation of the attack. Hoepner therefore ordered that the panzer corps would storm the enemy position on the morning of 15 May.

As expected, the fighting along the Dyle Position was fierce. It lasted the whole day on 15 May, and even into the night in the northern sector. The French line of resistance mostly followed the Leuven–Gembloux railway line. It had been skilfully laid out and was well-built, making excellent use of the terrain. Our tanks and motorised infantry were frequently unable to detect the defenders until they were within close

range. The destructive fire of enemy artillery and anti-tank guns
slowed down the attacking forces considerably as they attempted to
cross the Wavre–Gembloux road, which lay a little in front of the
Dyle Position. Stukas and German artillery were supposed to destroy
the enemy artillery, but this did not come to pass. The result was that
our attack was brought to a standstill. There were a few spots to the
north of Gembloux where we had penetrated the enemy position, and
the 3rd Panzer Division had made some good progress, but the major
breakthrough we had hoped for, despite the bravery of our troops,
did not occur.

In hindsight, it can be said that there had not been enough time the
previous day to properly prepare for what would clearly be a difficult
attack. The 4th Panzer Division had carried out an assault that was
more well-coordinated than that of its northern neighbour, but the
unfavourable terrain in its sector put it at a disadvantage from the very
beginning. The fortress of Gembloux protruded to the east. It thereby
restricted and slightly outflanked the advance of the panzer division,
which was stopped dead when it reached the railway line. The fighting
deteriorated into a number of small skirmishes that went back and
forth. German casualties were high. Our troops, attempting as they
were to advance on flat terrain, were vulnerable against the French
artillery. We feared for some time that the commander of the panzer
brigade of the 4th Panzer Division had been killed by enemy artillery
fire whilst leading the attack. His vehicle was hit, and his body was
unable to be found. Only in the evening, long after nightfall, did he
manage to return to ground under German control. The panzer brigade
had in the meantime been ordered to retreat by the panzer division.
The withdrawal had been slow and had been exposed to enemy fire
the whole time. In recognition that little progress had been made, that
casualties had been heavy, and that few reserves were available, the 4th
Panzer Division ordered the cessation of the attack shortly before noon.
General Hoepner declared that the attack would not be renewed until
its execution had been planned carefully.

An organised and united attack failed to take place in the sector
of the 3rd Panzer Division. The tanks had been held back whilst the
motorised infantry sought to create holes in the enemy defensive line.

The tanks were then to punch through those holes. Unfortunately, the infantry attack disintegrated, and the Stuka and artillery support that had been anticipated did not materialise. Then, towards noon, the infantry attacked again and were able to set foot in Perbais, pushing the enemy out of the village. Our troops were surrounded there, but they held on to the ground they had taken. It was much later when the reserve battalion of the panzer division arrived with a panzer company under its command, with the task of taking the village of Ernage, which lay just to the south of Perbais. The seizure of Ernage would hopefully enable contact to be made with the 4th Panzer Division. Our troops persevered with the utmost courage against the heavy enemy defensive fire and succeeded in taking the village. They pushed further to the west, going through Cortil-Noirmont and reaching the high ground that lay beyond. These troops had therefore achieved a breakthrough that extended 4 kilometres into the enemy's main defensive area. The enemy launched waves of powerful counter-attacks, supported by tanks, against the southern flank of the battalion before nightfall. They all failed due to the bold measures taken by the commander of the III Battalion of the 3rd Rifle Regiment. He did the best he could to maintain a firm hold of the position that had been reached. Elements of the II Battalion of the 3rd Rifle Regiment had arrived to secure the northern wing, while the 6th Panzer Regiment had sent forward reinforcements that were able to help repel the French counter-attacks from the south.[63]

The 3rd Panzer Division had made unexpectedly good progress on 15 May, but it soon ordered that the advance come to a stop. It had become dark in the meantime, so any further push was unlikely to succeed. It would have been too much to demand of the exhausted troops that they continue fighting into the night. Nevertheless, the panzer division saw to it that the rest of its motorised infantry and artillery moved forward overnight so that they would be able to support the renewed advance in the morning. When the commander of the III

---

[63] Good descriptions of the individual battles along the Dyle Position are contained in Colonel (ret.) Hermann Zimmermann, *Der Griff ins Ungewisse* (Neckargemünd: Vowinckel, 1964).

Battalion of the 3rd Rifle Regiment became aware of the divisional order to halt, he withdrew his forces to the high ground east of Cortil-Noirmont in order to create a better defensive front against the enemy counter-attacks he expected would take place after dawn. After this small withdrawal was completed after midnight, the fighting died down and the battalion commander went to the regimental command post to give his report.

Those at the command post initially found it hard to believe that the III Battalion had advanced so far into enemy territory. The brigade and divisional headquarters were also surprised. They had given up too soon on the idea that the attack would succeed, probably because their left-hand neighbour, the 4th Panzer Division, had already come to a standstill. They had decided that the attack would only be renewed once careful preparations had been made. The III Battalion had still been advancing at the time this decision was made, following the request that had been made by General Hoepner in the afternoon for the exploitation of the success at Perbais. Elements of the 6th Panzer Regiment had arrived in Ernage in the afternoon and had taken many prisoners, and it was the III Battalion of the 3rd Rifle Regiment that had been trying to take full advantage of the situation for the purpose of achieving a decisive breakthrough. Yet the brigade and divisional headquarters were by then probably considering going over to the defensive. A momentary breakthrough had in fact been achieved, but the headquarters of the panzer corps, despite its frequent requests for news, only found out about it the following morning. General Hoepner did not at that time reproach the 3rd Panzer Division for its conduct. After the failure of the attack, he had to focus on its renewal in the entire area of the panzer corps. This renewed attack had to be planned carefully, a view also taken by the Sixth Army, for it had not pushed forward to any appreciable degree on any of its other fronts. But General Hoepner was clearly dissatisfied with the 3rd Panzer Division. When the commander of the Sixth Army expressed his intention of awarding the divisional commander the Knight's Cross of the Iron Cross in recognition of the successful breakthrough, General Hoepner requested that it be given instead to the commander of the III Battalion of the 3rd Rifle Regiment, as it was the battalion commander himself who had performed well and achieved the success. None of this is to say that the divisional commander was not highly capable. He would receive the Knight's Cross later in the war.[64]

The situation on the morning of 16 May proved to be quite a surprise. Reconnaissance units of the panzer corps could find no evidence that the enemy was present. He must have withdrawn under cover of darkness. General Hoepner immediately ordered that the enemy be pursued along the entire front of the panzer corps. Reinforced reconnaissance units and advance detachments were to be sent ahead, while the 20th Motorised Infantry Division would be brought forward at once to the area near and to the south of Gembloux. This division, whose commander was to report to the corps command post as soon as possible, had thus far been on standby and was now to be employed on the southern wing of the front of the panzer corps. The 4th Panzer Division had borne the brunt of the fighting the previous day, so Hoepner visited its headquarters to discuss the situation with its commander. It had to be decided whether it could still be utilised at the front for now or whether it would best be placed in reserve.

The advance forces of the panzer corps moved forward throughout the day. On the northern wing was the 35th Infantry Division. It had been positioned there in the early hours of 16 May and placed under the command of the panzer corps. The original intention was that it would help with the assault against the Dyle Position, but it now partook in the advance. On its left was the 3rd Panzer Division, and further to the left was the 4th Panzer Division, which, it was decided, would remain at the front. On the southern wing was the 20th Motorised Infantry Division. There was barely any resistance to begin with. Only a few obstacles and mines were encountered. After an advance of approximately 10 kilometres beyond the Dyle Position, heavy fighting broke out. It was likely that we were dealing with rearguard units, and it was not long before they were hurled back. By the evening, the northern and central sectors of the panzer corps

---

[64] Translator's note: The commander of the 3rd Panzer Division during the invasion of France was Major-General Horst Stumpff. He was eventually awarded the Knight's Cross on 29 September 1941.

reached the Brussels–Charleroi road, and we had managed to maintain contact with the neighbouring units on the right and left. The objective for 17 May would be the canal that connected Brussels and Charleroi. Enemy forces could be expected behind this canal. It was only now that our advance was truly in motion. All the troops pressed forward and were able, against increasing resistance, to reach the canal. Some of them even arrived there in the early morning. On the northern wing, Nivelles was occupied by the 35th Infantry Division. This city had been the first operational objective of the panzer corps that day. By the evening, all four divisions had set foot on the opposite bank of the canal. There was much discussion throughout the day between the Sixth Army and the XVI Panzer Corps as to whether the attack ought to continue towards the west (in the direction of Ath) or the south-west (in the direction of Mons and Binche). It was then in the late afternoon that the panzer corps received the order that it was to be withdrawn from the front and employed elsewhere. It would be relieved by the formation to its south, the XXVII Army Corps, while the 35th Infantry Division, remaining where it was, would be subordinated once more to the formation on the northern side, the IV Army Corps. The relief of the panzer corps was planned to begin on the night of 17/18 May, and its departure was planned for the morning of 19 May. The panzer corps would then be detached from the Sixth Army, a formation with which it had always worked so well and in such a comradely fashion.

(c) The advance on Flanders

1. *The transfer of the XVI Panzer Corps*

The panzer units of Army Group A, after they had forced the crossing of the Meuse in the Charleville–Sedan sector, had entered open French terrain on 16 and 17 May and were driving towards the coast of the English Channel, the ultimate objective of the operation! The OKH wanted this attack to possess the utmost striking power. The army group had to thrust into France, pivot to the north, drive to the coast, and encircle and annihilate the bulk of the English, French, and Belgian forces. In the process, the army group would need to secure its southern flank, which would mostly run along the Somme. Given that the success of the entire campaign depended upon the rapidity of movement of the southern wing, all the mobile forces would need to be concentrated there, as had been foreseen in the operational plan. The infantry alone would not be fast enough. Even the panzer formations in Belgium and Holland would need to be shifted to the decisive wing. This meant that the XVI Panzer Corps had to be relocated, although the headquarters of the Sixth Army was not particularly happy about this. Without the panzer corps in its sector, the fighting in Belgium would most likely progress more slowly. It might possibly favour the defensive efforts of the Western Powers. The French Cavalry Corps would be able to master the situation along its security line to the west of Hannut, and the Anglo–French front, which ran along the Dyle and stretched all the way to Antwerp, would probably be capable of resisting any assaults carried out by the German infantry. The Western Powers might thereby be able to maintain a deep operational field for conducting their defence. Only if this operational depth were to be lost would the enemy be forced into a narrow bridgehead, and this was what eventually happened at Dunkirk.

However, these larger operational questions and ideas are not the focus of this study. The operational use of the XVI Panzer Corps by the OKH is the centre of attention here, for it highlights quite clearly the many ways in which the panzer arm could be employed. It is worth noting that General Hoepner had been in favour of remaining in the sector of the Sixth Army for the time being. The panzer corps had demonstrated in Belgium how the panzer arm was superior to the infantry in terms of achieving penetrative power. It would have been a mistake at that moment to reposition the panzer corps behind the main attack wing, where it could very well have been left unexploited.

Yet what decision was taken? The OKH reserves were to be sent behind the main attack wing! It was early on 19 May that the panzer corps started to move southwards. Its task was to make contact with the left envelopment wing, Panzer Group Kleist (with the XXXXI and XIX Panzer Corps). The panzer group had crossed westwards over the Oise the previous day, its southern wing had occupied Saint-Quentin, and it was now striving to reach Arras and Péronne (on the Somme).

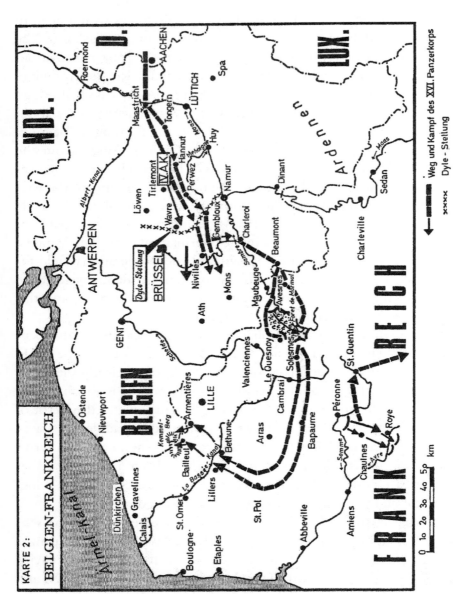

Map 2: Belgium and France

The distance from there to the coast of the English Channel was still approximately 100 kilometres! When the XVI Panzer Corps crossed the Sambre near and to the east of Charleroi, it came under the command of the Fourth Army (Colonel-General Günther von Kluge). Crossing the river proved to be difficult, so it was just the 4th Panzer Division that did so in the first instance. It went through Charleroi and Beaumont in the direction of Avesnes, which lay on the French side of the border. The 20th Motorised Infantry Division crossed the river to the east of Charleroi and followed the right wing of the 4th Panzer Division. The 3rd Panzer Division could only set off on the morning of 20 May, and it went along the same road that had been used by the 4th Panzer Division. The headquarters of the panzer corps had already been relocated to Sars-Poteries, which lay 7 kilometres to the north-east of Avesnes.

The panzer corps crossed paths with the front wave of the infantry divisions of the Fourth Army. They were following the panzer forces of the same army and were attempting to reach the battlefront that lay roughly along the Valenciennes–Cambrai line. They were also mopping up any remaining pockets of resistance along the way. The XV Panzer Corps (General Hermann Hoth) had crossed the Meuse at Dinant, driven through the terrain on which we now stood, and was at that moment in combat to the north-west of Cambrai. The 5th Panzer Division (of the XV Panzer Corps) had briefly captured Maubeuge, but the old French fortress had been retaken by the enemy once the panzer division had moved on. The fortress was conquered once more on 19 May, this time by the VIII Army Corps. A few forts on the front to the north and the north-west held out a little longer. They capitulated on 20 May. Only in the Forêt de Mormal, a large forested region to the west of Maubeuge and Avesnes, did there remain a strong enemy presence. The enemy forces there probably consisted of two North African divisions. The Fourth Army did not want its infantry to be delayed. It therefore ordered that its VIII Army Corps bypass the forest to the north and its II Army Corps to the south. On the evening of 19 May, the Fourth Army gave the XVI Panzer Corps the task of eliminating the enemy forces in the forest, mainly with the 4th Panzer Division. We were being asked to deal with an impenetrable area that was thickly populated with trees and brushwood. Only infantry forces would be capable of combing through the area quickly. Tanks would hardly be of use there. The 3rd Panzer Division and the 20th Motorised Infantry Division therefore had to be brought forward on 20 May so that all the infantry elements of the panzer corps could be employed for the difficult task. Fortunately, the 8th Infantry Division (of the VIII Army Corps) arrived on 21 May and was ordered to march through the forest from the north-east to the south-west, a distance of approximately 15 kilometres. Parts of the 3rd and 4th Panzer Divisions were to conduct a reconnaissance of the terrain further to the west as far as the Canal de l'Escaut, which connected Valenciennes and Cambrai. The mopping-up operation was carried out on 22 May and was finished in the afternoon, although not necessarily thoroughly. There were not many prisoners.

General Hoepner opposed the shift of the panzer corps to the western operational wing. It was being carried out because the German military leadership had become concerned about the danger to the outer flank, but Hoepner saw it as a delay of three or more days in which his troops were being used for a task for which they were ill-suited. What was supposed to be a swiftly executed sideways movement had become a wasteful utilisation of panzer forces. The panzer corps was merely a tool for the Fourth Army and was exploited most ineffectively. Most of the enemy forces in the Forêt de Mormal escaped detection. The lesson to be drawn here is that such a task requires considerable time and ought to be conducted by the infantry.

The commander of the panzer corps consulted with the headquarters of the Fourth Army while the forest operation was still underway. He managed to obtain its approval for the assembly of both panzer divisions to the south-west of the forest in the late afternoon of 22 May so that they would be able to attack to the west early on 23 May. The 20th Motorised Infantry Division was still being employed elsewhere and had, unfortunately, been detached from the panzer corps. While the panzer divisions were still in the process of being assembled in the area of Le Quesnoy and Solesmes (west of the Forêt de Mormal) on the evening of 22 May, the panzer corps faced the prospect of its forces being weakened further. An armoured attack had been launched by the English on 21 May.

Heading southwards from Arras, it had taken the 7th Panzer Division (of the XV Panzer Corps) by surprise and was attempting to push eastwards towards Cambrai on 22 May. That evening, the commander of the Fourth Army was considering sending the XVI Panzer Corps westwards from the area south of Cambrai towards Bapaume (to the south of Arras). General Hoepner spoke with Colonel-General von Kluge over the telephone and was told that a reinforced rifle regiment of the 4th Panzer Division might be left behind in the vicinity west of Solesmes in case the English managed to push as far as Cambrai. Depending on how the situation developed overnight, the commander of the Fourth Army stated that it might still be possible to dispatch the entire panzer division to Bapaume. The situation certainly must have been confusing for the Fourth Army that night.[65] At one point we were informed that the regiment would have to remain behind; at a later point we were notified that the whole panzer division would be allowed to set off. At dawn, the panzer division was preparing to roll forward. Advance detachments were already on their way to Bapaume. It was at that moment that a radio message was received from the headquarters of the Fourth Army. The reinforced rifle regiment was once more ordered to stay behind. What were we to do? We had lost telephone and radio contact with the panzer division. I drove off in an armoured car with the authority to stop some of the elements of the panzer division. It was a slow drive through the assembly area of the panzer division, but I reached one of the departure points where, fortunately, the divisional commander was to be found. I was able to convey the order to him just in time, but, when I returned to the headquarters of the panzer corps, General Hoepner greeted me with the words: 'Well, it gets to march once more!' He was referring to the regiment that had just been told to stay where it was. It had been a complicated and critical situation. General Hoepner did not want to see his panzer corps split up into smaller components, although it can also be understood that Colonel-General von Kluge had been

---

[65] It turned out that the fighting to the south of Arras was already under control on 22 May. The English and French measures were poorly coordinated, and the situation there was soon to be resolved in our favour.

concerned about the possibility of an enemy attack prising open a gap in the front of the Fourth Army.

2. Over the La Bassée Canal to Kemmel

The advance of both panzer divisions to the area of Bapaume took place without further interference from friend or foe. They arrived there in the course of the morning, and the headquarters of the panzer corps was shifted to Achiet-le-Grand, 6 kilometres to the west of Bapaume. We received an urgent order in the afternoon to the effect that the panzer corps was to pivot to the north-west as soon as possible and head in the direction of Saint-Pol. The panzer divisions had already stopped for rest and resupply, so we decided that the time of their departure would be at 0315 hours on 24 May. Road reconnaissance units would set off in advance. The temporary objective of the 4th Panzer Division would be Avesnes-le-Comte (20 kilometres west of Arras), and that of the 3rd Panzer Division Saint-Pol (30 kilometres north-west of Arras). After issuing these orders, General Hoepner left in the late afternoon with the corps troops and positioned the headquarters of the panzer corps in Brias (4 kilometres north of Saint-Pol). He wanted to obtain for himself a picture of the situation where the rest of the panzer corps was soon to arrive. General staff officers from both panzer divisions were ordered to Brias early on 24 May so that they could be appraised of the situation and assigned new objectives.

The panzer corps moved into the new attack front that was being formed. The Allied forces in the north had been encircled and were about to be put out of their misery. The line of encirclement on the western side ran from La Bassée along the La Bassée Canal through Béthune, Aire, and Saint-Omer, and finally to the coast of the English Channel in the vicinity of Gravelines. The panzer corps was assigned an attack sector 20 kilometres in width, extending eastwards from Béthune to the zone north-west of Lillers. To the left of the XVI Panzer Corps was the XXXXI Panzer Corps (General Georg-Hans Reinhardt), which was under the command of Panzer Group Kleist. The only unit initially in the sector allocated to the XVI Panzer Corps was SS Division Totenkopf.[66]

---

[66] SS Division Totenkopf was a motorised infantry division.

On the opposite side of the canal were English forces seeking to defend the southern part of the Dunkirk pocket.

The leading elements of the 3rd and 4th Panzer Divisions arrived at the front on 24 May and positioned themselves to either side of the SS division. The former was near Lillers and the latter near Béthune, and they started to explore the best points at which to cross the canal. Preparations for the attack were made on 25 May. English forces attempted that day to apply some pressure against both wings of the front of the panzer corps. Hostile tanks appeared before the 4th Panzer Division. Once our artillery assembled on 26 May and were topped up with ammunition, the final preparations were complete. The main attack was earmarked for early on 27 May, but preparatory raids were launched by the 4th Panzer Division and the SS division on 26 May at 2200 hours with the purpose of constructing bridges over the canal under cover of darkness. The raiding parties pushed far enough across the canal in order to secure the crossings.

The panzer formations on the western and south-western sides of the large pocket (Dunkirk, Lille, Diksmuide, Nieuwpoort) rolled forward early on 27 May. On the southern, eastern, and north-eastern sides, the infantry units of the Fourth and Sixth Armies pressed forward. The XVI Panzer Corps was to attack towards the north-east with the objective of arriving on either side of Armentières. General Hoepner had the command post of the panzer corps placed in the village of Hinges, from where he had a good view of the surrounding terrain. The village stood on high ground with the canal far below immediately to the north and east. The entire attack sector on the northern side of the canal could be seen. Nobody could possibly wish for a more ideal command post!

English resistance was tough. The terrain was filled with hedges and ditches, and the fighting soon split up into numerous skirmishes around villages, farmsteads, and small woods. Progress was slow. We had to fight tooth and nail for every inch of ground. The 4th Panzer Division pushed forward approximately 14 kilometres that day. SS Division Totenkopf was a little further behind, but it managed to take Vieille-Chapelle. The 3rd Panzer Division was temporarily placed under the command of the formation on the left, the XXXXI Panzer

Corps, so that a united effort could be made to advance through the Forêt de Nieppe, an extensive forested region. The panzer division was once more subordinated to the XVI Panzer Corps on 28 May. The enemy's resistance then diminished slightly. We could see that he was taking a few steps backwards. The Sixth Army was approaching from the north-east, so we had to take care to ensure that German forces did not fire at one another. For that reason, a change in the direction of advance of the XVI Panzer Corps was ordered. It was to pivot to the north and proceed on either side of Bailleul towards Kemmelberg, which rose high above the surrounding flat terrain. The 251st Infantry Division was at that moment placed under the command of the panzer corps. This would enable the densely populated area to be combed through properly without holding back the panzer divisions.

Armentières was occupied by the 4th Panzer Division on 29 May. The panzer division remained there and slightly to the south while the IV Army Corps approached from the east. This sealed the fate of the French forces in the industrial area of Lille and Roubaix. The army corps took Kemmelberg from the east, while the panzer corps, going through Bailleul, established contact with the army corps from the south. With the south-eastern corner of the enemy pocket sliced off, the forces there soon surrendered. Mopping-up operations were conducted on 30 May, and the panzer corps, with its two panzer divisions, was from that point withdrawn from the fighting around the Dunkirk pocket. The 3rd Panzer Division returned to Lillers, whilst the 4th Panzer Division continued to remain in the vicinity of Armentières, its troops having a well-deserved rest.

The encirclement and destruction of the Allied forces in the north had been successful. The panzer arm had been skilfully employed and had clearly been superior to the enemy in combat. It had quickly become apparent that our infantry could not perform well on their own against a strong enemy. They required the support of our tanks. This was demonstrated by the fact that the advance of Army Group B through Belgium proceeded quite slowly after the departure of the XVI Panzer Corps. The debate between Hitler and the OKH regarding whether or not the panzer formations ought to halt before

THE CAMPAIGN IN FRANCE IN 1940 • 95

Dunkirk between 24 and 26 May has been much discussed since the end of World War II.[67] General Halder noted down the following in his war diary on 25 May: 'A complete inversion has taken place. I wanted Army Group A to be the hammer and Army Group B the anvil. Now Army Group B has become the hammer and Army Group A the anvil. Since Army Group B is facing a solid front, we can expect that its advance will be slow and will shed much blood.'[68] Army Group B would only have infantry with which to attack. Their striking power was insufficient. The panzer formations were all in the zone of Army Group A, most of them with Panzer Group Kleist, yet Hitler, it seemed, no longer wanted them to attack.

A remark should be made about the legend of the Halt Order. As is clear from Halder's note in his diary, the OKH wanted to deliver the *coup de grace* against the Dunkirk pocket with the powerful and superior panzer forces from the west. It wanted Army Group A to be the hammer! Hitler, allegedly, wanted to go easy on the use of the panzer forces and therefore preferred that the main strike in the final phase be carried out by the Sixth Army from the east. After much debate from 24–26 May, Hitler finally agreed at noon on 26 May that the attack by the panzer arm could commence from the early hours of 27 May. The participation of the XVI Panzer Corps in this attack has been described.

Did the decision to halt the panzer formations put us at a disadvantage in our efforts to eliminate the Dunkirk pocket? The answer to this question is 'no'. Panzer Group Kleist had been successful thus far against a particularly strong enemy, but its units had become quite dispersed. These units needed to be reorganised and reassembled so as to be able to carry out a sustained and vigorous attack with no setbacks whatsoever. Such

---

[67] On this topic, see the documents that have been compiled in H. A. Jacobsen, *1939–1945: Der Zweite Weltkrieg in Chronik und Dokumenten* (Darmstadt: Wehr und Wissen, 1959), 125–28. Included are entries from the war diaries of the OKW, the OKH, and Army Group A. See also H. A. Jacobsen, *Dünkirchen: Ein Beitrag zur Geschichte des Westfeldzuges 1940* (Neckargemünd: Vowinckel, 1958); in English as *Dunkirk: German Operations in France 1940*, trans. Geoffrey Brooks (Havertown, PA: Casemate, 2019).

[68] Halder's war diary, 25 May 1940.

reorganisation and reassembly had to take place on 25 May and possibly also on 26 May. This was certainly the time required for the XVI Panzer Corps to arrive and reinforce the front. In any case, the attack could barely take place before 27 May, for it was throughout the day on 26 May that strong elements of the army artillery moved into position. It is therefore neither convincing nor correct when General Kurt von Tippelskirch makes the following claim in his book on World War II: 'Hitler's Halt Order allowed the bulk of the British Expeditionary Force to be rescued along with a part of the French forces that had also been encircled. This order has been the subject of intense debate ever since. It is certain that it originated with Hitler, that it was supported by Keitel and Jodl, and that it was opposed unsuccessfully by the commander in chief of the army.'[69] But there was in fact no unnecessary loss of time. The assembly of forces for an attack always requires time, and this was something the commander in chief of the army gained Hitler's approval for.

The campaign in France was being conducted by the OKH. When Hitler gave the order that the panzer formations were to halt temporarily, it was not only an important moment but also the first time he had personally intervened. According to the records of the OKW, the OKH, and Army Group A, the reason for this intervention was an OKH order which foresaw placing the Fourth Army under the command of Army Group B so that it could play a leading role in the final phase of the battle of Dunkirk. The attack from the south was to be coordinated closely with that from the east. The details were to be planned carefully so that German troops would not inadvertently fire at one another. All the men were especially sensitive to this. It had thus been agreed beforehand that Kemmel would be the meeting point between the IV Army Corps and the XVI Panzer Corps, and that there would be constant radio communication between these two formations. Recognition signals and aerial surveillance were also used to good effect. Such measures could be difficult across army group

---

[69] Kurt von Tippelskirch, *Geschichte des zweiten Weltkriegs* (Bonn: Athenäum, 1951), 94. Unfortunately, this claim by Tippelskirch was made too soon. Not all the relevant documents were available to him at the time he wrote it down. Despite this error, his book still provides a good general overview of World War II. Tippelskirch's assumption was, in essence, correct.

boundaries, and it was because of this that the OKH had decided to subordinate the Fourth Army to Army Group B. Hitler learnt of this only on 24 May when he was paying a visit to Army Group A, and it was then that he decided to intervene. It seems that the headquarters of the army group made it clear to Hitler that, although it had wanted time to regroup, it now felt somewhat excluded from the final phase of the battle. The OKH had issued the order to halt as a military necessity before this final phase could be executed. Hitler had approved this. He would have hardly decided on his own that the panzer arm needed time to regroup and to find terrain suitable for continuing the attack. He lacked the understanding and insight necessary for such a decision. But, with the transfer of the Fourth Army, he now felt as if he had been shut out from the details of the decision-making process. His vanity had been injured. He therefore issued his own Halt Order and then cancelled it a few days later.

(d) The attack against the Weygand Line

1. *The attack plans*

The Weygand Line was the French defensive front that had been formed to the south of the terrain through which the panzer thrust had swept. It extended from the coast of the English Channel and joined up with the well-built Maginot Line to the south-east of Longuyon, in Lorraine. It led through the Forest of Argonne, partially along the Aisne, and then along the Somme through Pronne and Abbeville. The French General Maxime Weygand had ordered that the line was to be built with all the means that were available and defended with all the forces that could be gathered. The degree to which construction could be completed would depend on how much time there was before the German onslaught commenced. Towns, villages, and woods along the line were to be held fast. Open areas between those points were to be mined and covered with anti-tank fire. It was General Weygand's plan to put into practice a most important defensive idea: to allow the attacking German tanks through, to separate them from the following German infantry, to counter-attack the German tanks, and to bring the entire German attack to a standstill!

The German attack therefore had to be carried out soon. Each passing day allowed the French more time to enhance the defensive capability of the Weygand Line. Since the panzer formations would have to execute the main strike, they would need to be relieved from their tasks in the north as quickly as possible and redeployed in the south. The moment at which this redeployment was to occur had to be chosen carefully. The panzer arm was still urgently required for the annihilation of the Dunkirk pocket, but it had to be ready for the beginning of the attack in the south, which was planned for 5 June. The OKH handled this well. The greatest possible victory was achieved in the north with the panzer formations, but they were nevertheless ready in time for the assault against the Weygand Line.

Army Groups A and B were to conduct the attack from the north against the Weygand Line. Army Group C stood opposite the Maginot Line and was only to set off once the panzer forces of the other two army groups had penetrated deep into enemy territory and thrust south-eastwards into the rear of the French forces that held the Maginot Line. This thrust into the rear of the last strong enemy bulwark was the main objective of the operation. If carried out successfully, it would determine the outcome of the entire campaign in France in our favour. Under the command of Army Group B were the Fourth and Sixth Armies; under Army Group A were the Ninth, Second, Twelfth, and Sixteenth Armies.[70] The boundary between Army Group B (in the west) and Army Group A (in the east) would be roughly to the north of Soissons. Army Group B was to start its advance on 5 June. Its first objective would be the lower Seine downstream from the confluence with the Oise. Army Group B would therefore be on the other side of the Oise from where the Paris defensive position lay, which stretched around the northern side of the city from the Oise to the Marne. The strongest panzer forces would initially be allocated to Army Group B, and they would attack from three bridgeheads that had already been established over the Somme: the XV Panzer Corps from Abbeville, the XIV Panzer Corps from Amiens, and the XVI Panzer Corps from

---

[70] Translator's note: This was the order in which the formations were lined up from west to east.

Péronne. The infantry would attack between these bridgeheads. The point of main effort of Army Group A would lie with the Twelfth Army to the north-east of Rheims. Panzer Group Guderian stood there in readiness to strike with the XXXIX and XXXXI Panzer Corps. The OKH would reserve for itself the decision as to when Army Group A would roll forward. It wanted to be able to assess the development of the situation in the zone of Army Group B before making this decision. Another important reason why Army Group B would set off first was that its forces would be assembled before those of Army Group A. The route from north to south was shorter in the area of Army Group B. The tentative date for the commencement of the advance of Army Group A was 9 June. When that time came, it was possible that some of the panzer forces of Army Group B might be transferred to Army Group A.

Those involved could certainly sense that the time available for regrouping was short. The XVI Panzer Corps had been withdrawn from the fighting in the vicinity of Dunkirk throughout the day on 31 May. General Hoepner, who, like his staff, had counted on a brief pause, intended to see for himself on 1 June how the fighting was unfolding near Boulogne and Calais. It is hard to imagine why! We were at that time only 80 kilometres away from both places. He and I set off on this reconnaissance trip in an armoured car early on 1 June.[71] Our first destination was Boulogne. Progress was slow through Saint-Omer. Captured Belgian cavalry forces were riding through the town. We changed our plans and headed for Calais. The fighting there had almost drawn to a conclusion. The citadel, along with the rest of the city, was in a sorry state. Stuka raids had caused a lot of damage. The city seemed to be deserted. No civilians were to be seen. No shops were open. We then drove to Boulogne under glorious sunshine. There were several sunken ships in the harbour, and a part of the old city wall had been reduced to rubble. Otherwise, it was rather peaceful in Boulogne. The people were going about their daily activities, and

---

[71] A commander and his chief of staff rarely travelled together. If both men were to be killed at the same time, the leadership of the formation they led would be put at a serious disadvantage.

the German soldiers in the city did not seem to draw any attention. We enjoyed a good breakfast there, something that had not at all been possible in Calais. What could have been better than drinking schnapps after that? General Hoepner was a connoisseur of French cognacs, and he chose on this occasion a Grand Marnier. He was adamant that it was the best liqueur, recalling fondly his time in Metz as a young officer making several trips across the border into France! We then departed Boulogne and made a small detour through Étaples to the well-known resort town of Le Touquet. A number of bathing beauties were on the beach there. After that, we returned to the headquarters of the panzer corps in Béthune.

The god of war had intervened in the meantime. The panzer corps had been ordered to assemble in the bridgehead over the Somme near Péronne, and its headquarters was to be shifted to Combles, a village to the north-west of Péronne. The first general staff officer of the panzer corps had already departed for the new headquarters in the early afternoon. General Hoepner followed early on 2 June. On this day and the next, both panzer divisions drove from Lillers and Armentières via Arras to the new attack front. The 3rd Panzer Division reached the area north of Combles and the 4th Panzer Division that north-east of Péronne. Hoepner visited the commander of the 33rd Infantry Division. This formation currently held the bridgehead and was going to be placed under the command of the panzer corps for the attack. During his visit, Hoepner took the opportunity to study the terrain to the south of the Somme.

2.   The attack from the Péronne bridgehead

For the attack, the XVI Panzer Corps was placed directly under the command of the Sixth Army. It was not at that stage subordinate to Panzer Group Kleist. The only formation initially under the command of the panzer group was the XIV Panzer Corps, which was to advance from the Amiens bridgehead. The Péronne bridgehead was quite narrow: only 7 kilometres in width and 5 kilometres in depth. This would make the approach and assembly of the panzer divisions difficult. Many of the combat troops would have to remain on the north bank of the river to begin with. There was just not enough room in the bridgehead. Parts of the Somme Valley were muddy, and there were many arms of the river in the area. This meant that our forces had to cross two or more bridges on their way to the assembly zone. The valley lay within reach of long-range French artillery. Upon clambering over the high ground of the south bank of the river, it was possible to see the enemy's forces in the distance. His positions ran along the old army road that connected Amiens with Saint-Quentin. Our line of attack would need to cut through this east–west road. So as to be able to take the enemy by surprise, it was best that we make our preparations at night and that reconnaissance and other measures be carried out carefully. Our artillery would need to be concealed. They would be opening fire from terrain that could be seen by the enemy, which meant that they could only be employed at the commencement of, not before, the attack.

The enemy was indeed taken by surprise. Large numbers of men from the French 19th Infantry Division were captured. This division had been withdrawn from the Maginot Line in order to defend the Péronne sector of the Weygand Line. It had been a fully intact division, had positioned itself behind well-built emplacements, and had fought bravely against the advance of the XVI Panzer Corps.

The original plan of the commander of the panzer corps had been for both panzer divisions to lead the attack, but he had changed his mind after seeing how little room there was in the bridgehead. He decided that the 33rd Infantry Division, given that it was already in the bridgehead, would be committed to the attack from the outset. With two of its infantry regiments, it would be allocated to the sector on the left. The 3rd Panzer Division would assume responsibility for the sector on the right. The 104th Infantry Regiment was already in that sector and so would be transferred from the 33rd Infantry Division to the 3rd Panzer Division. The 4th Panzer Division was ready, but it would be held in reserve. Except for the artillery, which was to play an important part in the attack with its preparatory fire, there was very little that could be moved to the south bank beforehand. Despite the difficult situation in the bridgehead, preparations were complete by the time the attack was scheduled to begin. That time was 0515 hours on 5 June. General Hoepner's main concern was to ensure that the troops in the rear would be able to cross the Somme as soon as possible after the start of the advance, for they would be urgently needed at the front. Of high priority was the elimination of the enemy artillery. The corps artillery commander would be responsible for the concentration of our own artillery fire against the French guns. We hoped that this would be enough to suppress French artillery fire until well after our advance was underway. We also hoped that the enemy would fail to notice our movements through the Somme Valley prior to the attack. Fortunately, his artillery remained silent.

This attack from the Péronne bridgehead is particularly interesting because we had learnt of, and believed that we were prepared for, the enemy's new anti-tank tactics. We had taken this intelligence into consideration when planning the advance, and it helped to ensure our success. To shed light on how this played out, the attack of the 3rd Panzer Division will be examined closely. The panzer division moved forward with its panzer and rifle brigades. On the flanks (mostly on the western side) were the infantry. The panzer brigade punched through the enemy front in two waves. It was to bypass any villages and charge into the rear of the enemy's position. Its primary task was the destruction of the French artillery, the greatest enemy of our infantry. The rifle brigade would initially accompany the panzer brigade, but it would then remain behind to annihilate the points of resistance, which were mainly in the villages. It had at its disposal a panzer company, what might be regarded as a third wave of tanks. In short, the panzer units were to destroy the enemy artillery while the rifle units were to take the heavily fortified villages.

The panzer brigade drove surprisingly quickly into the rear of the enemy position. Within two-and-a-half hours, it had already destroyed 14 French batteries amidst heavy fighting. Both regiments of the panzer brigade had advanced approximately 8 kilometres and were standing in the vicinity of Chaulnes, a small market town with a railway junction. There was also a large artillery nest there. On the instructions of General Hoepner, who was at that moment at the command post of the 3rd Panzer Division, the panzer brigade was radioed an order from the panzer division to advance further towards the hills that lay south of Chilly and Hallu, as it was believed that the enemy was establishing a new line of resistance in that area. This objective lay 5 kilometres away. The panzer brigade, though low in fuel and ammunition, reached it in an hour. On the following morning, three enemy batteries fell into the hands of the panzer brigade. With that, the French artillery in the attack sector of the 3rd Panzer Division had been put out of action.

Yet the 3rd Rifle Brigade was still a long way behind! The French infantry had remained camouflaged in the villages and allowed the German tanks to drive past, but they put up stiff resistance against the approaching rifle brigade. Although the rifle brigade, as directed, bypassed the enemy-occupied villages of Fay (on the right) and Belloy (on the left), it encountered fierce resistance near the larger village of Estrées-Deniécourt. This village lay on high ground along a 1.5-kilometre stretch of the aforementioned road connecting Amiens and Saint-Quentin. The rifle brigade soon came to a halt. The French infantry had skilfully prepared their defensive measures. They had lodged themselves not directly on the outskirts of the villages but rather in gardens and fields that lay slightly in front of them. Because of this, our artillery fire and Stuka raids against these villages had been practically worthless. The rifle brigade was harassed by powerful defensive fire not only from ahead (Estrées-Deniécourt) but also from the left flank (Belloy). Additional forces were needed to gain control of the situation. Belloy would have to be captured, and this took place towards 1500 hours; 600 enemy soldiers were taken prisoner. The attack against Estrées-Deniécourt had been renewed at 1400 hours with artillery support. Some of the rifle units infiltrated the village, but they soon came to a stop. They were pulled out so that the recently arrived reserve battalion could attack. From 1620 hours, German artillery fire rained down on the village for half an hour. The rifle units and the accompanying panzer company then launched a simultaneous assault on a wide front. The assault swept through the hotly contested village, which was firmly in our hands by 1700 hours. We had taken 700 prisoners. Our pioneer troops cleared the ground in and around the village of about 1,000 mines.

In the meantime, towards noon, the commander of the panzer corps had issued the order to the 4th Panzer Division to advance. Its panzer brigade was to proceed roughly along the boundary between the 3rd

Panzer Division and the 33rd Infantry Division with the goal of striking as far into enemy territory as had the 3rd Panzer Brigade. Like the 3rd Panzer Division, the 4th Panzer Division had to deal with enemy artillery. The 33rd Infantry Division had ground to a halt due to the French guns and had suffered heavy losses. Rifle units of the 4th Panzer Division partook in the fighting for Belloy and seized the fiercely defended village of Berny, which was situated 2 kilometres to the south-east of Estrées-Deniécourt. This helped the 33rd Infantry Division to get going again. By the end of this difficult but successful day, the front line of the rifle and infantry units lay roughly 4 kilometres to the south of the road connecting Amiens and Saint-Quentin. The panzer units had pushed far beyond this front. Chaulnes and several other villages were still in the hands of the enemy.

The rifle and panzer units of the 3rd Panzer Division were finally reunited on the morning of 6 June. The battlefield in the sector of this panzer division had been cleared of any remaining enemy forces. Both panzer divisions continued the southward advance and reached the upper course of the Avre on either side of Roye that same day. The 33rd Infantry Division almost reached Nesle. SS Division Verfügungstruppe had in the meantime been placed on the west wing of the panzer corps, for the enemy had been increasingly applying pressure there throughout the day.[72] It was not yet clear whether this enemy was a retreating force or a new attacking one. It was probably the former.

We crossed the Avre on 7 June, after which we won a number of individual tank battles against the enemy. The infantry had caught up on both wings by then, and so it was decided that the panzer corps could be withdrawn from the front on 8 June. There was no desire for the panzer arm to run aground on the Paris defensive position. It was the view of the OKH that the time had come for Army Group A to be reinforced. The advance by this army group was scheduled to commence on 9 June.

It was thanks to the panzer arm that the attack from the Péronne bridgehead could be carried out quickly and successfully. The inferiority of the infantry as an attacking force was demonstrated by the slow

---

[72] SS Division Verfügungstruppe was a motorised infantry division.

progress of the 33rd Infantry Division. If enemy artillery remained untouched, the chances for the infantry were slim. This led to the creation of the assault gun formations later in the war. Their support of infantry attacks became indispensable, but views remained divided throughout the war over the ideal size of such a formation within an infantry division. The reason for this split view was, on the one hand, the emphasis placed by the panzer arm on the need to concentrate all armoured elements against a point of main effort, and, on the other, the justifiable demand by the infantry for assault guns so that it could remain an effective fighting force. General Hoepner would occupy himself with this question ever since the advance from the Péronne bridgehead. The weakness of the infantry in the attack would become clearer during the advance on Leningrad and quite obvious during the assault on Moscow. Based on his experiences, Hoepner was in favour of a limited but organisationally committed allotment of assault guns to the infantry divisions without abandoning the fundamental idea of the concentration of armour in the panzer arm.[73] It should be remembered that the infantry still comprised the largest part of the army, as the ratio of infantry troops to panzer troops was roughly six to one. Their needs could not be neglected entirely.

As far as the employment of the panzer arm was concerned, the advance from the Péronne bridgehead was a triumph. General Hoepner had been in full agreement with the commander of the 3rd Panzer Division as to how the advance had to be conducted. The enemy artillery had been the primary objective of the panzer attack, while the enemy infantry, despite the difficulties, had to be tackled by our rifle units. These rifle units had only a few tanks at their disposal. It is worth pointing out that the initial trouble encountered by the rifle units made us discuss the possibility of bringing back elements of the 3rd Panzer Brigade. We dismissed this idea, as the 4th Panzer Division was still in reserve and was therefore able to help. This leads to the question as to what could have been done in this situation had there

---

[73] Even by the time of the beginning of the campaign in Russia, the infantry divisions did not always have assault guns at their disposal. They were allotted on a case-by-case basis. It was only later in the war that each infantry division was regularly assigned an assault-gun battery of 10 assault guns.

been no panzer reserve. The answer is that some of the panzer units that had charged ahead would have most likely needed to return. This would suggest that the commitment of all our armour well in front of the infantry was a mistake. The long-range thrust of tanks certainly created an image of tremendous striking power, but the effect of withdrawing some of those tanks, had it been necessary, would have been demoralising. There might of course have been some situations where such a withdrawal was unavoidable. This would have demanded of a panzer commander excellent leadership and the ability to reorient his forces without delay. Not every panzer commander could do this well. In the attack from the Péronne bridgehead, it would have been possible for one panzer battalion, but not more, to be redirected for the purpose of hastening the mopping-up efforts of the rifle units. However, the continued advance of the 3rd Panzer Brigade was the correct course of action on this occasion. Victory had not eluded us. The commander of the panzer corps was pleased with the performance of his troops.

(e) Over the Marne to the Rhône

1. The attack over the Marne

By the early hours of 9 June, the XVI Panzer Corps had been released from the combat zone to the south of Roye by the IV Army Corps. The three divisions of the panzer corps drove eastwards, pausing overnight in Saint-Quentin. They could not stay there for long. The advance of Army Group A commenced on the evening of 10 June, so the panzer corps continued southwards that night, its two panzer divisions crossing the Aisne and assembling to the south of Soissons. SS Division Verfügungstruppe remained behind to begin with. The panzer corps was placed under the command of Panzer Group Kleist at that time. According to the plan of the OKH, the panzer group would be on the west wing of the army group and would be used to provide extra momentum to its advance.[74]

---

[74] Panzer Group Kleist remained subordinate to Army Group B until 14 June. From 15 June, it came under the command of Army Group A.

Aside from the XVI Panzer Corps, the XIV Panzer Corps (General Gustav Anton von Wietersheim) also belonged to Panzer Group Kleist. The XIV Panzer Corps had been withdrawn from its attack zone to the south of Amiens and had followed the XVI Panzer Corps towards the east. The two panzer corps could therefore be placed alongside one another. The infantry on the adjoining wings of the army groups (the 1st Mountain Division under Army Group B and the 81st Infantry Division under Army Group A) had forced the crossing over the Marne on 11 June. The XVI Panzer Corps was to go over the river there on 12 June with the objective of thrusting towards Montmirail. The most difficult aspect of this task was not the enemy, for his power of resistance had diminished, but rather the state of the bridges over the Marne and the traffic congestion to the north of the river.

Panzer Group Kleist ordered that a pontoon bridge that had been constructed by the 81st Infantry Division would be made available to the XVI Panzer Corps on 12 June. This pontoon bridge lay 10 kilometres upstream from Château Thierry. However, it required reinforcement before it could be used by tanks. The 4th Panzer Division would cross the Marne there whilst making allowances for the supply traffic of the 81st Infantry Division. For the 3rd Panzer Division, the panzer corps would construct a bridge in Château Thierry itself. This bridge was to be ready early on 12 June. Yet there were delays at both bridge sites. Although the troops were ready, heavy rain and wind forced them to wait. The 4th Panzer Division could finally cross the river at 1030 hours, while the 3rd Panzer Division could only do so at 1300 hours. This did not at all go smoothly. Troops came from all directions and sought to join the march columns. This caused overcrowding, but we had to ensure that the forces that most urgently needed to cross the river did so first. This demanded that special measures be taken. The byways from which more troops had been emerging were closed so that the march columns could continue to move forward without interruption. The sudden arrival of a flak corps from the west in the early afternoon threatened to cause significant disruption. Unaware of the situation in our area, its two eastbound march columns wanted to cross the direction of advance of our march columns. That was impossible! The flak formations had to wait until our combat troops had moved further south. Some of the flak troops were a little annoyed, but their commander understood that the wait was necessary.

It was because of this incident that General Hoepner, at a later stage, expressed his opinion most clearly that any flak formations in the combat zone of the army ought to be subordinated to the corresponding army units. There should be no more than one commander in charge of any particular sector of the front![75] Hoepner regarded the subordination of the flak to the Luftwaffe to be incorrect. He did not mince his words when he told this to the OKH.

The new command post of the panzer corps stood on the high ground to the north of Château Thierry, close to the road of advance of the 3rd Panzer Division. General Hoepner made his way there early on 12 June. He wanted to observe and, if necessary, intervene in the crossing of the Marne. Given the conditions, it could be foreseen that not everything would run smoothly. Yet the bad weather made it difficult to see much from the command post. Nothing whatsoever could be seen on the south bank of the river. Our awareness of what was happening there was entirely dependent on the reports we received, but we seldom received such reports. We were only aware of the constant stops. Traffic near the command post was often at a standstill. General Hoepner considered this to be most unsatisfactory. It was good that both panzer divisions had conducted reconnaissance beforehand, but this was no guarantee that the situation on the south bank was at that

---

[75] General Hoepner wrote a report of his experiences in Poland and France and submitted it to Colonel-General Halder on 27 July 1940. He had the following to say about units in the combat zone that were not under the command of the army: 'The greatest obstacles for rapid movement in Belgium and France were the air, air signal, and (especially) flak units and columns that were not subordinated to the army. They would often run into the march columns of the army and would ignore any agreements, requests, or orders that were made. They would even try to overtake our columns, thereby causing the worst traffic congestion. It is imperative that flak units crossing the movement and combat zone of an army formation must be placed under the command of the headquarters of that army formation. Flak corps and flak brigade headquarters are in fact superfluous. They are incapable of effective leadership, and they are disruptive rather than helpful. It would be best if flak staff officers were incorporated into the headquarters of army formations.'

moment under control. Hoepner became increasingly impatient as the afternoon wore on. After denying the flak corps passage through the area of the panzer corps, he decided to cross the river himself. He wanted a clearer picture of the progress that had been made and to see what the enemy was doing. Despite the delays, he hoped that the panzer corps could still reach its objective for the day, which was the Petit Morin in the vicinity of Montmirail. Driving ahead with some reconnaissance units, Hoepner drew the conclusion that the enemy, lacking in forces and having no will to fight, had been unable to establish a new defensive front. The spearheads of both panzer divisions managed to reach the Petit Morin in the evening. The command post of the panzer corps was set up in a small, somewhat remote chateau that lay halfway between the Marne and the Petit Morin. The presence of the chateau had been pointed out to General Hoepner by a patrol unit of the 3rd Motorised Reconnaissance Battalion. Our thoroughly wet clothes could be dried by the fireplace there, and we could of course warm ourselves up too. I only arrived there long after nightfall, as there had been more traffic congestion on the south bank of the Marne, but we could still be satisfied with the progress that had been made in the end.

2.   The Seine

Panzer Group Kleist assigned the crossing of the Seine as the next task to be undertaken. Once this was done, an eastward-facing front was to be established along the Seine between Troyes and Romilly so as to cut off enemy forces retreating from the north-east. The next river to be crossed before reaching the Seine was the Grand Morin. General Hoepner did not believe there would be much resistance along the Grand Morin, but he expected crossing the Seine would be a greater challenge. The Seine was a wide river, with multiple arms and several long stretches converted into canals. The panzer corps would be significantly delayed if the enemy blew up the bridges that led over the river. General Hoepner thought it highly likely that this was what would happen. He knew that rebuilding the bridges would take a long time and that any element of surprise would thereby be lost. The possibility existed that elements of the panzer corps would need to veer further to the west so that they could try to cross the river at another location with greater success. For now, a rapid advance was of the utmost importance. Any chance of striking into the rear of a shattered enemy had to be exploited. The most important precondition was that the Seine itself be reached at the earliest possible moment. The objectives for 13 June were the bridges over the Seine in Marcilly, Pont, and Nogent. These bridges lay 50 kilometres away. The 3rd Panzer Division would head for Pont and Nogent; the 4th Panzer Division for Marcilly. Three advance detachments would be sent on ahead, each heading for a different bridge and each accompanied by a staff officer. These staff officers were to let Hoepner know by radio whether the bridges were seized intact.

The Grand Morin posed no problems for the panzer divisions when they crossed it on 13 June. The advance detachments approached the Seine at dusk and, once it was dark, captured all three bridges. The enemy had been taken by surprise. He put up some resistance, albeit in a disorganised manner. Despite his preparations to blow up the bridges, they had fallen into our hands intact. General Hoepner was informed of the good news. It would no longer be necessary for elements of the panzer corps to veer to the west.

The continued thrust of the panzer corps to the south on 14 June could only be carried out at half strength. As mentioned, Panzer Group Kleist had directed that an eastward-facing front would be established along the Seine between Troyes and Romilly in order to cut off an enemy retreat. It had been the hope of the commander of the panzer corps that the 13th Motorised Infantry Division, which had just been placed under his command, would be able to undertake this task. However, by 13 June, the spearhead of this division had only reached Montmirail. This meant that the Troyes–Romilly obstacle line would have to be set up by the 4th Panzer Division on 14 June. Once the 13th Motorised Infantry Division arrived near Troyes, which would probably be on 15 June, the 4th Panzer Division would be free to continue its southward drive. The 3rd Panzer Division would initially be on its own. Despite the fierce fighting overnight near Nogent and Pont, the 3rd Panzer Division pushed forward approximately 60 kilometres on 14 June. The panzer troops were far in front of the infantry. Closer to the 3rd Panzer Division was the

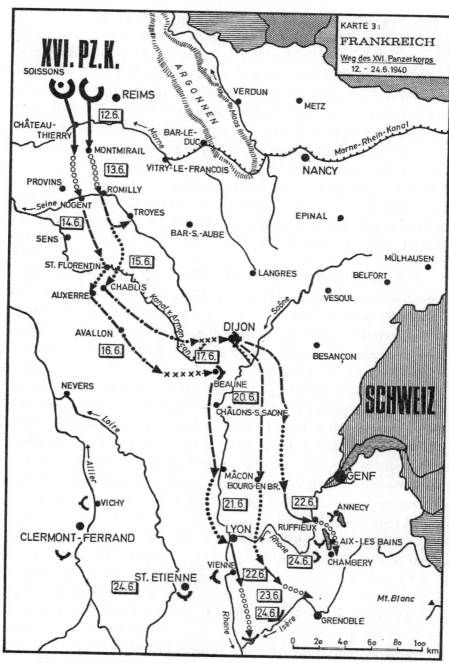

Map 3: France: The Path of the XVI Panzer Corps, 12–24 June 1940

leading formation of the XIV Panzer Corps, the 10th Panzer Division, which had crossed the Seine to the south of Provins on 14 June. Its next objective was Sens, and, after that, it would head towards Joigny in the Yonne Valley. Meanwhile, the 3rd Panzer Division would advance on Auxerre, the main city in the western part of Burgundy. Behind the 10th Panzer Division was the 9th Panzer Division, and behind that SS Division Totenkopf. All these divisions seemed to offer sufficient striking power for the continued advance. Nevertheless, more German forces were on their way. In the area of the XVI Panzer Corps, behind the 13th Motorised Infantry Division, was SS Division Verfügungstruppe. Panzer Group Kleist was also considering placing SS Motorised Infantry Regiment Leibstandarte Adolf Hitler under the command of the XVI Panzer Corps.

3. *Pivoting eastwards towards Côte-d'Or*

The subordination of Panzer Group Kleist to Army Group A came into effect on 15 June. The advance of the panzer group thus far had been directed towards the western part of Burgundy and the upper Loire. The eastern wing of Army Group B had thereby been able to make good progress by following in the wake of the panzer group. However, the decisive thrust into the rear of the Maginot Line was soon to be executed by Panzer Group Kleist in conjunction with Panzer Group Guderian. The latter had advanced over the Aisne north-west of Rheims and attacked towards the south-east along and to the east of the valley of the upper Marne. Its western wing had reached Vitry-le-François on 13 June and Bar-sur-Aube on 15 June. It was the intention of Panzer Group Guderian to advance through the eastern part of the Plateau de Langres towards Besançon and Belfort, and to approach the Swiss frontier in that area. Panzer Group Kleist would pivot to the south-east so as to widen and reinforce the panzer phalanx that was approaching Switzerland. This would prevent the escape of enemy forces withdrawing from the Maginot Line. The panzer group would advance through and to the south of Dijon, the capital of Burgundy, after which, depending on the development of the situation, it would head towards the Rhône Valley (Lyon) and the upper Loire.

In the area of the XVI Panzer Corps, the 3rd Panzer Division was initially on its own in pushing further to the south. It launched a surprise attack on Saint-Florentin in the early hours of 15 June. This town, barely 3 kilometres across, was an important junction which lay on the Armançon, and we suspected that there was a large enemy camp there. Several bridges in the town led over five watercourses, including the Burgundy Canal, which connects the Loire with the Rhône. These bridges, as well as a railway bridge, had to be taken before the enemy destroyed them. Under cover of darkness, the spearhead of the panzer division, the II Battalion of the 3rd Rifle Regiment, seized the town and all its bridges in time. French infantry and motorised groups attempted to flee, but they were swiftly captured. Ever since we had crossed the Marne, our surprise raids had been causing the enemy great confusion and had been helping us to maximise our success. Unfortunately, the courageous battalion commander was severely wounded during the fighting in Saint-Florentin, but his battalion was nevertheless victorious. Although there were small groups of French soldiers who fought fiercely, it was generally the case that the enemy's will to fight had been broken. Even so, it should be remembered that we were deep in enemy territory. This was not where the bulk of the French Army was to be found. It was expected that the panzer divisions ought to be able to advance rapidly, gaining as much territory as possible and annihilating any points of resistance that stood in their way. Long-range reconnaissance was the most important activity at that time. This would alert us as to whether large numbers of enemy forces were on their way and would therefore give us time to prepare our encounter with them.

The 3rd Panzer Division pressed further on 15 June. It reached Auxerre and even sent an advance detachment as far as Avallon, which lay 50 kilometres to the south-east. In the meantime, the 4th Panzer Division had managed to catch up. It had been released from the obstacle line near Troyes by the 13th Motorised Infantry Division and charged forward 80 kilometres in a single day, a true indication of the determination of the troops. The panzer division occupied Chablis, a town which lies 20 kilometres to the east of Auxerre and produces the famous white wine that is named after it.

Throughout 16 June, the panzer corps gradually swept around to face eastwards. By the end of the day, the spearheads of both panzer divisions were in the foothills of the western part of Côte-d'Or. The 4th Panzer Division stood approximately 30 kilometres to the west of Dijon, while the 3rd Panzer Division was near Arnay-le-Duc, roughly 35 kilometres west of Beaune (known for its red burgundy). The panzer corps was now in the area where enemy forces were expected to appear as they withdrew from the Maginot Line. We had already encountered some smaller groups that were in retreat. General Hoepner had been with one of the advance detachments in the afternoon the moment it clashed with French tanks. Although his unarmoured vehicle could not partake in the fighting, he dismounted so that he could at least better follow what was happening. The administrative officer who was accompanying him, a cavalry captain of the reserve, was lightly wounded by a machine-gun bullet. He had probably not crouched low enough while on his way to the ditch beside the road, but he was lucky. The bullet had gone through his leather belt and was stuck in the flesh of his rear. He remained oblivious to this until later in the day when someone in the officers' mess pointed out the hole in his belt. The bullet was easily removed by the doctor. The cheerful captain, an older man who had fought in World War I, was delighted with the souvenir he had inadvertently collected. That alone was reason enough for a drink in friendly comradeship. We could of course also be happy with the distance we had covered that day. It would surely not be too long before the campaign was over!

Dijon and Beaune were occupied on 17 June. Reinforced reconnaissance units drove further south and south-east towards the Saône and the Doubs. The Belfort Gap was blocked by the German panzer arm. Only here and there could a small number of French troops escape. General Hoepner set off for Dijon in the afternoon, shortly after the enemy there had surrendered. He wrote about his visit to the city in a report on the campaign: 'In the prefecture of Dijon on 17 June, I heard a radio announcement at 1730 hours in which Philippe Pétain conceded defeat and declared that France must lay down its arms. It was a historical moment!' The headquarters of the panzer corps had been set up in a chateau near Pont-de-Pany, 18 kilometres to the west of Dijon. This chateau had only a few days before been the headquarters of the French Second Army Group, responsible for defending most of the length of the Maginot Line. The letter paper of its commander, General André-Gaston Prételat, was still to be found in his study. The chateau sat peacefully amidst a beautiful country estate on wooded hills, and the terrace offered an excellent view of the terrain of Burgundy to the east. The staff officers of the panzer corps were there when they heard the words of Marshal Pétain, who in 1918 had celebrated the triumph of France and who now had to acknowledge that the military power of his country had been crushed. It was a momentous occasion, although most of the listeners probably felt some measure of sympathy for the brave yet defeated enemy.

4. To the Rhône, the Alps, and the Isère

The fighting was not yet entirely over, but the advance of the panzer corps became much easier. On 18 and 19 June, German forces reached the Swiss border. On the orders of Panzer Group Kleist, the panzer corps had created an obstacle line on 18 June on the western side of the Plateau de Langres, roughly along the Dijon–Troyes road. The 13th Motorised Infantry Division covered the southern stretch and SS Division Verfügungstruppe the northern. The number of French troops taken prisoner increased considerably.

The panzer forces were reorganised on 20 June. Panzer Group Kleist was returned to Army Group B and was given the task of occupying French territory along the Atlantic coast as far as the Spanish frontier. The reinforced XVI Panzer Corps remained in its current operational area with the 3rd Panzer Division, the 4th Panzer Division, the 13th Motorised Infantry Division, Infantry Regiment Großdeutschland, and SS Motorised Infantry Regiment Leibstandarte Adolf Hitler. Placed under the command of the Twelfth Army (Colonel-General Wilhelm List), the panzer corps was to thrust southwards via Lyon and then, to the east of the Rhône, 'advance from the rear towards the alpine road that leads through Montgenèvre, over Mont Cenis, and along the Little St Bernard Pass'. This route of advance was in accordance with the wishes of our Italian ally, who hoped that it would make his push into France easier. However, the panzer corps had to be prepared for the possibility that it might need to drive towards Marseille instead. Depending on how the situation developed, the panzer corps might also be needed for the occupation of territory to the west of the Rhône.

The panzer corps started its southward advance in the early hours of 20 June. The 3rd Panzer Division was on the eastern side of the Saône and was heading towards Bourg-en-Bresse. It would then cross the Rhône upstream from Lyon. The 4th Panzer Division and Infantry Regiment Großdeutschland were advancing directly towards Lyon, while SS Motorised Infantry Regiment Leibstandarte Adolf Hitler followed behind and slightly to the right. The 13th Motorised Infantry Division, no longer needed by the Dijon–Troyes obstacle line, also marched southwards. It would proceed through Chalon-sur-Saône and position itself on the east wing of the panzer corps.

By the evening of 23 June, the headquarters of the panzer corps was based in Lyon. The units of the panzer corps stood to the south and south-east of the city and were ready for further operations. On the right wing was the 4th Panzer Division. Its headquarters was based in the old Roman city of Vienne, 28 kilometres to the south of Lyon. The panzer division had established a line of security along the Isère, stretching from the confluence with the Rhône to a point approximately 30 kilometres upstream. The south bank was occupied by the enemy. Assault squads were prepared to strike westwards over the Rhône, where more enemy forces were to be found. A small bridgehead had therefore been set up on the other side of the river, west of Vienne. To the east of the panzer division was a roughly 30-kilometre gap which could only be covered by reconnaissance units.

At the other end of that gap was the 3rd Panzer Division. It stood near the bend in the Isère that was 15 kilometres downstream from Grenoble. In the vicinity of Voreppe, the panzer division had encountered strong enemy forces which were determined to put up a fight. Not far beyond were the Alps, which in that area rose to a height of 1,700 or 1,800 metres. Any further advance would require careful preparation. The front of the panzer division extended northwards from there along the foot of the mountain range as far as the hills to the west of Chambéry.

The bulk of the 13th Motorised Infantry Division had crossed the Rhône near Ruffieux, while a smaller group had done so near Groslée. The main group had occupied the spa town of Aix-les-Bains, which lay on the east bank of Lake Bourget, on 23 June. The division now wanted to march through Chambéry from the north and west and approach the Isère at a point approximately 40 kilometres north of Grenoble. This would enable an attack to be carried out against the rear of the enemy forces in the area. It was on that day that the 13th Motorised Infantry Division met with the leading elements of the 1st Mountain Division. They would work in conjunction with one another so as to push further into the hills and eliminate any French forces they encountered. They were at that stage already at an altitude of 1,500–1,800 metres. Taking effect from noon on 24 June, Group Kübler was formed by merging the 1st Mountain Division and the 13th Motorised Infantry Division. This group was led by the commander of the mountain division and was directly subordinate to the panzer corps.[76]

Infantry Regiment Großdeutschland was at that time in Lyon, while SS Motorised Infantry Regiment Leibstandarte Adolf Hitler stood to the west of the Rhône. The latter had approached Saint-Étienne on 23 June and occupied the industrial town on 24 June.

It was at 1235 hours on 25 June that the armistice took effect on all fronts. The campaign had come to an end. In the evening, the staff of the panzer corps enjoyed a hotel banquet with fine French food and a bottle of 1840 vintage Cognac. The troops finally had a chance to take some time off for the first time since the campaign had begun. They could pass the time in the beautiful city of Lyon and spend in a trice the military pay that they had accumulated. General Hoepner visited the divisions near Aix-les-Bains, Grenoble, and Vienne. The weather was splendid, and everyone was in high spirits. Hoepner, who had been invited by the commander of the 4th Panzer Division to visit Vienne, decided that he would make his way to the old Roman city by water. His small entourage made use of a couple of assault boats that belonged to

---

[76] Translator's note: The commander of the 1st Mountain Division was Lieutenant-General Ludwig Kübler.

the corps pioneer battalion to travel along the Rhône. The surrounding countryside was stunning, although there were some obstacles along the way. Our progress was slowed considerably by the rubble from a large road bridge that had been detonated upstream from Vienne. We eventually reached our destination at the beginning of July. We were welcomed by the divisional first general staff officer, a competent man in the military field who also possessed great knowledge of antiquity. He gave us a tour of the city, showing us the beautiful Roman temples, the amphitheatre, and many other remnants of the past. This experience concluded with a meal at the world-famous gourmet Restaurant de la Pyramide. The internationally recognised founder of this praiseworthy restaurant, Monsieur Point, was not present, although Madame Point saw to it that we were looked after.[77] There was a small mishap when the waiter brought an oversized platter of fish baked in marvellously browned pastry. The platter crashed to the floor as he tried to lay it down on the table between me and General Hoepner. Madame Point sprang into action. To our delight, a new platter with an identical meal was produced a short time later. We could continue to enjoy the evening. There was no reproach and no anger. No word was said. Madame Point perhaps looked a little pale for a short time, but that was all. On the way back to Lyon, this time in an armoured car, France was naturally the main topic of conversation. Friedrich Sieburg's question as to whether God was to be found in France could very much be answered in a positive sense.

This was one of our last experiences in France. As Lyon lay to the south of the armistice line, German troops near and to the south of the city had to be withdrawn. This withdrawal was the final military task of the campaign to be carried out by the panzer corps. On 5 July, the formation was relieved of duties in France, and it was back in Berlin four days later.

---

[77] Fernand Point, the father of modern French cuisine, died in 1955.

CHAPTER 3

The Advance on Leningrad in 1941

(a) Preparations and operational plans

1. The starting position of Army Group North

At the beginning of the campaign in Russia in June 1941, Colonel-General Erich Hoepner was the commander of Panzer Group 4.[78] Together with the Sixteenth Army (Colonel-General Ernst Busch) and the Eighteenth Army (Colonel-General Georg von Küchler), Panzer Group 4 was subordinate to Army Group North (Field-Marshal Wilhelm Ritter von Leeb). There were two panzer corps under the command of Panzer Group 4. The first was the XXXXI Panzer Corps (General of Panzer Troops Georg-Hans Reinhardt) with the 1st Panzer Division, the 6th Panzer Division, the 36th Motorised Infantry Division, and the 269th Infantry Division. The second was the LVI Panzer Corps (General of Infantry Erich von Manstein) with the 8th Panzer Division, the 3rd Motorised Infantry Division, and the 290th Infantry Division. In panzer group reserve was SS Division Totenkopf. This meant that the panzer group had at its disposal a total of three panzer divisions, three motorised infantry divisions, and two infantry divisions. The assembly zone of the army group was the northern

---

[78] In recognition of the performance of the XVI Panzer Corps during the campaign in France, Hoepner had been promoted to colonel-general on 19 July 1940. The headquarters of the panzer corps officially ceased to exist on 15 February 1941, as its staff and personnel were augmented for the activation of Panzer Group 4. A new XVI Panzer Corps was not created.

area of East Prussia. The attack of the panzer group itself would be launched from the narrow area to the north of the Memel, on either side and to the east of Tilsit.

Army Group North was the northernmost of the three army groups assigned to the campaign in Russia. According to the *Barbarossa* plan drawn up by the OKH on 31 January 1941, Army Group North was to carry out the following task:

> Enemy forces in the Baltic region are to be annihilated. The Russian fleet will be deprived of its strongpoints through the occupation of the Baltic harbours as well as of Leningrad and Kronstadt. For help in the execution of this task, the OKH may decide to divert strong elements of the mobile forces of Army Group Centre from their drive towards Smolensk.

This support of the relatively weak Army Group North would depend on the development of the situation. While the point of main effort of the entire operation would initially lie with Army Group Centre, the possibility existed that panzer forces would pivot from the central sector of the front to the northern one.

The deployment of enemy forces in the sector of Army Group North was quite different to that in the sectors of Army Group Centre and Army Group South. Most of the Russian forces in those other sectors were concentrated rather close to the frontier. This was especially the case in the Białystok salient, which protruded far to the west, threatening southern East Prussia and northern Poland. Army Group Centre would need to undertake the difficult task of conducting a large double envelopment against this salient. Russian forces in the former Baltic states of Lithuania, Latvia, and Estonia, on the other hand, were distributed in far greater depth. The reserve formations of the enemy in the northern sector were to be found in old Russian territory, in the area to the east of Pskov. We had identified defensive fortifications along the border, particularly on either side of Tauroggen, so a degree of resistance would need to be overcome there. However, there did not appear to be any strong enemy groups in the vicinity of the frontier. As a result, Army Group North would probably not have the opportunity to envelop and eliminate Russian forces on a large scale. However, with the enemy unprepared for war at that stage, a rapid advance deep into his territory might be possible.[79] Each weak group of enemy forces might perhaps be taken by surprise and destroyed one after another! This would require that we move much more quickly than the enemy. Any clash we had with his forces would need to be followed up with a swift thrust.

We did not yet know to what degree our Finnish ally would actively partake in the war against Russia.[80] It was possible that Army Group North would have to infiltrate far into enemy territory on its own. Nevertheless, the commander of the army group decided to concentrate his panzer forces in the central zone of his attack front. The line of attack would be towards the north-east, and the superior mobility of the panzer formations would be exploited to achieve as deep a penetration as possible. They would thereby end up well in front of the slower infantry units. It could not be foreseen to what extent this would succeed. Much would depend on the degree to which the enemy was taken by surprise and the degree to which he put up resistance. The army group hoped that the concentration of its meagre panzer forces would maximise the chances of victory. Initial thoughts about allocating some panzer units to the infantry armies, be it on the right to help the Sixteenth Army over the Neman in the vicinity of Kovno or on the left to help the Eighteenth Army over the Western Dvina in the vicinity of Riga, had been quickly dismissed.[81] Such ideas were at best stopgap solutions. In the plan envisioned by Field-Marshal von Leeb, the offensive of the army group would resemble a wedge whose spearhead would be Panzer Group 4 and whose increasingly deep flanks would be covered by the infantry armies. It was important that the spearhead of this wedge maintain

---

[79] We on the German side presumed that the Russian leadership was distrustful of the populations of the recently occupied Baltic countries, and that this was why it did not yet feel confident enough to establish a more permanent defence in those countries.

[80] In the winter of 1939–40, Finland had put up tough resistance, but was nevertheless defeated, in its defensive war against a Soviet offensive. Finnish forces were therefore somewhat reserved and only started their advance towards Leningrad from 11 July 1941. The German panzer units had by that stage already pushed beyond Pskov in their drive towards Leningrad.

[81] The Neman was the name for the Memel on the Russian side of the border.

its momentum for as long as possible so that it could drive deep into enemy territory. All the striking power at the disposal of the panzer group had to be committed to the thrust to the north-east. Any subsidiary tasks that would divide the attention of the panzer group and cause it to be split up into smaller elements had to be avoided. The panzer group was therefore to be relieved of the need to carry out any security measures on the flanks. Such measures would be undertaken by the infantry armies, which meant they would have to place the main emphasis of their advance on their inner wings. This would in fact work to their advantage. A rapid thrust by the panzer group would help pull along the neighbouring formations. The point of main effort of the Sixteenth Army would therefore be on its left wing, with Dünaburg as its objective; that of the Eighteenth Army would be on its right wing, the idea being that it could then envelop the Baltic region from the east.

The specific task to be carried out by the army group was formulated in an order issued by Field-Marshal von Leeb on 5 May 1941:

> The objective of the operation is the annihilation of enemy forces in the Baltic states and the seizure of the Baltic ports, and thereupon the conquest of Leningrad and Kronstadt. On B-Day at Y-Hour, Army Group North will break through enemy lines along the border and, with Panzer Group 4 in front, cross the Western Dvina between Dünaburg and Rembate (halfway between Jakobstadt and Riga). After crossing the river, the army group, still led by Panzer Group 4, shall advance rapidly to the north-east. The bulk of the army group will drive around the southern side of Lake Peipus. This will prevent enemy troops in the Baltic states from fleeing eastward and will create the preconditions for pushing on towards Leningrad. In order to achieve this overall objective, it is imperative that every opportunity to forge ahead be exploited, thus denying the enemy time to construct a defensive front further east.

The operational objective of Leningrad lay 800 kilometres away. The ground that would have to be covered between the border and the first intermediate objective, the Western Dvina, amounted to 300 kilometres, about the same distance that had been covered in the drive to the coast of the English Channel during the campaign in France. The second intermediate objective, the southern end of Lake Peipus (near Pskov), corresponded to 550 kilometres. The assignment of such long-range objectives before the commencement of the campaign in Russia clearly highlights the confidence with which the commander of the army group assessed our prospects of success. Everything depended on a rapid advance that should not be held up. Strike the enemy once with a devastating blow and keep going! The commander of the panzer group would fully commit himself to this approach.

2. The plans of the commander of Panzer Group 4

The army group order of 5 May 1941 elaborated on the task for the panzer group:

> With the strong support of the inner wings of the Sixteenth and Eighteenth Armies, Panzer Group 4 is to break through the enemy border zone between the Neman and the Tilsit–Riga road and, before long, the Dubysa sector between the mouth of the river and Saule. Panzer Group 4 shall then thrust to the Western Dvina and establish bridgeheads between Dünaburg and Jakobstadt. The point of main effort, so far as the situation allows, will be in the area of Dünaburg.

It was of the utmost importance that the Western Dvina be reached and crossed quickly, which meant that the bridges over the river had to be taken intact. If the enemy were to blow up those bridges, especially the two in Dünaburg, we would experience a loss of time of at least three days. While we constructed new bridges across the wide river, the enemy would have ample opportunity to establish a strong defensive area behind it. We would thereby be robbed of the ability to launch any further surprise attacks. The chances of victory would then fade away. The urgency of the 300-kilometre rush to the Western Dvina could not be overstated!

The border fighting could not be permitted to hold our offensive in check. We had to punch through the frontier and thrust deep into enemy territory. The Dubysa sector lay roughly 75 kilometres from the frontier and offered the enemy a potentially favourable defensive position.[82] If the momentum of the offensive were to be maintained, the panzer group, on the first day alone, would need

---

[82] The Dubysa was a right tributary of the Neman, flowing into it roughly halfway between the border and Kovno.

to reach the Dubysa and secure bridgeheads on the other side. It was important that the bridges remain untouched. Once on the other side of the river, the panzer group would have more room to manoeuvre. The panzer divisions under its command would then have to charge on ahead. They could not afford to be delayed under any circumstances. Should it be necessary to eliminate strong resistance and mop up the battlefield, the infantry divisions would undertake this task.

For the advance over the border, Colonel-General Hoepner placed the LVI Panzer Corps on the right and the XXXXI Panzer Corps on the left. The LVI Panzer Corps would thrust from the narrow assembly area north of the Memel towards the east and would head towards the Kovno–Dünaburg road via the junction in Kedainiai. The 290th Infantry Division was already to the north of the Memel and was committed to the defence of the border. This left room for only one mobile division (the 8th Panzer Division) to assemble to the north of the river. Everything else had to remain to its south. The 8th Panzer Division would be assigned just a 5-kilometre stretch of the frontier. However, the area was forested and would enable the panzer division some degree of flexibility. The German tanks would be camouflaged and would most likely be able to take the enemy by surprise. The 3rd Motorised Infantry Division would have to follow the 8th Panzer Division over the border. Only on the other side of the Dubysa would the divisions of the panzer corps be able to spread out. Meanwhile, the XXXXI Panzer Corps would be able to advance on a wider front. The 269th Infantry Division would be on the eastern wing, the 6th Panzer Division in the middle, and the 1st Panzer Division on either side of the Tilsit–Saule–Riga road. This panzer corps had to gain ground to the north to begin with so that it could then pivot to the north-east and head towards the Western Dvina. The enemy border forces in the sector of the XXXXI Panzer Corps were probably stronger than those in the sector of the LVI Panzer Corps. Russian entrenchments had been spotted not only on the main road but also to the south and south-east of Tauroggen. The reserve division of the XXXXI Panzer Corps, the 36th Motorised Infantry Division, had to start on the south bank of the Memel.

Panzer Group 4 assigned Dünaburg as the main objective that had to be reached on the Western Dvina. The city was to be captured by the formation that was the closest and that could therefore, foreseeably, arrive there the soonest. This formation was the LVI Panzer Corps. However, Colonel-General Hoepner would reserve for himself the decision as to whether this task should be handed over to the XXXXI Panzer Corps. It would depend on the development of the situation. There were Russian armoured reserves in the vicinity of Jonava. If they attacked the southern flank of the panzer group, it might slow the progress of the LVI Panzer Corps. In a situation like this, enemy tanks cannot simply be bypassed. The panzer units would need to attack and destroy them. This was one of the main reasons for the existence of the panzer arm.

A significant disadvantage that confronted the panzer group from the outset was the lack of mobile reserves! The mobility of the panzer forces and the element of surprise could only be fully exploited if there were strong reserves. This is because if a situation arose somewhere on the front that could be used to our advantage, the commitment of reserves at that point could prove decisive. Ideally, a third of the available combat strength of a formation would be in reserve to begin with and would then be employed in specific locations for the attainment of ambitious objectives. The enemy would probably be unable to match us in terms of initial strength and mobility, but the lack of reserves could be a severe handicap for the panzer group once it was far in front of the infantry units. The panzer group might have increasingly limited opportunities and might even find itself held back by an anxious superior headquarters. Colonel-General Hoepner was immediately aware of this disadvantage and had requested that he be allocated a third panzer corps. However, not even one more mobile division was available. The quantity of mobile forces was relatively meagre when considered alongside the immensity of the task that was being demanded of them. Moreover, the point of main effort of the entire campaign in Russia as envisaged by the OKH would not be in the direction of Leningrad. Consequently, we could not expect that further forces would be allocated to Army Group North. Hoepner decided that the best he could do was to hold SS Division Totenkopf in reserve in the starting position. He would then at least have something at his disposal in the event of an unforeseen development. Yet it was not a real reserve, as it would need to be given to the LVI Panzer Corps the moment a breakthrough in the direction of Dünaburg had been achieved. Hoepner considered that he might then be able to fall back upon the 36th Motorised Infantry Division, which belonged to the XXXXI Panzer Corps. It would by no means make up for the lack of a third panzer corps, but there was at least the chance, in accordance with the *Barbarossa* plan, that mobile forces would be diverted from Army Group Centre towards Leningrad at a later stage.

(b) Rush to the Western Dvina[83]

On the morning of 22 June 1941, at 0305 hours, Panzer Group 4 rolled forward across the frontier. The commander of the panzer group was at the headquarters of the XXXXI Panzer Corps. It was expected that the greatest enemy resistance would be in the sector of this formation, especially in the vicinity of Tauroggen. That turned out to be the case. Nevertheless, the panzer corps overcame this resistance that very morning and was soon advancing further to the north. As planned, the enemy had been taken by surprise. He did not have a chance to take any counter-measures, be they offensive or defensive. Meanwhile, the LVI Panzer Corps had ploughed eastwards through weak enemy resistance and had reached the Dubysa. By the evening, the most important bridges across the river had been seized intact.

It would be revealed on 23 June to what extent we would have to deal with Russian counter-measures. We needed to gain an impression on this question early in the day. The panzer wedge was deep yet narrow, with the 8th Panzer Division already far to the east. The XXXXI

---

[83] The description of the advance on Leningrad will be limited to the plans and decisions made by Colonel-General Hoepner. The effects of the actions of the panzer group will also be explored. A more detailed description of this advance, based closely on the available documents of the headquarters of Panzer Group 4, is contained in Walter Chales de Beaulieu, *Der Vorstoß der Panzergruppe 4 auf Leningrad 1941* (Neckargemünd: Vowinckel, 1961); in English as *Leningrad: The Advance of Panzer Group 4, 1941*, trans. Linden Lyons (Havertown PA: Casemate, 2020).

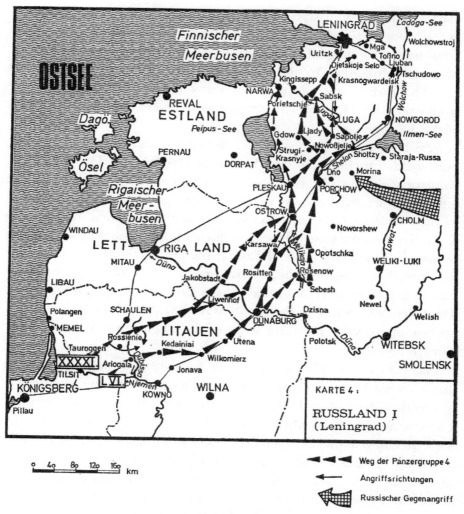

Map 4: Russia (Leningrad)

Panzer Corps would start to veer from the north to the north-east or east, but the degree to which it would do so would depend on how the situation unfolded. Behind the 8th Panzer Division, the 3rd Motorised Infantry Division would probably reach the Dubysa that day. The earliest it could partake in any fighting to the east of the river would be 24 June. This was the consequence of the narrowness of the assembly area!

Aerial reconnaissance spotted a Russian tank formation moving northwards from Jonava towards Kedainiai at 0400 hours. This formation, constantly observed by our aircraft, reached Kedainiai and proceeded further to the north or north-west. It was strange that it paid no attention to the 8th Panzer Division, which was at that moment approaching Kedainiai from the west. The enemy formation consisted of somewhere between 200 and 350 tanks. Whatever the precise number, it could not be ignored, especially if there were further forces following it. There was even a group of enemy tanks on the left wing of the panzer group. They were assembling to the south-west of Saule, although they ended up heading towards the right wing of the Eighteenth Army (I Army Corps).

The presence of the Russian tank formation from Jonava meant that Colonel-General Hoepner was confronted with the question as to whether the eastward advance towards Dünaburg should continue. The enemy formation would need to be destroyed, but would this be with or without the involvement of the 8th Panzer Division? Could the thrust towards Dünaburg be put on hold temporarily? This would amount to the abandonment of any chance of taking the enemy forces in the city by surprise. They would have plenty of time to blow up the bridges there! Hoepner thus decided that the LVI Panzer Corps was to continue with its advance to the east. Dünaburg would remain its objective. By nightfall, the 8th Panzer Division stood about 10 kilometres away from Kedainiai. It would now be up to the XXXXI Panzer Corps to eliminate the Russian tank formation. This formation had advanced to the north-west and had clashed with the 6th Panzer Division by the Dubysa in the afternoon. There did not seem to be any further enemy forces on their way. Aerial reconnaissance spotted no vehicles that evening on the Jonava–Kedainiai road. The LVI Panzer Corps would therefore commit only a small number of security forces against the enemy tank formation; otherwise, the bulk of this panzer corps would proceed with the charge towards Dünaburg.

In this situation, the enemy formation (the Russian 2nd Tank Division) conducted itself in the way Colonel-General Hoepner had hoped and expected. The tank division had approached the Dubysa in the vicinity of Raseiniai and attacked the German panzer forces there. It achieved some initial success against the 6th Panzer Division on the late afternoon of 23 June, but was soon forced to defend itself and was pushed back. In the ensuing battle of Raseiniai, between 24 and 26 June, the XXXXI Panzer Corps enveloped and fully annihilated the tank division. More than 200 tanks were captured. The rest were destroyed.

Both panzer corps were working together effectively. The drive on Dünaburg was proceeding according to the operational plan. Early on the morning of 24 June, at 0345 hours, the 8th Panzer Division advanced through Kedainiai without encountering any enemy resistance. Wilkomierz, which lay 50 kilometres further to the east, was occupied in the late afternoon. The Kovno–Dünaburg road had thereby been reached. The reconnaissance units of the panzer division, now with this good road at their disposal, advanced another 15 kilometres in the direction of Dünaburg. The remaining distance to the city was 125 kilometres! On 25 June, towards 1500 hours, Utena was occupied. The distance to Dünaburg was still 70 kilometres! Despite the multitude of enemy counter-attacks and the increased activity of Russian bomber aircraft, the panzer division made rapid progress along the road. The enemy's best efforts were not enough to bring the spearhead of the panzer division to a halt. Its advance continued into the night. The objective was ever closer! Our panzer units even overtook some retreating enemy forces. A couple of assault squads were assigned to the 8th Panzer Division so that they could exploit this situation.[84] They drove ahead of the panzer division, infiltrated the city of Dünaburg at 0630 hours on 26 June, and occupied the

---

[84] Translator's note: The troops of the two assault squads consisted of fluent Russian speakers. They were dressed in Russian uniforms and would approach the bridges in Dünaburg on captured Russian trucks.

two bridges over the Western Dvina. Heavy fighting broke out at both sites, one a road bridge and the other a railway bridge, but the tanks of the panzer division soon arrived and were able to intervene decisively. Dünaburg fell into our hands with the road bridge intact. The railway bridge had been partially detonated and lightly damaged, but could still be used.

The first intermediate objective of the panzer group had been reached at its most important point. We would be able to cross the large river without delay. However, the penetration of the Western Dvina front would only be effective if the bridgeheads could be expanded and secured against Russian counter-attacks. Even before the tank battle of Raseiniai had been brought to a conclusion, Colonel-General Hoepner had assigned to the XXXXI Panzer Corps as its next task the crossing of the Western Dvina between Illuxt and Jakobstadt. The latter was the next location downstream from Dünaburg that had a bridge over the river. Ferries rather than bridges were used in Illuxt and Liwenhof. There were only stragglers before the front of the panzer corps once the envelopment battle had come to an end. As far as we could ascertain, there appeared to be neither entrenchments nor enemy troops on the other side of the river.

The enemy had failed to exploit the Western Dvina as a naturally strong defensive line. Our advance had been fast; his reactions slow. The thought had occurred to Colonel-General Hoepner on the morning of 26 June that the XXXXI Panzer Corps, in whole or in part, might be able to cross the Western Dvina via Dünaburg. However, it would be better for the rest of the panzer group, and indeed for the entire army group, if there were several bridgeheads along the river between Dünaburg and Jakobstadt. This would enable the infantry formations, advancing as they were on a wide front, to cross the river quickly. The lack of an enemy presence not only before the XXXXI Panzer Corps but perhaps also on the other side of the river had to be fully exploited. The chances of a swift advance were good. It was probably the case that the enemy would focus his defensive efforts near Dünaburg and Riga. Consequently, the area in between might be where a breakthrough could be achieved, a significant benefit of which was that the line of advance from that area would lead to Ostrov and Pskov.

The XXXXI Panzer Corps thrust forwards and over the Western Dvina. By 30 June, bridgeheads had been established over the river near Liwenhof and Jakobstadt. Military bridges had been constructed in both towns. Both bridgeheads were expanded and united on 1 July. By the end of the day, the united bridgehead was 30 kilometres in depth. As expected, there was little enemy resistance, so the continuation of the attack was likely to go well.

Russian counter-measures were indeed limited to the combat zone around Dünaburg. The enemy was using all the means at his disposal in an attempt to retake the city. The most critical day of the battle was 28 June. The LVI Panzer Corps was temporarily on the defensive. Its eastern front had been pierced by the enemy. Nevertheless, with more German forces entering the bridgehead, the Russian attacks were unable to enjoy lasting success. During the course of 29 and 30 June, the bridgehead was expanded so that it was 30 kilometres in depth. It was via Dünaburg that the Sixteenth Army intended to cross the Western Dvina, and its leading elements had already arrived in the bridgehead.

The rapid thrust of Panzer Group 4 to the Western Dvina had been successful. Several bridgeheads had been established across the river, providing a firm foundation from which further operations could be conducted in the direction of Leningrad. This success had been achieved more quickly than had been anticipated. The operations up to the river had been executed precisely in accordance with the order that had been issued by Army Group North on 5 May 1941: 'it is imperative that every opportunity to forge ahead be exploited, thus denying the enemy time to construct a defensive front further east'. The infantry armies would now be able to exploit the success of the panzer group. Their inner wings could cross the river without delay at those points that the panzer group had reached. Colonel-General Hoepner was of the view that, so as to be able to reach Leningrad, the advance should continue in the manner that had been outlined in the army group order. In practice, this meant that the panzer group would once more charge well in front of the infantry wave and be on its own in the depths of enemy territory. Yet the task of the infantry would remain the same. They were to follow in the wake of and thereby secure the flanks of the advance of the panzer group. Field-Marshal von Leeb agreed with Colonel-General Hoepner's view. The panzer group would continue its dash towards Leningrad without awaiting the arrival of all the infantry. After all, the panzer group was ready to go, whereas the assembly of the infantry would require more time.

(c) Through Latvia to the Stalin Line

Although the panzer group did not need to await the arrival of the infantry, there was another factor that might possibly hold it back. That factor was the supply. East Prussia had thus far been the area from which supplies had been transported to the front, but this would become more difficult with the panzer group well beyond the Western Dvina. The supply lines would be too long. The journey from Tilsit to the Western Dvina and back was already 600 kilometres! The necessity of establishing a supply base on the Western Dvina had been foreseen from the outset, although resupplying the troops would still demand a certain amount of time. The size of the supply gap had to be taken into account when making a decision about the resumption of the advance. The next objectives were Opochka and Pskov, both of which lay more than 250 kilometres away from the Western Dvina. The flow of supplies to the panzer group would need to be secure across that distance. On 29 June, after careful consideration, Colonel-General Hoepner informed Field-Marshal von Leeb that 2 July was the day on which both panzer corps could resume the advance. The army group therefore issued orders to that effect. This allowed enough time for the resupply of the panzer group. The expenditure of ammunition in the defence of the Dünaburg bridgehead against Russian attacks had been considerable. The replenishment of this ammunition had caused the quartermaster of the panzer group quite a headache, but he managed to master the situation.[85]

With the early seizure of Dünaburg, the idea had arisen at the head-quarters of the panzer group of an immediate push to the north-east in the direction of Rositten. However, the Russian counter-attacks near

---

[85] The quartermaster oversaw the supply services of the panzer group.

Dünaburg had soon dashed any hopes of pursuing this idea. The LVI Panzer Corps felt unprepared to send reinforced reconnaissance units towards Rositten, even though this would ease the resumption of its advance. The enemy was too powerful and could not be defeated by the panzer corps on its own.[86] If the panzer corps was to continue to the north-east at that moment, its supply lines would be endangered. Aside from that, the 290th Infantry Division, which belonged to the panzer corps, only arrived in the Dünaburg bridgehead on 1 July. Until the arrival of the Sixteenth Army, this infantry division was the only formation available that could release the mobile forces of the panzer corps whilst keeping the enemy at bay. But the Sixteenth Army would hardly arrive before 4 July.

The commander of Panzer Group 4 had decided that the advance over the Western Dvina would be conducted on a wide front. This would be possible thanks to the tremendous success in establishing multiple bridgeheads along the river. He had also decided that the second leap of the advance would be carried out with both panzer corps simultaneously. He did not want one or the other to press on ahead by itself. He had anticipated that the enemy would concentrate his efforts in the vicinity of Dünaburg. An early assault in the direction of Rositten would have been insufficient to take the enemy by surprise. What was needed was a perfectly executed second leap!

On the morning of 2 July, the panzer group resumed its advance. The objective of the LVI Panzer Corps, on the right, was Novorzhev (70 kilometres north-east of Opochka); that of the XXXXI Panzer Corps, on the left, was Ostrov and Pskov. As early as the evening of the following day, the northern wing of the XXXXI Panzer Corps (the 1st Panzer Division) had entered old Russian territory and stood only 12 kilometres to the west of Ostrov. By the evening of 4 July, Ostrov had been occupied by the 1st Panzer Division. The road bridge over the Velikaya had fallen into our hands intact. The enemy forces in the vicinity of the town had been completely unprepared for an attack from where the 1st Panzer Division had approached. Russian

---

[86] The bulk of the enemy's forces stood to the east of Dünaburg. It was from that direction that most of his counter-attacks were launched.

tank reserves near Pskov did not have a chance to intervene. They were ready for combat, but the relatively weak forces of the 1st Panzer Division had been too fast for them. Only on 5 July did the Russian tanks strike ruthlessly towards Ostrov, but they were repelled after more than 140 of them were destroyed. The situation had been more difficult for the 6th Panzer Division, for it encountered a well-prepared line of enemy fortifications on either side of the Dünaburg–Ostrov road in the vicinity of the Russo–Latvian border. Nonetheless, this defensive line soon collapsed, probably because Ostrov itself had already fallen.

The LVI Panzer Corps had reached the Russo–Latvian border on 4 July. On the other side of that border was an unexpected and impenetrable obstacle. This obstacle was not the enemy, for he had fled; rather, it was forest and marshland. The small number of narrow roads that led through this terrain, if they could be called roads, were so cluttered with bogged-down and abandoned Russian vehicles that any carefully thought-out plan to block the roads could not have done a better job at slowing the progress of the panzer corps. Many of the troops of the 8th Panzer Division dismounted and advanced on foot, struggling through to Krasnoi by the evening of 5 July. They had to wait for more than two days for their vehicles to arrive, as several kilometres of corduroy roads had to be built for those vehicles beforehand.[87]

On the night of 4/5 July, the LVI Panzer Corps radioed a report of the conditions it had encountered to the headquarters of Panzer Group 4. In the early hours of 5 July, while I went to visit the XXXXI Panzer Corps in Ostrov, Hoepner set off for the command post of the LVI Panzer Corps to discuss how the push to the east would proceed. It was clear that the LVI Panzer Corps could not advance through marshy terrain without a significant loss of time. The 8th Panzer Division might now be able to go through Krasnoi, but the other two mobile divisions of the panzer corps had no choice other than to drive northwards through Ostrov. This would also involve a loss of time, as both divisions would

---

87 Translator's note: Corduroy roads were roads formed by tree trunks laid across impassable muddy or swampy areas.

have to advance along the main road one behind the other, but it would nevertheless bring them towards their next objective in the north-east, Porkhov, more quickly. Hoepner was aware that this change of plan meant that the panzer group would be giving up Opochka as an objective. The roads and terrain in that direction were simply no good. The 8th Panzer Division would continue towards Novorzhev via Krasnoi and would secure the right flank of the panzer group, but the main thrust would now head through Porkhov (LVI) and Pskov (XXXXI) in the direction of Leningrad.

The drive through the Baltic region had been even faster than the rush to the Western Dvina. The enemy had failed to anticipate the line of advance that would be taken by the XXXXI Panzer Corps. The bulk of his defences had been concentrated in the vicinity of Dünaburg. The few forces he had near Ostrov had been swiftly overcome. Had the panzer group attempted only to advance from the Dünaburg bridgehead, it would have hardly been able to take the enemy by surprise. Despite the tremendous strength that would have been in that bridgehead, the units of the panzer group, with only a narrow front before them, would have been compelled to move forward one at a time to begin with. This would have been too slow. The Russian leadership had been prepared for a German advance from Dünaburg and had attempted to carry out counter-attacks in that area. The tank reserve group near Pskov, a constant source of concern for the leadership of the panzer group, had been held back. What would have been more natural than for the enemy to send this tank reserve group along the main road in the direction of Rositten and Dünaburg? But this did not happen, and the panzer group made a rapid advance that surprised even its own leadership. The 1st Panzer Division had covered more than 125 kilometres in the space of a single day! With the enemy caught unawares, the panzer arm had achieved a great success. The Stalin Line had been penetrated on 4 July.[88] Colonel-General Hoepner had assessed the situation correctly and had made the best choice as to

---

[88] The Stalin Line had only been occupied at the most important locations, e.g. to the south-west of Ostrov and further south near Sebezh. In between lay the deliberately neglected region of forest and marshland, a natural obstacle for the German forces.

how to approach Ostrov. The result was the greatest gain in territory in what was thus far the shortest amount of time.

(d) Approaching Leningrad

1. *The prospects for approaching Leningrad*

Panzer Group 4 had reached the Ostrov–Pskov area with great rapidity. Could this situation be exploited with an immediate renewal of the advance towards the operational objective of Leningrad? The panzer group would only be able to draw upon the forces at its disposal. Not even the motorised elements of the infantry armies would be close enough to provide support. The infantry armies had only started to cross the Western Dvina on 4 July. As a result, they stood approximately 250 kilometres behind the panzer group. This distance would increase if the panzer group were to push on at once. Would such a course of action be possible? How great would the danger be? Colonel-General Hoepner was in favour of continuing without delay, as it seemed to him that the enemy had not yet managed to organise a coordinated defence. The infantry armies nevertheless had to endeavour to advance their units as quickly as possible, especially, as before, on their inner wings. He requested of Army Group North more aerial reconnaissance as well as more armour-piercing and anti-aircraft weaponry. He also wanted reinforcements of machine-gun battalions so that the flanks could be better protected. 'So as to ensure that the full force of the panzer group can surge forward in one united effort, it is important that the panzer group not be burdened with the responsibility for the right flank,' wrote Hoepner in a report on 6 July outlining his assessment of the situation. Field-Marshal von Leeb had requested such a report, for he was expecting a visit from the commander in chief of the German Army, Field-Marshal von Brauchitsch, at the command post of the army group on 7 July for a discussion on the continuation of operations.

Field-Marshal von Leeb faced at that moment a difficult decision. Could the panzer group be released for the final and decisive 300-kilometre drive towards Leningrad? Or were other demands like the encirclement of Russian forces in the Baltic region more important? We were on the verge of taking Pskov, which would render the escape of those Baltic forces around the southern end of Lake Peipus impossible. If their escape around the northern end of the lake was to be prevented, might that be where the panzer group ought to be sent? The commander of the army group decided that the drive on Leningrad would continue. Hoepner, in his report, had recommended 9 July as the day on which the advance could resume. If Leningrad fell, the fate of the Baltic enemy would be sealed. The Eighteenth Army would commit a few units to a frontal attack against this enemy, but the bulk of its forces would sweep around the southern end of Lake Peipus in the wake of the advance of the panzer group. For the security of the right flank of the panzer group, it seemed as if Leeb would see to it that sufficient forces from the Sixteenth Army were available.

Brauchitsch agreed with Leeb's recommendation on 7 July that the panzer group proceed in the direction of Leningrad. There were potentially many risks, but both the army group and the panzer group believed that this was the best course of action. The forces available to the panzer group were indeed quite meagre, especially when the vastness of the terrain is taken into consideration. The third panzer corps that Hoepner had requested would have helped in a situation like this, but such a formation did not exist. Nonetheless, he was of the view that the two panzer corps under his command would have just enough strength to break through to Leningrad. The flanks would become ever more extended and exposed, especially on the right, but this could not be allowed to diminish the striking power of the panzer group! This was the one and only opportunity to achieve what had been sought-after since the commencement of the campaign, namely, to rapidly approach Leningrad and, perhaps, to bring about a decisive victory there.

2. *The failure of the first attempt to break through to Leningrad*

After the thrust on Leningrad had been approved by Field-Marshal von Brauchitsch on 7 July, the army group ordered that it commence on 10 July. The panzer group therefore set off on that day from the Ostrov–Pskov area, making use of the two main roads that led to

Leningrad. On the right was the LVI Panzer Corps, which was to advance via Porkhov, Soltsy, and Novgorod; on the left was the XXXXI Panzer Corps, which would drive through Luga. While the XXXXI Panzer Corps would be able to employ all four of its divisions, the LVI Panzer Corps could only commit the 8th Panzer Division and the 3rd Motorised Infantry Division to begin with. Additional forces had not yet arrived. Unfortunately, the commander of the LVI Panzer Corps, despite the agreement that had been reached on 5 July, had permitted SS Division Totenkopf to push in a completely different direction. This division had been fighting near Rosenov, on the southern wing of the panzer corps. It had been the idea of the leadership of the SS division to advance to the south-east through Sebezh, circle behind the enemy to the north, go through Opochka, and then re-establish contact with the panzer corps. It is worth pointing out that Colonel-General Hoepner had regarded this idea as one that could not be carried out. The difficulties presented by the terrain had led to the decision to send SS Division Totenkopf and the 3rd Motorised Infantry Division directly to the north via Ostrov. However, General von Manstein had concluded that the idea of the SS division was worth pursuing. The result was that the SS division had found itself in heavy fighting and had ground to a halt even before it had reached Sebezh.[89] Manstein had still believed that the advance of the SS division had good prospects. Hoepner had expressed his doubts on 6 July, but Manstein had remained adamant on 7 July that the advance of the SS division should continue and that the most difficult hurdle had been overcome. With Manstein so certain that the SS division could succeed, Hoepner could not easily order that its advance on Sebezh, which was already underway, be called off. Nevertheless, Hoepner made his opinion quite clear when he spoke with Manstein over the phone:

> Colonel-General Hoepner once more expressed his view that the prospects of success for SS Division Totenkopf did not look good. He emphasised, as he had done before, his lack of enthusiasm for the current commitment of the LVI Panzer Corps along a 120-kilometre front between Sebezh

---

[89] SS Division Totenkopf suffered such heavy losses in the fighting near Sebezh that its three infantry regiments had to be reorganised into two.

and Ostrov. The panzer corps must be brought northwards as soon as possible.[90]

SS Division Totenkopf subsequently made slow progress. It journeyed an arduous 200 kilometres to the north, finally re-establishing contact with the LVI Panzer Corps on 14 July in the vicinity of Soltsy. Regrettably, Manstein had in the meantime decided that the 290th Infantry Division would also be sent to the south-east so that it could help with the fighting near Sebezh. This infantry division ended up so far away that it was eventually detached from the panzer corps and placed under the command of the Sixteenth Army. It would be sorely missed by the panzer corps.

The panzer group advanced effortlessly on 10 July, crushing all enemy rearguard units that stood in its way. As early as 11 July, though, it was becoming apparent that the drive along the two main roads could not be carried out quickly enough. The terrain favoured enemy resistance, and it became increasingly impossible for the panzer arm to bring its superior firepower and offensive capacity to bear. The panzer group had entered the rather impenetrable forested region that extended across both roads of advance all the way to the outskirts of Leningrad. Thick undergrowth and marshy ground prevented our tanks from straying from the roads. They had to remain in their columns. Only the small number of leading tanks could be employed for tactical combat, but their losses were high, dangerously exposed as they were to the well-hidden enemy. Circumstances like these reduced not only our speed but also the chances of victory! Such terrain, especially the Volkhov swamps to the south-east of Leningrad, no longer existed in Central Europe and was unusual even in central and southern Russia.

The XXXXI Panzer Corps had pushed beyond Novoselye (80 kilometres north-east of Pskov) on 11 July and had advanced another 30 kilometres to Zapolye on 12 July. It was there, on what was essentially an island in the middle of marshland, that the panzer corps came to a halt. From there, it could only crawl forward at the tempo of an infantry

---

[90] From my situation report at 1000 hours on 7 July regarding the use of SS Division Totenkopf.

formation amid combat. Similar conditions were encountered by the LVI Panzer Corps on the road to Novgorod. There was ever-growing enemy resistance, with the Russian leadership sending reinforcements by rail from Leningrad to Dno via Soltsy to stop the German advance. The spearhead of the panzer corps (the 8th Panzer Division) was compelled to conduct a small retreat on 15 July. Confronted with strong enemy forces on its right flank, near and to the east of Porkhov, it was unable to attack further in its weakened state. SS Division Totenkopf had just arrived, so elements of it were committed to the Porkhov area. This division would remain under the control of the panzer corps, even though the commander of the panzer group would have liked to have kept it as a reserve unit. The 290th Infantry Division was by then no longer under the control of the panzer corps, yet infantry forces were urgently needed on the southern wing. Colonel-General Hoepner made a request to the army group to this effect, and he was informed that the I Army Corps of the Eighteenth Army was on its way. It was at that moment to the south of Pskov and could be in the vicinity of Porkhov from roughly 17 July.

3. *A change of plan*

The extensive woodlands caused severe difficulties for Panzer Group 4, more so and at an earlier stage for the XXXXI Panzer Corps than for the LVI Panzer Corps. As early as 11 July, the question had arisen as to how and where the panzer arm could be utilised more effectively. It was even being considered whether the plan for a rapid thrust on Leningrad ought to be given up altogether. The current lines of attack along the main roads would bring about slow progress at best. Both panzer corps were restricted in their freedom of movement and were therefore incapable of enveloping the enemy or taking him by surprise. Their spearheads were too thin, and their flanks were vulnerable. Our tanks would be committed to worthless security tasks on the flanks until the infantry divisions arrived to strengthen the front and engage in heavy fighting. In the meantime, the enemy would enjoy all the advantages. Even a pair of tree trunks across the road with a small number of enemy troops placed on the other side would be incredibly difficult for the panzer formations to overcome. And the enemy had prepared several such obstacles. He would be in control of the situation and could determine where the fighting would take place.

In an effort to find better terrain for our tanks, the maps were studied very carefully at the headquarters of Panzer Group 4 as well as at the headquarters of the XXXXI Panzer Corps. We identified a stretch of 50–80 kilometres of good terrain between Narva and Leningrad on the south bank of the Gulf of Finland. The layout and development of that area resembled something that could be expected in Central Europe. There was a road network there which appeared to offer decent, if not excellent, possibilities for our panzer forces in combat. What remained uncertain was how best to get there. The area lay at least 100 kilometres to the north. There did not seem to be a single good road that led there unless the panzer corps was to swing back around the western side of Lake Peipus.[91] Reconnaissance had to be carried out at once so that the best roads could be found. It was discovered that the entire area to the north, all the way to the lower Luga, was free of enemy forces aside from a few weak units on the east bank of Lake Peipus. It would be possible to reach and cross the lower Luga via a number of narrow forest and country roads. As the weather was still dry, any marshy stretches of road would be able to be improved. If one panzer corps was to be shifted to the left, should the other risk the same course of action? The combined efforts of both formations would be indispensable for the decisive battle before Leningrad. However, even a short period of rain could endanger the pivot towards the lower Luga.

The search for suitable roads was not the only challenge that Hoepner had to take into consideration when contemplating the rotation of the panzer group to the north; the other was the opinion of the OKH that the main line of approach on Leningrad should be from the south–east so that any attempt by Russian forces to escape could be prevented. It will not be discussed here whether an approach from the south–east was necessary or practical, even though it can be said with certainty

---

[91] This solution was recommended by the commander of the XXXXI Panzer Corps on 12 July 1941. Colonel-General Hoepner had requested General Reinhardt's assessment of the situation so that he could present it to the chief of staff of Army Group North.

that the Russian leadership would have never evacuated Leningrad, as it would have simply facilitated our occupation of the city; nor will it be discussed whether the forces of Army Group North would have been capable of carrying out such an approach. On the question as to whether the panzer group could have advanced on Leningrad via Novgorod and Chudovo, the answer is most clearly in the negative. It would have had to commit so many forces to flank security near Lake Ilmen and along the Volkhov that there would have been nothing left with which to approach the outskirts of Leningrad. For this reason, it was decided by 12 July that the LVI Panzer Corps would no longer attack towards Novgorod. It would instead commit its forces where the new point of main effort lay. The efforts of the commander of the panzer group between 13 and 16 July to place SS Division Totenkopf in reserve is to be understood in this context. He did not want it to be tied down to fighting on the right flank. Unfortunately, this initial measure to bring the LVI Panzer Corps to the north alongside the XXXXI Panzer Corps could not be carried out. Given the absence of the 290th Infantry Division, SS Division Totenkopf was the only unit available that could provide protection on the right flank (near Porkhov and along the Shelon). There is no doubt that the 290th Infantry Division would have been best suited to this task of defending the flank and that it would have thereby enabled the rest of the LVI Panzer Corps to maintain greater mobility. Colonel-General Hoepner wanted to manage with as few forces on the right flank as possible, and he was even prepared to conduct a tactical withdrawal there. He did not believe that the enemy could easily pursue such a withdrawal. The northern wing of the Sixteenth Army would soon be in the area to provide the security that was needed, and the eastward attack of the I Army Corps through Porkhov that had been promised by the army group was supposed to take place in the near future.

Hoepner reached the decision that the XXXXI Panzer Corps would indeed pivot to the north. There was barely any enemy presence in that direction. The panzer corps would cross the lower Luga and would then exploit the good terrain on the north bank for a powerful thrust on Leningrad. It had been difficult for Hoepner to make this decision, and he had done so in the expectation that the entire panzer group would in due course be committed in this direction. After all, it was the full strength of the panzer group that would be needed to ensure that we could lunge as far as Leningrad. Despite any reservations he may have had, Hoepner ultimately had to act in accordance with his convictions. There were few commanders who would have been capable of understanding the difficulty of the situation and of taking responsibility for what needed to be done. The average commander would have lacked the courage to make his own decision. He probably would have submitted to the directives of the superior headquarters rather than to the demands of the terrain.

Field-Marshal von Leeb agreed with the decision that had been taken by Colonel-General Hoepner. The field-marshal stated in a telephone conversation on 13 July that it was 'necessary to find and pierce through the enemy's weak point', in this case the lower Luga. But his unease could be detected in what he had to say next: 'The army group depends on the panzer group, so the latter must not become worn out.' The panzer group was a long way ahead in a promising yet risky situation. At any rate, the headquarters of the panzer group was filled with confidence!

Once it turned northwards, the XXXXI Panzer Corps made excellent progress. There was no noteworthy enemy resistance. By 15 July, the panzer corps had already established a couple of bridgeheads over the Luga, with one held by the 1st Panzer Division near Sabsk and the other by the 6th Panzer Division near Porechye. On the left flank of the panzer corps, the 36th Motorised Infantry Division eliminated what few enemy forces remained. The bridges in Sabsk and Porechy had been taken intact, and there was almost no enemy presence on the north bank. The panzer corps had emerged from the marshy terrain and had only to advance through 20 kilometres of forest before reaching the road network that would take it the final 100 kilometres to Leningrad. Even though there was little enemy resistance, the panzer corps could not continue at that moment. A few days would be needed to top up supplies and improve the supply road, which branched off from the main road near Novoselye and stretched more than 150 kilometres to the Luga bridgeheads. All the construction and pioneer forces of the panzer group were assigned to work on the supply road. Colonel-General Hoepner hoped to be able to grant the XXXXI Panzer Corps freedom of action on 20 July or, if not, by 22 July at the latest. In the meantime, he would do everything he could to move the LVI Panzer Corps to the north.

It is worth stepping back for a moment to examine the situation across the entire front of the panzer group in the middle of July. Near Zapolye, on the Pskov–Leningrad road, the 1st Panzer Division had been relieved by the 269th Infantry Division on 14 July. The incredible march performance of this infantry division, although aided by the transport vehicles of the XXXXI Panzer Corps, is worthy of recognition. It ensured that the three mobile divisions of the panzer corps would be free to attack from the Luga bridgeheads! Once it was in Zapolye, the 269th Infantry Division came under the command of the LVI Panzer Corps. It was Hoepner's plan that the mobile divisions of the LVI Panzer Corps would at first be shifted to the road leading to the town of Luga and that they would later be placed behind the XXXXI Panzer Corps as a second wave for the assault over the Luga River. The attack on the town of Luga would then be left to the infantry. The road to Luga and the railway line that ran alongside it needed to come under German control, for both would be essential for the flow of supplies once the assault on Leningrad was underway. Hoepner had originally thought that the I Army Corps could be committed to the Luga road, but its advance via Porkhov had come about on the request of the army group. It had become clear that the Sixteenth Army could no longer fulfil the role it had been given of covering the southern flank of the panzer group.[92] If the army corps was able to assume responsibility for this role, the entire panzer group might still be able to attack from the Luga bridgeheads. This would have to happen soon. Any delay would allow the enemy time to create and reinforce a defensive front against the bridgeheads. The strength of the panzer corps was hardly more

---

[92] So as to support Army Group Centre in its offensive towards Moscow, the OKH decided in the middle of July that the Sixteenth Army needed to place the emphasis of its advance on its right wing. This was in stark contrast to what had been envisioned in the operational plan of Army Group North. The result was that the Sixteenth Army was unable to protect the southern flank of Panzer Group 4 for approximately three weeks.

than two-thirds of what it had originally been. Now was the moment for action!

(e) Panzer Group 4 is ordered to stay put

1. *A change in the point of view of Army Group North*

What the panzer group had just achieved was tremendous. It had advanced a long way in a short period of time and now stood on the lower Luga, poised to leap further towards the ultimate operational objective. However, the army group was growing increasingly concerned about its overextended front. It was inclined to think that a continuation of the advance at that moment was beyond the capability of the panzer group. Aside from the I Army Corps (of the Eighteenth Army), there was nothing that the army group could place alongside the southern wing of the panzer group. This was the very wing that might be exposed to danger if the panzer group immediately pushed further towards Leningrad. The formation on the northern wing of the Sixteenth Army, the X Army Corps, had veered away from the north-east to the south-east on 14 July so that it could work in conjunction with the XXVIII Army Corps to encircle Russian forces near and to the south of Novorzhev. This would last a whole week and would thereby increase the gap between the Sixteenth Army and the exposed wing of the panzer group. Although the operational plan of Army Group North had envisioned that the point of main effort of the Sixteenth Army would be on its northern wing, the OKH now demanded that this effort be shifted to the southern wing. The reason for this was that the OKH wanted the Sixteenth Army to cooperate closely with Panzer Group 3 (of Army Group Centre). In fact, it can be said that Field-Marshal von Leeb had already taken measures that were for the benefit of Army Group Centre. The point of main effort of the Sixteenth Army had never been fully placed on its northern wing. Now, in the middle of July, it was indisputably on the southern wing. The commander of Army Group North was deliberately supporting the plan of the OKH for a main thrust on Moscow. He wanted to help his close friend and chief of staff of the OKH, Colonel-General Halder, as much as was within his powers to do so. Yet this decision by

Army Group North to focus on the south came at the very moment that Panzer Group 4 wanted to strike to the north in the direction of Leningrad!

The close friendship between Leeb and Halder has been mentioned here so that the generosity of Army Group North in its decision to prioritise Moscow can be understood. It can also be understood that the army group had multiple factors to take into consideration. For the panzer group, Leningrad was the main objective, and Hoepner was certain that the city could be taken if he had six mobile divisions available for the task. For the army group, however, Leningrad was one of many considerations. Moscow was another such consideration, and an important one too. The result was that the army group and the panzer group were bound to have divergent views on how to assess the situation and how to act. For example, while the army group was of the belief that the enemy was 'putting up tough and united resistance', the panzer group thought that the enemy, helped by the terrain, was still employing stopgap measures that did not represent any real danger.[93] In any case, we could not afford to hand over the initiative to the enemy. Another example was the concern of the army group about the recent reorganisation within the Russian high command, with Marshal Kliment Voroshilov now in charge of the headquarters of the hostile army group based in Novgorod. The panzer group, on the other hand, was more interested in what forces the enemy possessed and what their level of training was. Several auxiliary formations had appeared before the front of the XXXXI Panzer Corps, including officer cadet units and proletarian divisions from Leningrad. Yet the panzer corps remained in the Luga bridgeheads for the time being. This was because the panzer group was acting in accordance with the wishes of the army group to proceed more slowly. We at the headquarters of the panzer group still thought that the advance would be renewed shortly, probably on 22

---

[93] Paragraph 1 of the order of Army Group North from 15 July 1941 stated: 'The enemy appears to be putting up tough and united resistance before the front of the army group.' This order was the first indication to the panzer group that there had been a change in the point of view of the army group, for it declared that the panzer group was to hold back for the time being. This would shape the character of the fighting for roughly the next three weeks.

July rather than 20 July. Little did we know that the halt ordered on 15 July would last as long as three-and-a-half weeks. The Luga bridgeheads would have to be held until 8 August. If such a prolonged halt, as well as the extended absence of the infantry of the Sixteenth Army, had been intended from the beginning, it would have been best to evacuate the bridgeheads so as to reduce the attrition on the forces of the panzer corps. Maintaining the Porechye bridgehead in particular proved to be costly for our troops. But even the army group had not anticipated that there would be so long a wait before the renewal of the advance. The panzer corps could very well have been used during that time for the seizure of Narva, which lay only 50 kilometres away from the Porechye bridgehead. This would have cut off the route of retreat for Russian forces in Estonia. The army group had not considered this solution, as it would have meant sending the panzer group away from rather than towards Leningrad.

2. The consequences for Panzer Group 4

The desire of the army group to hold back had such an impact on the panzer group that even the planned shift of the LVI Panzer Corps to the north was made dependent on the satisfactory development of the situation in the south. While the panzer group viewed the approach of the I Army Corps as an opportunity to provide security on the southern wing and release the LVI Panzer Corps for action in the north, the army group wanted both of these corps to combine their efforts for a renewed push in the direction of Novgorod. Between 17 and 25 July, both corps pressed forward approximately 40 kilometres to the east against reinforced enemy units. However, no decisive breakthrough was achieved. This advance came to a standstill almost 10 kilometres before the western tip of Lake Ilmen. It was unable to make further progress and had to await the arrival of the infantry formations on the northern wing of the Sixteenth Army that were still on their way from the south-west.

The LVI Panzer Corps had been drawn away from what had been the intended point of main effort of the panzer group. With its forces split in two, the panzer group had been rendered incapable of pushing northwards from the Luga bridgeheads. The XXXXI Panzer Corps lacked the necessary strength on its own to execute the 100-kilometre thrust on Leningrad. Both flanks would be dangerously exposed. On the right would be the bulk of the enemy's forces; on the left, the Russian 8th Army would be retreating along the coast from the Baltic region towards Leningrad. The flanks would somehow have to be protected. Such a task would require the commitment of three mobile divisions, leaving nothing with which to conduct the assault on the city itself. Under such circumstances, it was not worthwhile for the XXXXI Panzer Corps to advance from the Luga bridgeheads. The panzer corps would be needlessly putting itself in danger. The commander of the panzer group had gained the impression that the army group had not fully comprehended or had at least considerably underestimated the difficulties that had to be overcome. Too much was being expected of the panzer arm. It almost seemed as if there was a prevailing belief that there was nothing our tanks could not do. It is of course true that they frequently achieved the incredible, and they would do so again when they eventually did strike northwards from the Luga bridgeheads. But they could not perform miracles. They only ever succeeded if they could operate in favourable terrain and, most importantly, if they could take the enemy by surprise.

Colonel-General Hoepner and the troops under his command were at all times eager to renew the advance. The wait for three-and-a-half weeks was agonising, but there was nothing he could do until the LVI Panzer Corps was once more in his hands. This panzer corps had been under the direct control of the army group throughout the second half of July, and it was now to be assigned the task of carrying out the attack on either side of the road that led to the town of Luga. Subordinated to the panzer corps was the 3rd Motorised Infantry Division and the 269th Infantry Division, and it was intended that another infantry division (the Police Division) be placed under its command. In the meantime, on 2 August, the 8th Panzer Division was made available to the panzer group. It was placed in panzer group reserve and positioned behind the XXXXI Panzer Corps. Unfortunately, SS Division Totenkopf would be in army group reserve, although Field-Marshal von Leeb indicated that it might possibly be placed at the disposal of the panzer group at a later stage. Hoepner constantly strove to arrange the allocation of as many units as possible to the planned attack from the Luga bridgeheads. He wanted the eventual renewal of the advance to possess the utmost power and to be decisive in nature!

Just as great as the struggle for mobile forces was the tug-of-war over the date for the renewal of the advance. This date was initially postponed from 20 July to 22 July, but then it was put off until 26 July, 28 July, 3 August, 4 August, 7 August, and finally 8 August. When the panzer group pushed forward on that final date, it had to do so without the help of the Luftwaffe. German aircraft were instead supporting the advance on Novgorod. Field-Marshal von Leeb, who was not always free to act independently, left it up to Colonel-General Hoepner to decide at the last moment whether to postpone the attack another one or two days. Such a postponement might perhaps be advantageous if the weather was good and the Luftwaffe was available. However, the commander of the panzer group remained committed to 8 August. He was convinced that the attack had to go ahead after such a long wait. Any further delay would worsen the chances of success. Besides, preliminary measures had already been taken by the panzer group from noon on 7 August for the renewal of the advance. Forces had been moved into position and preparatory attacks had been carried out. A withdrawal at that moment might have been seized upon by the enemy. Something else that may have played a role in Hoepner's decision was the fact that he wanted to get the hesitant army group going again. It was best that our offensive regain momentum at once. The enemy could not be allowed the opportunity to strengthen his defence or even to surprise us with a counter-attack.

(f) The reorganisation of the forces of Army Group North

Although the army group had made it clear as early as the middle of July that it intended to reorganise its forces for the assault on Leningrad, the actual redistribution of those forces only took place gradually. This was one reason why the panzer group was so significantly delayed in renewing its advance. But the greatest effect was on the Sixteenth Army. Assigned an ever-changing series of tasks that generally drew it further towards the south, the Sixteenth Army was unable to exert its influence in the north. The leadership of the army group had developed a tendency to focus on secondary tasks. It had therefore lost sight of its primary objective. When the commander of the army group did have a chance to turn his attention to the north on 22 July, it was his plan to place the X Army Corps (the northernmost formation of the Sixteenth Army) and a further infantry division on the right wing of the panzer group. He was of the view that the advance in the direction of Novgorod had the best prospects of progressing rapidly.[94] But it was only a short time later that Leeb changed his mind and decided that the area to the south of Lake Ilmen, near Staraya Russa, was more important. The X Army Corps would therefore be sent there instead. The task of protecting the right flank of the panzer group would have to be given to next formation that was expected to arrive from the south, the XXVIII Army Corps. However, the two divisions of this army corps were still a long way behind! The capriciousness of the god of war always seemed to be impacting the development of the situation in the northern sector of the Eastern Front. The OKH was greatly interested in Staraya Russa. Panzer Group 4 would find itself in action in the vicinity of this town later in the year, although the results there would be disappointing.

Perhaps the one advantage that arose from the frustratingly long wait was that the infantry formations had a chance to catch up to the panzer units. Elements of the Sixteenth Army could therefore be counted upon to help with the advance on Leningrad once it resumed. It was the plan of Field-Marshal von Leeb that the Sixteenth Army constitute the right wing of the attack front on Leningrad. It would advance in the direction of Novgorod and then approach Leningrad via Chudovo, thereby freeing the panzer group of the need to proceed along this route. The northern attack wing of the Sixteenth Army would be made up of the I and XXVIII Army Corps, creating a total of five and one-third infantry divisions and one motorised infantry

---

[94] In accordance with the wishes of Army Group North, the leadership of Panzer Group 4 decided on 22 July that it would push forward on the right wing before doing so on the left.

division (SS Division Totenkopf). To the left of the Sixteenth Army would be Panzer Group 4. The panzer group would be responsible for a front 160 kilometres in width and would have four infantry and five mobile divisions under its command. In the right sector of the panzer group, on either side of the road to the town of Luga, was the LVI Panzer Corps with the 269th Infantry Division, the Police Division, and the 3rd Motorised Infantry Division. In the central sector of the panzer group, the Luga bridgeheads, was the XXXXI Panzer Corps with the 1st Panzer Division, the 6th Panzer Division, the 36th Motorised Infantry Division, and the 1st Infantry Division. Behind this central sector was the 8th Panzer Division in panzer group reserve. In the left sector of the panzer group, south of Narva, was the XXXVIII Army Corps with the 58th Infantry Division. The main attack of the panzer group would most clearly proceed from the Luga bridgeheads. It was foreseen that the 8th Panzer Division would be committed there once the attack was underway. The enemy had prepared a number of defensive lines in depth before the bridgeheads, so our attack there would be difficult. Nevertheless, Colonel-General Hoepner was confident that we would succeed. If that did indeed turn out to be the case, Field-Marshal von Leeb indicated that he might send us SS Division Totenkopf for additional support. Yet this was not a firm promise. We at the headquarters of the panzer group thought that the commander of the army group was more inclined to give SS Division Totenkopf to the Sixteenth Army so as to hasten the push in the direction of Novgorod. This would be in accordance with the wishes of the high command for the placement of the point of main effort on the right for the approach on Leningrad. Colonel-General Hoepner was concerned that this would split up the forces of the army group without any benefit. The terrain to the south-east of the city was particularly unfriendly. Also, with so few forces at its disposal, the army group would have best created just one point of main effort. This would have to be placed where the most progress had been made and where the terrain ahead looked good. In other words, the bridgeheads over the lower Luga had to be our focus. It was from there that we had the best chances of launching and sustaining a rapid advance. We therefore decided that this attack front would be reinforced with the

1st Infantry Division. It was placed inside the Porechye bridgehead and would attack towards the north-west in the direction of Kingisepp in order to help the XXXVIII Army Corps with its own advance. It would simultaneously push northwards so as to protect the flank of the XXXXI Panzer Corps.

The attack of the LVI Panzer Corps towards the town of Luga would be difficult. The area was filled with forests, lakes, and marshland. Aside from that, there was a large Russian training ground near the town. We could expect to run into extensive defensive fortifications as well as several anti-tank ditches, obstacles, and minefields. The Russian 41st Rifle Corps stood there with three divisions (later five divisions) under its command. It was in a good position to resist our advance, and its supply was secure with Leningrad to its rear. Despite the enormity of the challenge, it was imperative that the panzer corps fight its way through the town of Luga in the direction of Leningrad. The road along this line of advance would be important for the flow of supplies on the German side once the assault on Leningrad commenced. There would be no alternative supply route! The other main road that led to Leningrad, via Novgorod and Chudovo, would be less safe. Much of this road ran alongside the Volkhov River, behind which the enemy lay. For the support of the attack of the LVI Panzer Corps, it was envisaged that the XXVIII Army Corps would be able to be utilised. It was just arriving from the south and would be placed on the eastern wing in due course.

The elimination of the enemy's centre of resistance in the vicinity of the town of Luga was of high priority. Colonel-General Hoepner decided that this could be done most quickly by striking towards the town from the north. The enemy would thereby be dislodged from the rear. The forces to approach from the north would need to come from the XXXXI Panzer Corps. Once this formation reached Krasnogvardeysk, elements of it would foreseeably circle to the right to make this approach. Progress would probably be slow. Krasnogvardeysk was situated 100 kilometres to the north of the town of Luga, and the road that connected the two was surrounded on either side by forests and marshland.

It would be difficult to secure a supply route through such unfriendly terrain. The Luga–Leningrad road was what we needed to gain control of, but we could assume that the enemy would do the utmost to hold on to it. The road via Novgorod and Chudovo was in good condition, although, as mentioned, it would not be free from danger. The third, and at that time the only, supply route was the one that led to the XXXXI Panzer Corps on the lower Luga. It was only a temporary route and was too easily affected by the weather conditions. Fortunately, supplies continued to flow along this route to the degree that was needed until the road through the town of Luga came under our control. Not at any stage did the enemy manage to attack our temporary route.

The importance of the flow of supplies in the considerations of the panzer group cannot be overstated. While we wanted to press forward as much as possible, the establishment and security of supply lines demanded our constant attention.

(g) The attack from the Luga bridgeheads succeeds but cannot be exploited

1. *The attack succeeds despite great difficulty*

At 0900 hours on 8 August, the four divisions of the XXXXI Panzer Corps pushed forward from the Luga bridgeheads. Aerial support was impossible due to heavy rain. The fighting was heavy too. It was in fact the most fierce and costly fighting our troops had endured to date. The reactions of the Russian troops were astonishingly fast and powerful, especially before the Porechye bridgehead. The enemy concentrated his artillery and mortar fire there and conducted multiple counter-attacks. The 6th Panzer Division made no progress whatsoever, yet it lost one-third of its combat troops on just that first day of the attack! The 36th Motorised Infantry Division, whose initial task it was to advance to the north-west from the Sabsk bridgehead and establish contact with the 6th Panzer Division, only managed to move forward a short distance. Only on the outer wings of the bridgeheads was there some degree of success by nightfall. But the panzer corps did not consider this to be enough. Casualties had been so heavy that it looked as if the attack might fail altogether. It was questionable whether the 6th Panzer Division could keep going with the forces it had left. In his report to the panzer group late that first evening, the commander of the panzer corps ended his appraisal of the situation with the following words: 'The XXXXI Panzer Corps will halt at and fortify the line that has been reached and will go over to the defensive.'

Colonel-General Hoepner felt compelled to intervene at that moment. Both he and the commander of the panzer corps had been aware from the outset that there would be strong enemy resistance. In the three-and-a-half weeks during which we had been at a standstill, the Russians had created a deep and dense network of defensive positions, obstacles, anti-tank ditches, and minefields in front of the narrow bridgeheads. This network was bound to be difficult to overcome, particularly in the unfriendly terrain near the Porechye bridgehead. Even the army group had been made fully aware of the situation beforehand. Hoepner telephoned Reinhardt after midnight and urged him to persist with the attack. The outer wings of the panzer corps had made some progress, so an attempt should be made on the next day at the very least to exploit this. Both men held one another in high esteem. They had fought together since the campaign in Poland. Hoepner had at that time been the commander of the XVI Panzer Corps and Reinhardt of the 4th Panzer Division. The battle in the vicinity of the lower Bzura had been just as critical as the position we were in now. The bond of trust between the two men back then had helped to ensure that the situation could be mastered, and it was perhaps the case that they both remembered this now. General Reinhardt therefore declared that he was ready to attempt a continuation of the attack.

It was difficult for Hoepner to have to urge a commander so high in his estimation to keep going. Was it possible that the enemy had become too strong, as was what seemed to be the conclusion of the panzer corps? Were we sacrificing the lives of our men in vain here? It was not unjustifiable that such questions might arise. And now Hoepner was countermanding the order of the commander in charge of the panzer corps! Although a tough call to make, Hoepner regarded it as necessary. But then the commander of the army group telephoned at 0700 hours and spoke of his intentions of drawing upon the forces of the panzer group for the offensive on the right wing. He wondered whether the advance of the XXXXI Panzer Corps ought to indeed be brought to a halt. So even the army group wanted to hold back rather than push forward! Yet Hoepner did not halt the advance. And with the XXXXI Panzer Corps fighting on its own at that moment, he thought it crucial that the LVI Panzer Corps drive forward with all the energy it could muster.

The reason for the difficulties encountered in advancing from the Porechye bridgehead became apparent later. According to evidence gathered from POWs, the Russians had ordered an attack for midnight on 8 August so as to eliminate the bridgehead. This explained the enemy's concentrated artillery and mortar fire, his high expenditure of ammunition, the tenacity of his infantry, and his immediate execution of a counter-attack. Had our own attack not already begun, the enemy would have disrupted our preparations in the confined space of the bridgehead with his heavy fire and mass of ground troops. A situation could have arisen in which the German side was put at a disadvantage from the word go. The Porechye bridgehead might even have been lost. We could therefore count ourselves lucky that we had not further delayed the commencement of the offensive.

For several hours on 9 August, we waited anxiously for news from the front. It eventually became clear that the 1st Panzer Division was making progress. On 11 August, elements of the panzer division had advanced northwards out of the woodlands and into terrain that was ideal for combat. They enveloped and destroyed the enemy resistance near Porechye and then, on 12 August, continued to the north and northwest. By 13 August, the entire XXXXI Panzer Corps was once more advancing on Leningrad. The enemy forces had been utterly decimated. Only a few weak elements remained before the front of the panzer corps. Not a single Russian unit seemed to be intact. Brand new tanks had been disabled and captured; it was the first time that their crews had sat in tanks. The prospects of a breakthrough to Leningrad were good. We just needed the forces to carry it out! We were once more of the view that, despite our success, we were too weak on this front. The 3rd Motorised Infantry Division and SS Division Totenkopf needed to be brought forward quickly!

The commander of the panzer group thus made further efforts to obtain the allocation of these forces from the army group. After the 8th Panzer Division, as planned, had been committed to the attack front of the XXXXI Panzer Corps on 11 August, Colonel-General Hoepner described to Field-Marshal von Leeb the situation that had arisen and the necessity of exploiting it. In particular, Hoepner requested that he be given SS Division Totenkopf, a possibility that had been mentioned by Leeb on 6 August. Yet the field-marshal now felt unable to make the SS division available. It was engaged in combat on the right wing and could only be released in the event of good progress there. The field-marshal wanted the advance on Novgorod to gain more momentum, whereas that in the north was already rolling forward and did not, in his view, need further help. The XXXXI Panzer Corps had entered open terrain, had relatively few enemy forces to oppose it, and had only another 50 kilometres to go before it reached Krasnogvardeysk. It was the preference of the commander of the army group that a pincer attack be carried out against Leningrad. However, the right pincer still had a considerable distance to cover, and the terrain in front of it would not encourage rapid progress. Hoepner followed up his request of 11 August with a written appraisal of the situation on 12 August. He sent it to the army group, but any decision regarding the transfer of the SS division was put off.

All the panzer group could do was to make the best use of the forces at its disposal. It would have to push its only other mobile division, the 3rd Motorised Infantry Division, to the front as quickly as possible. The division was not being used to its full potential in the forest fighting in the sector of the LVI Panzer Corps on the way to the town of Luga. It would be better sent to the sector of the XXXXI Panzer Corps and could very well be the unit to strike southwards from Krasnogvardeysk into the rear of the Russian 41st Rifle Corps. Colonel-General Hoepner therefore ordered early on 13 August the detachment of the 3rd Motorised Infantry Division from the front before Luga so that it could move into the area of the XXXXI Panzer Corps. The LVI Panzer Corps was scheduled to be relieved by the L Army Corps on 15 August, with the latter to take over the attack on the town of Luga and the former to be released for a second strike, behind the XXXXI Panzer Corps, against Leningrad. With the transfer of the 3rd Motorised Infantry Division, the planned shift of the LVI Panzer Corps, the approach of the L Army Corps, and the small chance that SS Division Totenkopf would become available in the future, it was beginning to look as if the panzer group would have the forces it needed to attack the town of Luga from the rear whilst also launching a decisive assault against Leningrad.

2. *Panzer Group 4 is stopped for the second time*

Field–Marshal von Leeb visited the command post of the panzer group early on the morning of 15 August. This command post was about to be shifted to a position further north, near Lake Samro, so as to be near the attack sector of the XXXXI Panzer Corps. While most of the staff of the headquarters of the panzer group set off along the supply road for the new command post, Colonel-General Hoepner stayed behind in the old command post in Strugi Krasnye for his meeting with the field-marshal. Hoepner informed Leeb that the panzer corps was moving forward and that it had good prospects of success. It ought to be able to reach Krasnogvardeysk and Krasnoye Selo in two days. It might even be able to make it as far as the outskirts of Leningrad. There were only weak enemy forces resisting the advance of the panzer corps. Most of them were the scattered elements of units that had been destroyed. The first infantry regiment of the 3rd Motorised Infantry Division was to be detached that day and sent behind the panzer corps. The detachment of the second infantry regiment would take place in another two or three days. With the arrival at that moment of the L Army Corps, the LVI Panzer Corps would soon be ready to follow in the wake of the XXXXI Panzer Corps. Hoepner made yet another request for the allocation of SS Division Totenkopf. Enemy resistance remained strong in the vicinity of the town of Luga, so Hoepner wanted the attack from the north against the town to be as powerful as possible. If the L Army Corps was left to deal with the Russian 41st Rifle Corps on its own, it might be several weeks before the road could be safely used by German supply traffic.

The commander of the army group expressed satisfaction with the development of the situation and agreed with the plans that had been made by the commander of the panzer group for the continuation of operations. Nevertheless, he was not prepared at that stage to assign the SS division to the panzer group. It was clear to Colonel-General Hoepner that Field-Marshal von Leeb still had in his head the idea of a point of main effort on the right, especially due to the fierce fighting taking place at that time to the south of Lake Ilmen near Staraya Russa. However, there was not yet any indication that the situation had become critical. The units of the X Army Corps were to the east and south of Staraya Russa and were being attacked by a determined enemy from the south. The commander of the army group wanted to wait and see how the situation there unfolded. Hoepner could be reasonably happy with how the meeting had gone as he drove to the new command post afterwards. The 130-kilometre trip took six hours. Although he was in an all-terrain vehicle, the roads were not in the best condition. He was glad when the trip came to an end. It was a sunny summer afternoon, and the new command post was situated near the peaceful Lake Samro amidst beautiful scenery.

The tranquillity was interrupted towards 1800 hours by an order from the army group that 'hit us like a bombshell'. The panzer group would be required to hand over the LVI Panzer Corps and the 3rd Motorised Infantry Division to the Sixteenth Army. This order was issued 'due to the deep penetration achieved by the enemy south of Staraya Russa'.[95] SS Division Totenkopf was to be placed under the command of the LVI Panzer Corps and committed to the area south-west of Staraya Russa. The task of the LVI Panzer Corps would be to confront and annihilate the strong Russian forces that were attempting, by heading towards Dno, to outflank the southern wing of the X Army Corps. With this decision, the panzer corps would no longer be taking part in the battle for Leningrad. One-third of the forces of Panzer Group 4 had been taken away at what was probably the most crucial moment.

---

[95] From my report at noon on 16 August 1941 regarding the handing over of the LVI Panzer Corps.

It suddenly looked as if the panzer group would not reach Leningrad after all. Great risks had been taken to approach the city as quickly as possible, but the forces that were needed for the final push were no longer available. It had at one moment been the case that the advance on Leningrad could be carried out with ease; in the next moment, that was not the case. The panzer group was too weak. All that could be done now was to await the arrival of the infantry. The XXXXI Panzer Corps had fought exceptionally hard, but its success could not be exploited. The most it could do was to aim for small tactical victories. An effort could still be made to strike the rear of the Russian 41st Rifle Corps, albeit with much greater care than before, as the deep flanks of the panzer corps would be vulnerable. It can therefore be said that the intervention of the army group effectively compelled the panzer group to come to a halt. As I wrote in my report on 16 August 1941:

> This is the second time that the army group has stopped the panzer group from achieving its objective. The first occasion was on 18 July when we wanted to strike northwards from the Luga bridgeheads; now it is when we want to fully exploit the breakthrough of the XXXXI Panzer Corps. The enemy currently has no forces opposing the panzer corps … Whether the severely worn-out divisions of the panzer corps will be able to continue to push forward after giving the enemy time to regroup is by no means certain.

This indicates how bitterly disappointed we were by the intervention of the army group. Our disappointment was all the worse given that the field-marshal had only that morning (15 August) approved of our plan to reinforce the XXXXI Panzer Corps. We had been led to believe that only SS Division Totenkopf would be held back. Now, as it turned out, the panzer group would have to slow down, and the Russian leadership would be granted another three weeks in which to prepare for the defence of Leningrad. Only on 9 September would Army Group North be ready to attack the outer defensive ring of the city.

3.   *Was the intervention of Army Group North necessary?*

It was only on the morning of 15 August that the panzer group had learnt about the existence of a combat zone in the vicinity of Staraya Russa, but the commander of the army group had made no indication that the situation there had become critical. As a result, his decision in the late afternoon to detach the LVI Panzer Corps from the panzer group came as a complete surprise to us. Yet Field-Marshal von Leeb ought to have been aware well before then as to how the situation near Staraya Russa was unfolding. Russian forces, including a motorised division and cavalry units, had been pushing through a gap in the front to the south of Staraya Russa since 13 August. These forces were in the deep flank of the X Army Corps on the evening of 14 August. It seemed as if they were aiming to strike the rear of this army corps, for they were pushing in the direction of Morina, which lay 25 kilometres to the east of Dno (on the railway line that connected Dno and Staraya Russa). The Sixteenth Army had committed emergency forces to the area, including the reconnaissance battalion of SS Division Totenkopf, in an attempt to regain control of the situation. Field-Marshal von Leeb would have known of this before his meeting with Colonel-General Hoepner. It explains his unwillingness to make the SS division available to the panzer group. The SS division would have been the only mobile formation near Staraya Russa. Upon his return to the headquarters of the army group in Pskov that afternoon, the field-marshal discovered that the fighting power of the X Army Corps had decreased so considerably that he regarded it as necessary to order the LVI Panzer Corps to render assistance. He must have been fully conscious of the negative impact such a measure would have had on the panzer group, but he was unable to find another solution. As it turned out, the OKH had made available to Army Group North the XXXIX Panzer Corps (from Panzer Group 3) for the crisis near Staraya Russa. It would, however, take a few days for this panzer corps to arrive. Yet even the LVI Panzer Corps could not be expected to conduct an immediate counter-attack to the south-west of Staraya Russa. It would hardly be ready before 19 August. The situation near Staraya Russa must have been truly disastrous if the army group thought it necessary to deprive Panzer Group 4 of an entire panzer corps! On the evening of 15 August, Leeb telephoned Hoepner to express his regret that such a decision had to be made. He had given the order 'only with the utmost reluctance'. He said that he hoped that those elements of the 3rd Motorised Infantry Division that had not yet been detached might still be allowed to remain with the panzer group. Perhaps he thought this possible given that the XXXIX Panzer Corps would soon be on its way to the army group.

Field-Marshal von Leeb had not considered the allocation of even a few elements of the XXXIX Panzer Corps to Panzer Group 4 as compensation for the loss of the LVI Panzer Corps. The entire XXXIX Panzer Corps would be committed to the right, meaning that it was to approach Leningrad via Novgorod and Chudovo. We at the headquarters of the panzer group were inclined to think that the field-marshal had not fully appreciated the success of the breakthrough of the XXXXI Panzer Corps. He was increasingly preoccupied with the problem of creating a point of main effort on the right. As he and the high command saw it, the XXXIX Panzer Corps was supposed to bring about a decisive outcome by attacking Leningrad from the south-east. Such a plan was flawed.

Colonel-General Hoepner regarded the detachment of the LVI Panzer Corps to be a mistake. It could very well have been used to maximise the success of the attack that had been launched from the Luga bridgeheads. To abandon the advance on Leningrad, an objective for which we had striven so hard since the beginning, due to what could only be a diversionary attack (Staraya Russa) would result in the initiative being taken by the enemy. The Russian leadership would be able to congratulate itself for such a result. It had obtained for Leningrad a reprieve of three weeks. Hoepner had not yet been informed of the allocation of the XXXIX Panzer Corps to the army group. Had he been aware of this, he could have tried to dissuade Field-Marshal von Leeb from employing it to the south-east of Leningrad. The terrain there was not ideal for tank battles. It was for that reason that the difficult decision had been made in the middle of July to pivot the XXXXI Panzer Corps to the north in the direction of the lower Luga. The army group had agreed with this decision, but it now failed to exploit the success that had been achieved.

(h) The panzer arm before Leningrad

1. *The success of the left wing*

Panzer Group 4 was severely weakened by the detachment of the LVI Panzer Corps. The result was the deceleration of the attack wing (the XXXXI Panzer Corps), for there were no longer any reserves to follow in its wake and protect the flanks. The northern flank in particular would be increasingly exposed to danger, as the Russian 8th Army was at that time retreating from Narva towards Leningrad. Until the arrival of the Eighteenth Army, which was pursuing the retreating formation, the XXXXI Panzer Corps would have to rely on its own forces to secure the northern flank. The 36th Motorised Infantry Division, the 6th Panzer Division, and elements of the 1st Panzer Division were committed to this task. In the meantime, the panzer corps slowly pushed forward into the area to the west of Krasnogvardeysk. Only a small number of forces were available for essential reconnaissance tasks to the east of the Luga–Leningrad road. It was extremely difficult for the panzer corps to scrape together any attack forces at all. The only remaining formation it could use was the severely depleted 8th Panzer Division. On 20 August, this formation reached the area south of Krasnogvardeysk and then turned to the right so as to approach the town of Luga from the north. Russian forces were still holding out in the vicinity of the town, but the position that the panzer division had reached ensured that they could no longer be supplied.

Even though the panzer corps was advancing much more slowly, the fact that it was still moving at all could be regarded as progress. On 31 August, the 8th Panzer Division finally made contact with the leading elements of the L Army Corps approximately 25 kilometres to the north of Luga. The Russian forces retreated into the marshland east of the main road and struggled northwards along the corduroy roads that they had built. They were later surrounded in the so-called Luga pocket and were forced to surrender. More than 20,000 men fell into captivity. It took several days for the road to be cleared and repaired, and the bridge over the Luga River had to be reconstructed. It was with a great sense of relief that our supply units could begin to make use of this vital road from 3 September. Colonel-General Hoepner was probably more relieved than anybody else. One-and-a-half months had passed since the decision had been made to pivot the XXXXI Panzer Corps towards the lower Luga. If the town of Luga had not been approached from the north, the enemy troops in the vicinity would not have been dislodged. Rather, they would have been a thorn in the side for any German advance via Novgorod and Chudovo.

Now that the road through the town of Luga was under the control of the panzer group, the most important task to be undertaken was the rapid advance of the L Army Corps towards Krasnogvardeysk.[96] The army group wanted to launch the assault on Leningrad with the strongest forces possible. Field-Marshal von Leeb and Colonel-General Hoepner discussed the situation during a meeting at the command post of the panzer group near Lake Samro on the morning of 27 August. It was the plan of the field-marshal that the XXXIX Panzer Corps, at that time near Tosno, would approach Leningrad on the right wing.[97] Under the command of this panzer corps was the 12th Panzer Division and the 20th Motorised Infantry Division.[98] Next to the XXXIX Panzer Corps would be the XXVIII Army Corps with the 96th, 121st, and 122nd Infantry Divisions. Both the XXXIX Panzer Corps and the XXVIII Army Corps were concentrated into one larger formation and designated Group Schmidt.[99] For the assault on Leningrad, it was intended that Group Schmidt would be subordinated to Panzer Group 4. The Sixteenth Army would in the meantime keep its front facing to the east. It was the task of Group Schmidt to attack Leningrad from the south-east. The L Army Corps and the XXXXI Panzer Corps were to approach the city from the south and south-west. On the left wing would be the XXXVIII Army Corps (of the Eighteenth Army). Unfortunately, despite the wishes of the commander of the panzer group, the LVI Panzer Corps was no longer available. After the victorious conclusion of the counter-attack south of Staraya Russa, the LVI Panzer Corps was to remain to the south

---

[96] Krasnogvardeysk lay on high ground and was formerly known as Gatchina, the location of one of the main palaces in the time of the tsars. The town had now been developed by the Russians into a defensive strongpoint.

[97] Tosno was situated on the Chudovo–Leningrad road, approximately 50 kilometres south-east of Leningrad.

[98] The third mobile division of the XXXIX Panzer Corps was the 18th Motorised Infantry Division, but it had to be left behind to cover the northern flank and the Volkhov River. This division was soon placed under the command of the I Army Corps.

[99] General of Panzer Troops Rudolf Schmidt was the commander of the XXXIX Panzer Corps.

of Lake Ilmen and was given the task of pushing further eastwards. The army group hoped that it would be able to gain territory in the direction of the Valdai Hills.

The commencement of the attack on Leningrad was earmarked for 9 September. The forces on the western wing moved forward that very day. Their goal was to tighten and seal the ring of encirclement that was forming around the city. To the south-east of Leningrad, they were to push as far as the south bank of the Neva. To the south of the city, they needed to take the Duderhof Heights. This high ground had been the location of the parade ground in tsarist times. To the west of the city, our troops would be required to reach the Gulf of Finland in the vicinity of Uritsk. The eastern attack wing, which was to approach Leningrad from the south-east, was not yet ready to advance. This will be examined shortly.

The western attack wing met with success. The panzer forces achieved the most, concentrated as they were for the drive on the Duderhof Heights. The XXXXI Panzer Corps had taken possession of the high ground there on the evening of 11 September, with the 1st Panzer Division and the 36th Motorised Infantry Division already thrusting further to the north in the face of little resistance. Leningrad lay ahead, now in clear view. However, we lacked the forces needed to exploit this success! It had been the intention of the commander of the panzer group to send in the 8th Panzer Division at the final moment. He thought that it might even possess sufficient power to be able to seize Leningrad, although Hitler had ordered that the city was only to be encircled. Unfortunately, the 8th Panzer Division was still taking part in the elimination of the Luga pocket and thereby the destruction of what was left of the Russian 41st Rifle Corps. The enemy forces in the pocket fought tenaciously and tied down German troops for a long time. Only on 14 September did the 8th Panzer Division become available. By then, though, the panzer group and the panzer division would be given entirely new tasks. They would no longer be involved in the assault on Leningrad.

On 15 September, the formation on the right wing of the XXXVIII Army Corps, the 58th Infantry Division, took Uritsk. It had thereby reached the Gulf of Finland. In the sector of the XXXXI Panzer Corps, any further thrust to the north had to be foregone. Only the 36th Motorised Infantry Division pushed onwards. The 1st Panzer Division had turned to the east in order to help the 6th Panzer Division and the L Army Corps in their push towards Detskoe Selo and Slutsk. The L Army Corps had been delayed by the fierce fighting around Krasnogvardeysk. It was not until noon on 13 September that this strongpoint fell into our hands, whereupon the L Army Corps could resume its advance on Detskoe Selo. Once this objective had been reached, a tight ring of encirclement had been established around Leningrad. No further progress was made after that, as the forces needed to infiltrate the city were lacking.

2. The failure of the right wing

The right wing comprised the I Army Corps with two and two-thirds infantry divisions and the XXVIII Army Corps with three infantry divisions. It attacked in the direction of Novgorod on 10 August, two days after the XXXXI Panzer Corps had commenced its advance. Both infantry corps were provided with air support as they struggled forward through woods and bushes against tough resistance. The I Army Corps seized Novgorod on 15 August, and from there it started to make faster progress to the north. However, it had to commit ever more troops to its right flank, for the enemy forces that had been in the vicinity of Novgorod had retreated eastwards over the Volkhov. Although the I Army Corps reached Chudovo, it was completely exhausted by the need to protect the flank. It had by then nothing left with which to continue in the direction of Leningrad, which still lay another 100 kilometres away.

It was at that time that the XXXIX Panzer Corps appeared. Its leading formation, the 18th Motorised Infantry Division, advanced on 25 August in conjunction with the infantry of the right wing of the XXVIII Army Corps towards Lyuban, 35 kilometres to the north–west of Chudovo on the road to Leningrad. The division was compelled to pivot to the north-east so as to repel enemy forces that had pushed westwards over the Volkhov. It was soon transferred from the XXXIX Panzer Corps to the I Army Corps and assigned to the security front along the river. As mentioned earlier, it had been the plan of the army group to subordinate Group Schmidt (with the XXXIX Panzer Corps and the XXVIII Army Corps) to Panzer Group 4 for the attack on Leningrad, while the Sixteenth Army would be assigned responsibility for the security of the eastern flank (with the I Army Corps along the Volkhov). However, the army group had yet to fully organise its forces along these lines.

The 12th Panzer Division took over as the spearhead of the XXXIX Panzer Corps from 25 August. It entered Tosno on 27 August (50 kilometres from Leningrad) and stood near Izhora by the end of the month (20 kilometres from Leningrad). It came to a stop after that. The headquarters of the panzer corps was of the view that any attempt by the panzer division to push on would be pointless, as the panzer division would have been on its own against the forces in Leningrad. The infantry of the XXVIII Army Corps had fallen behind, and the 20th Motorised Infantry Division, the second division of the XXXIX Panzer Corps, had swivelled to the north upon reaching Tosno. This division would approach the Neva downstream from Shlisselburg and was to destroy the weak enemy forces that stood in its path. It managed to carry out this task, but it was soon attacked by stronger Russian units from the north (over the Neva) and the east. These enemy forces gradually pushed forward on a wide front on the southern side of Lake Ladoga. In order to strengthen the defensive front against this enemy, the XXXIX Panzer Corps decided that the 12th Panzer Division would have to be sent there. Izhora had to be abandoned as a result, and the entire XXXIX Panzer Corps would have to miss out on the battle for Leningrad. The subordination of this panzer corps to the panzer group would not take place. The only formation that remained on the right wing for the assault on the city was the XXVIII Army Corps. Considerable demands had been placed upon this formation, as it had forced its way through marshy terrain and wooded areas against stiff enemy resistance. Its striking power had been severely depleted in the process. It was only ready to begin its attack on the city on 12 September, three days after our forces on the western wing had started to move forward. The army corps approached Slutsk and Detskoe Selo from the east. With few enemy forces to oppose it, the army corps soon stood on the outskirts of Slutsk. Nevertheless, it was still in a seriously weak condition. Colonel-General Hoepner requested of the army group at that time that the XXXIX Panzer Corps be assigned to relieve the XXVIII Army Corps. The panzer corps possessed greater striking power, and the army corps would be ideally suited for the defensive and security tasks in the forests and swamps near the Volkhov. The commander of the army group rejected this request on the grounds that the detachment of the panzer corps could not be carried out in the middle of a strong enemy attack. He added that the panzer corps was defending fiercely on a wide front and that it would take some time for the army corps to arrive. Although it had been his intention that the panzer corps play a role in the assault on Leningrad, this could no longer be the case.

With that, all hopes of an attack on the city from the south-east were dashed. It would be up to the western wing to carry out the decisive strike.

Yet the development of the situation in the combat zone of the XXXIX Panzer Corps required that another and final sacrifice be made by Panzer Group 4. The constant relief attacks conducted by the enemy in the vicinity of the Volkhov swamps caused Field-Marshal von Leeb great concern. Even though the Sixteenth Army had been able to assemble a few emergency units to plug the gaps that had appeared along the front, the situation continued to unfold so unfavourably that the field-marshal regarded it as imperative that the 8th Panzer Division be sent at once to the XXXIX Panzer Corps. He issued orders to that effect on 14 September. The panzer division was only just leaving the area where the annihilation of the Luga pocket had taken place, and Colonel-General Hoepner was hoping that he could use it to deliver the *coup de grace* against Leningrad. This was going to be the last chance to take the city, for the panzer group was soon to be transferred to Army Group Centre for the assault on Moscow. The date that had been set for the departure of the panzer group from Army Group North was 17 September. But with the allocation of the 8th Panzer Division to the XXXIX Panzer Corps, the thrust on Leningrad would be unable to continue. Hoepner cannot be blamed for feeling disappointed about this. He was required to hand over the final reserve force at his disposal, and it would be heading into terrain which, as he had previously pointed out to the army group, was no good for tanks. This situation also meant that the panzer division would not be available to the panzer group for the planned drive on Moscow.

Another prediction that had been made by Hoepner and that was now confirmed in practice was the precariousness of the flow of supplies along the road through Novgorod and Chudovo. On 10 September, the supply line of the XXVIII Army Corps had to be shifted from the road through Novgorod to that through Luga, as the former was too long and had become too slow. On 15 September, the supply line of the XXXIX Panzer Corps also had to be shifted to the road through Luga, for that through Novgorod had been blocked by enemy forces that had pushed beyond the Volkhov. It can only be imagined how unpleasant the situation would have been if all our panzer units had advanced via Novgorod! Without the rotation of the XXXXI Panzer Corps to the north and the subsequent advance of this formation from the Luga bridgeheads, the road through the town of Luga may very well have never fallen into our hands.

(i) Analysis of the advance on Leningrad

The study of the advance on Leningrad provides an opportunity to understand what can be achieved by a large panzer formation. Unlike the other three panzer groups in the initial stages of the campaign in Russia, Panzer Group 4 remained committed to a single operational objective and came within reach of that objective. The measures taken by our military commanders can therefore be evaluated in terms of how effective they were in propelling us toward that objective. The details of each situation can be reconstructed thanks to the records of the headquarters of the panzer group. This enables the assessment of the decisions of Colonel-General Hoepner in the context of the prevailing interests of higher levels of command.

It is important to understand the relationship between Panzer Group 4, Army Group North, and the OKH. The objective of the panzer group was Leningrad. The commander of the panzer group therefore did everything in his power to ensure a rapid advance towards the city. He had no desire for the forces under his command to be diverted from this objective. The success of the drive of the panzer group on Leningrad was also the primary focus of the army group to begin with. For the OKH, the most important objective was Moscow, and this inevitably had an impact upon the army group. The result was that the Sixteenth Army, whose point of main effort was supposed to be on its northern wing, was drawn ever further to the south. The army group was also influenced by the OKH in that it became increasingly fixated on the idea of creating a point of main effort on the right wing for the assault on Leningrad. Ever since the middle of July, then, the attention of the army group had been divided. The clear focus of the army group on Leningrad can be seen up until 10 July, for the panzer group was fully supported in its drive towards the city before then. After that date, the close relationship between Field-Marshal von Leeb and Colonel-General Halder played a central role in shifting the gaze of the army group towards Moscow. The field-marshal demonstrated that he was willing to place the interests of the OKH ahead of those of the army group. Unfortunately, this meant that the panzer group could not always rely on receiving the support it needed. Leningrad was only a secondary objective in the eyes of the OKH, even though Hitler attached it great importance. The OKH was therefore keen to prevent the diversion of forces from Army Group Centre to the north. Army Group North had to depend on what little it had for the attainment of its objectives. No additional forces would be allocated to it. Not even Panzer Group 3 was to be handed over, although such a measure had been foreseen as a possibility in the *Barbarossa* plan. Hitler even considered this possibility on multiple occasions in July, but nothing came of it. Instead, the forces of Army Group North would become increasingly involved in the fighting on the northern wing of Army Group Centre. The tendency of the Sixteenth Army to veer to the south is evidence of this development. By 2 July, the only infantry corps that Army Group North had in reserve, the XXIII Army Corps, had been transferred to Army Group Centre.

The demand of the OKH that the right wing for the assault on Leningrad be reinforced is a situation that can be interpreted somewhat differently. Hitler had requested that Leningrad receive greater attention, so it seems that the OKH was to some degree complying with this request.

The OKH did not want to irritate him under any circumstances. He had insisted on approaching the city on the right wing, even though such an approach would be too difficult given the nature of the terrain there. A fleeting glance at the map would not have revealed how troublesome the terrain would be for the XXXIX Panzer Corps later on. The OKH probably came to the conclusion in August that there was indeed a chance of seizing Leningrad and that it could take that chance by accommodating Hitler's request for an attack on the right wing. Yet the OKH also demanded of Army Group North that it reinforce the troops fighting in Estonia, as Hitler had said that he wanted Estonia to be occupied more quickly. It was in fact more important for the army group and for the entire German effort in the northern sector of the Eastern Front that a swift victory be achieved at Leningrad, but the focus of the OKH on Moscow continued to shape the conduct of operations. The OKH might not have revealed to Hitler that it favoured Moscow over Leningrad, but there is no doubt that the drive on Moscow was given priority.

The clash of conflicting priorities is something that can happen in everyday life. The more tense and critical a situation becomes, the stronger and more conflicting are the views that arise. In times of peace, this phenomenon is perhaps most apparent in politics, with opinions always differing on domestic, foreign, economic, and social policy. In war, differences of opinion are considerably more difficult, for they must be resolved amidst the constant pressure and uncertainty of the battlefield! These competing interests of Panzer Group 4, Army Group North, and the OKH should be borne in mind when assessing the decisions made by Colonel-General Hoepner during the advance on Leningrad. The most important questions he had to consider were, in short, the following: the rapid thrust, Staraya Russa, the right wing, and the role of the terrain.

The *rapid thrust* refers to the advance of the panzer group well in front of the infantry wave. The support of the infantry is essential in many situations, but time can be lost if their arrival must be awaited. Only a rapid thrust can exploit the element of surprise. Once the enemy is thrown off balance, he can be compelled to retreat whilst repeatedly being attacked and outflanked. Such a success was achieved by the panzer group. It lunged forward again and again before the enemy had a chance to recover. This method of attack enabled the panzer group to advance more than 600 kilometres into hostile territory. Field-Marshal von Leeb fully supported the rapid thrust at that time. The panzer group had leapt once to the Western Dvina and again to the Ostrov–Pskov area, so it looked as if the third and final leap to Leningrad might be executed just as easily. Field-Marshals von Leeb and von Brauchitsch set 10 July as the date on which the third leap would begin. So that the panzer units under his command could continue to make use of good terrain and thereby maintain combat superiority, Colonel-General Hoepner decided that the panzer group would pivot towards the lower Luga. The progress made by the XXXXI Panzer Corps proved this decision to be correct. No enemy forces stood in the way of the panzer corps. It would only need a short period to be resupplied before making the final dash to Leningrad. The commander of the panzer group was convinced that the city could be reached if all six of his mobile divisions were committed to this task. He was also certain that there would be sufficient infantry forces to ensure the protection of the flanks. This should have been enough to keep the enemy in a state of surprise all the way to the gates of Leningrad. The eventual attack on the city failed, but this was due to unnecessary delays that took place beforehand. It ought to have been possible for a tight ring of encirclement to be established around the city six weeks earlier. The army group would have then enjoyed much greater freedom of action at a much earlier stage, and the OKH could have sooner realised its plan for a reinforced assault on Moscow.

The commitment of the army group to the rapid thrust began to wane from the middle of July. It had become concerned about the unstable situation on the southern wing of the panzer group. Due to the influence of the OKH, the left wing of the Sixteenth Army had not made as much progress as expected. The army group was aware of this development early on, but the panzer group only perceived that there was something amiss at a later stage. When it seemed as if, for whatever reason, the arrival of the infantry would be delayed, Colonel-General Hoepner was of the view that the best solution would be a defensive position on the southern flank. The defensive power of the I Army

Corps would be sufficient for this task, and the terrain there would be suitable for defence. The view of the army group on this matter was quite different. It wanted to remain on the offensive on the southern wing so as to create favourable conditions for the subsequent thrust that would swing around to approach Leningrad from the south-east. An attack requires strong forces. Because the infantry formations were still on their way, the army group chose to keep the LVI Panzer Corps to the south. This split up the forces of the panzer group. Yet Hoepner was under the impression that this was only temporary and that he would soon be able to attack over the Luga. The army group expected that the operation in the direction of Lake Ilmen could be carried out quickly, but this did not turn out to be the case. It had never been the intention of the commander of the panzer group for the XXXXI Panzer Corps to advance on its own from the Luga bridgeheads. The panzer corps possessed too little striking power to reach Leningrad. If it had attempted such an advance, it would have only put itself in danger.

The four mobile divisions in the Luga bridgeheads eventually rolled forward on 8 August. By that time, Hoepner believed that a rapid success was possible. The 3rd Motorised Infantry Division had become available and was assigned the task of following in the wake of the advance from the bridgeheads. He was also counting on the allocation of SS Division Totenkopf to the panzer group in a short time. The situation looked much worse on 15 August when the LVI Panzer Corps was suddenly detached from the panzer group. The most that could be achieved was an attack against the rear of the Russian forces in the vicinity of the town of Luga. This brought about the opening of the vital supply road through the town and at the same time the acceleration of the advance of the L Army Corps on Leningrad. The army group did not attach great importance to this. Ever since the renewal of the advance of the XXXXI Panzer Corps on 8 August, the army group saw the panzer group as merely the left wing for an 'army group attack' on Leningrad. The panzer group could have carried out a powerful and decisive assault against the city on its own had it been significantly reinforced, but the army group failed to seriously consider this. The army group hoped for, and therefore devoted considerable resources to, a swift advance on the right wing. The OKH would have hardly concerned itself with the question of a rapid thrust and would have most certainly never dreamt of the idea of a 'panzer group attack' on Leningrad. While it would have been happy with the rapid advance of the panzer group in the initial stages of the campaign, it would have been less pleased to see that the XXXXI Panzer Corps had veered to the left, towards the lower Luga. The OKH would have much preferred that the entire panzer group remain on the right wing. This topic will be revisited shortly.

The commitment of many of the forces of the army group in the direction of Staraya Russa had the effect of depleting the strength of the panzer group and of putting the army group itself in quite a predicament. It had been the original intention of the army group that the X Army Corps be used on the right wing for the approach on Leningrad, but this formation ended up being sent further to the east, towards Staraya Russa. This was by no means a simple security measure; it was rather the preliminary stage of a major operation planned by the OKH. This operation would involve the establishment of a foothold in the Valdai Hills so that the southern wing of Army Group North could subsequently carry out an assault on Moscow in conjunction with the northern wing of Army Group Centre. It was decided that the LVI Panzer Corps would partake in and therefore give greater impetus to such an operation. This was why Colonel-General Hoepner was deprived of this formation at the very moment he needed it for a reinforced attack on Leningrad. The value that the OKH attached to the seizure of the Valdai Hills is demonstrated by the creation of a southern pincer that was also to head towards the area. This southern pincer was composed of the II Army Corps and, from Panzer Group 3, the LVII Panzer Corps. The result of this operation was the laborious occupation of what became known as the County of Demyansk.[100] This region was operationally meaningless and filled with terrain that made combat difficult. While there were many forests, marshes, and lakes, there were barely any roads. The region was later

---

[100] 'Grafschaft Demjansk', named after the commander of the II Army Corps, General Walter Graf von Brockdorff-Ahlefeldt.

encircled by Russian forces and had to be fiercely defended in the winter of 1941–42. There was no point in holding on to this position, but Hitler had insisted that it not be given up. The defensive fighting was costly in terms of men and matériel, yet the pocket had to be abandoned in the end anyway.

Colonel-General Hoepner was disappointed that the LVI Panzer Corps had been taken away from him. Panzer forces were being split up rather than concentrated. 'What are they supposed to do there?' was his question when he discovered where many of his tanks were going to be sent. If both panzer corps had been utilised for the advance on Leningrad, the situation there probably would have been resolved quickly and dramatically. After that, it would have been possible for contact to be established with the Finns. Hoepner felt that the decision to detach the LVI Panzer Corps from Panzer Group 4 was the result of a serious misjudgement of the situation. The OKH seemingly regarded the advance through the Valdai Hills in the direction of Moscow to be of such great importance that it was prepared to deprive us of the forces needed for the assault on Leningrad. The fixation on Staraya Russa was detrimental to what should have been the main operation. The headquarters of the panzer group always maintained its focus on Leningrad, but it felt somewhat abandoned by the OKH and Army Group North.

The higher levels of command strongly favoured an attack on Leningrad on the *right wing*. If the panzer group had advanced via Novgorod, it might very well have been able to approach Leningrad, but it would have also been exposed to enemy attack. Its room for manoeuvre would have been severely limited. To the right of the road was the Volkhov, and to the left was forest and swamp. The panzer group would have had to fight for its existence and would have had little opportunity to exploit its superiority in mobility. An advance by the panzer group via Novgorod therefore had to be ruled out. It might only have been possible if additional panzer forces were available to sweep around the southern side of Lake Ilmen and clear the area to the east of the Volkhov. Such a security operation would have demanded considerable forces, and there would have been no guarantee that it would be able to push as far as Lake Ladoga. The Sixteenth Army had already sent the I Army

Corps (three and two-thirds divisions) behind the Volkhov front. This army corps fought its way across 120 kilometres of the 200-kilometre width of the enemy front. It cannot be said with any certainty how many more security forces would have been needed in the difficult terrain to the east of the Volkhov, but it is hard to imagine that the army group would have had anything else at its disposal! Besides, there were no good roads that led around or to the north of Lake Ilmen. This restricted movement and supply. A major operation there would have been utterly hopeless.

Neither the panzer group nor the army group gave the idea of a large-scale operation to the east of the Volkhov serious consideration. Field-Marshal von Leeb viewed the drive of mobile forces via Novgorod as an operation that could only be carried out simultaneously with an infantry advance (of the XXVIII Army Corps) through the forests to the west of the road. This required the preparedness of strong infantry forces at the front, but that was not the case in the first half of July. There would have been a wait of three weeks for the arrival of the infantry. Any such wait would have meant the abandonment of a rapid thrust. The army group did not want this. It therefore allowed the panzer group to search for and pivot towards the area where the enemy was weakest. It did not at that time intend to detain German forces in the Luga bridgeheads for three weeks. As has been mentioned, the XXXXI Panzer Corps would have had a chance to seize Narva in that period. However, during those three weeks, the situation changed considerably from the point of view of the army group. Its conduct was increasingly influenced by the OKH. By the time the infantry arrived, the army group was determined that Leningrad be approached from the south-east. It was for this reason that the commander of the army group wanted to reinforce the right wing with elements of the panzer group. While Colonel-General Hoepner was still counting on being able to send the LVI Panzer Corps over the lower Luga, Field-Marshal von Leeb had already decided that this formation was to be placed on the right wing. The field-marshal had originally allocated the 8th Panzer Division and the 3rd Motorised Infantry Division to the LVI Panzer Corps in preparation for the thrust from the Luga bridgeheads, the importance of which he had thoroughly understood. However, his view was soon changed by the unfavourable development of the situation in the sector of the X Army Corps and by the influence of the OKH. The XXXIX Panzer Corps was allocated to the right wing, and it was decided that Leningrad would be encircled rather than taken. Yet the panzer group continued to pursue the possibility of a decisive outcome before Leningrad. We remained unaware of what precisely was going on in the minds of those at the headquarters of the army group. Our objective never changed, so we devoted all our energy to the attainment of that objective. Despite the differences in the points of view between the army group and the panzer group, there always remained a relationship of trust and mutual respect between their commanders. The field-marshal may have been making decisions whose reasons were difficult to fathom, but it is worth remembering that he did not at all times enjoy freedom of action and that he did not necessarily like the course of action he felt he had to take. He supported the panzer group as much as possible. When discussions were taking place at the end of July regarding the creation of a point of main effort on the right, the OKH was in favour of detaching some or all of the elements of the XXXXI Panzer Corps from the panzer group. This idea was rejected by the field-marshal, who knew that the panzer corps had prospects of success over the lower Luga. And the panzer corps was indeed successful. Not only did it strike the rear of the Russian forces near the town of Luga; it also helped to clear the strip of land near Narva, between Lake Peipus and the Gulf of Finland, of enemy forces. The detachment of this panzer corps from the panzer group could not have been easily carried out in any case, for there were no infantry forces close enough to assume responsibility for the Luga bridgeheads. The distance between the town of Luga and the combat zone near Narva was at least 125 kilometres. The defence of this sector required the commitment of considerable forces. Any attack would have been impossible without the XXXXI Panzer Corps. The town of Luga would probably not have been taken then.

Even a reinforced attack on the right wing would have still encountered difficulties due to the unfriendliness of the terrain. Sending the XXXXI Panzer Corps there would not have helped. No more than one panzer corps could be committed there anyway, as there would not have been enough room for the exploitation of the superior mobility of the panzer forces. They would have been more likely tied down to security measures along the Volkhov, and this was what happened to the XXXIX Panzer Corps in the end. An infantry corps would have been much better there. The panzer formations were needed where the chances of success were greatest. This was on the left wing.

The *role of the terrain* was an important consideration in the employment of the panzer arm. Bad roads were encountered in the Baltic region, and movement was often difficult there, but there was always enough room for manoeuvre to enable progress to be made. The first real difficulties arose when the LVI Panzer Corps, crossing the Russo–Latvian border, entered old Russian territory. The two major roads that led to Leningrad (one via Novgorod and the other via Luga) were especially problematic. Vast stretches of territory to the south-west of Leningrad were covered with forest and swamp. This was unusual even by Russian standards. There was little room for our panzer formations to be used effectively. Their striking power, mobility, and performance were reduced to an unbearable minimum! The panzer troops were advancing at the rate that would ordinarily be expected of the infantry. Despite the inferiority of the Russian forces, there were barely any opportunities on the German side for conducting an envelopment or achieving a breakthrough.

A solution had to be found if we did not want to forego a swift victory. The area to the south of the Gulf of Finland offered the best possibilities for the employment of tanks and the push on Leningrad. It was therefore towards that area the panzer group needed to advance. It was a difficult decision for the commander of the panzer group to make, but it was essentially dictated by the nature of the terrain. Although the higher levels of command may have decided that they wanted to place the emphasis on the right wing, Colonel-General Hoepner could not be convinced that this was a good idea. The terrain on the right wing presented too many dangers. The unfortunate development of the combat and supply situation there proved Hoepner's assessment to be correct. The headquarters of the panzer group would have much preferred our full effort to be committed to the terrain to the west of Leningrad. If this direction of advance on the city had been pursued from the outset, a tremendous and early victory could very well have been achieved.

The panzer arm was far more dependent on good terrain than was the infantry. Regrettably, the OKH gave barely any consideration to the terrain around Leningrad. Its thoughts revolved around Moscow.

CHAPTER 4

The Assault on Moscow in 1941

(a) Plans for the operation

From the middle of September 1941, the bulk of the German Army in the East made preparations to launch a powerful strike that would annihilate the enemy forces under the command of Marshal Semyon Timoshenko and would subsequently lead to the capture of Moscow – the military, economic, and political centre of power of Russia. Approximately 70 divisions, all of which had already advanced far into Russian territory, would be committed to this assault. The formations at the disposal of Army Group Centre (Field-Marshal Fedor von Bock) were, from south to north, the Second Panzer Army (Colonel-General Heinz Guderian), the Second Army (Colonel-General Maximilian Freiherr von Weichs), the Fourth Army (Field-Marshal Günther von Kluge), and the Ninth Army (Colonel-General Adolf Strauß). Accompanying the Fourth Army was Panzer Group 4 (Colonel-General Erich Hoepner), and accompanying the Ninth Army was Panzer Group 3 (General of Panzer Troops Georg-Hans Reinhardt). These formations stood along a line which followed, from the area south of Bryansk, the upper course of the Desna and then ran through the terrain on the eastern side of Smolensk, Velizh, and Velikiye Luki. It was already autumn, so the weather was bound to deteriorate soon. This would negatively impact the movement of our units, especially the motorised troops. But there was no choice. The attack had to be carried out. It was imperative that most of the enemy's forces be destroyed before the onset of winter; otherwise, the Russian leadership would possess sufficient strength to make it more difficult for the German formations to take up a defensive position. The OKH was convinced that it would be possible to reach Moscow and thereby bring about a decisive outcome to the war. Even Colonel-General Hoepner was of the view that a final attempt should be made to achieve victory. If the risk had been taken to venture into Russia in the first place, any opportunity to defeat the enemy should be ruthlessly exploited. This did not mean that he was not apprehensive. The experience on the Volkhov front seemed to suggest that Russian reserves were inexhaustible. German strength, on the other hand, was limited. We were lacking in reserves, and most of our divisions were at half strength. The combat troops of Panzer Group 4 had been given little or no chance to rest, for they had been required to make the tiring journey to their new assembly area right away. Excessive demands had been placed on the matériel of the panzer group, and there was also a shortage of replacement parts. But if it was true that the enemy was running out of reserve forces, as believed by Hitler and many in the OKH, the attempt to take Moscow had to be made.

The planned operation would involve a double envelopment across a front approximately 200 kilometres in width. Mobile forces were to encircle and eliminate the bulk of the Russian formations to the east of Smolensk so as to create the conditions for a thrust on Moscow. It was intended that the northern and southern pincers would meet at the town of Vyazma, which lay 150 kilometres to the north-east of Smolensk. In the south, Panzer Group 4 would attack from the area east of Roslavl, in the sector of the Fourth Army; in the north, Panzer Group 3 would attack from the area east of Velizh, in the sector of the Ninth Army. Once they had completed their envelopment manoeuvre, the panzer groups would maintain a westward-facing front on either side of Vyazma whilst the infantry of the Fourth and Ninth Armies crushed the encircled enemy from the south-west, west, and north-west. This would be the main operation. Further to the south, the Second Panzer Army and the Second Army would conduct a smaller encirclement operation at the same time against enemy forces in the vicinity of Bryansk.

The role of Panzer Group 4 in the main operation will be the centre of attention here. The panzer group was subordinated to and placed on the right wing of the Fourth Army, and from there it would execute a rapid advance as the southern arm of the pincer attack. To the north of the panzer group and under the command of the Fourth Army were the VII, IX, and XX Army Corps, but the point of main effort would lie with the panzer group itself. To carry out the task that it had been assigned, the panzer group was given:

- the XXXX Panzer Corps with the 2nd and 10th Panzer Divisions;
- the XXXXVI Panzer Corps with the 5th and 11th Panzer Divisions;
- the LVII Panzer Corps with the 19th and 20th Panzer Divisions, the 3rd Motorised Infantry Division, and SS Motorised Division Reich (corresponding to a motorised infantry division); and
- the 252nd and 258th Infantry Divisions (already in the attack zone on the Desna front).

The panzer group was also assigned the XII Army Corps (with the 34th and 98th Infantry Divisions) for the protection of its southern flank during the advance and the maintenance of contact with the Second Army on the right.

Most of the enemy forces in the attack sector of the panzer group lay behind the Desna. Only a handful of forces remained on the west bank of the river. The position of the front line there had come about in the wake of a counter-attack that had been carried out by the enemy in late August and early September and had made inroads against the southern side of the Yelnya salient. This salient was a good location for the concentration of German forces for the envelopment operation. The enemy had now established a defensive position in the area, and he was in the process of setting up a second defensive line 20–25 kilometres further back. It was not yet clear precisely where he intended to focus his defensive efforts. We assumed that there was a strong reserve group in the vicinity of Spas–Demensk and another near Vyazma.

The task of the panzer group was to penetrate the enemy front line, drive between and well beyond Kirov and Spas–Demensk, and wheel to the north to complete an envelopment manoeuvre. Colonel-General Hoepner planned to swing as far to the east as possible, with the outer wing going through Yukhnov, so that he could surround all hostile combat and reserve forces. However, the highest levels of command (Army Group Centre, the OKH, and Hitler) were averse to the idea of a large encirclement like the one that had taken place in the battle of Smolensk. They feared that the line of encirclement might become overstretched and that the mobile forces committed to the task might thereby be exposed to danger. The commander of the Fourth Army, Field-Marshal von Kluge, who was inclined to agree with the plan of the commander of the panzer group, convinced his superiors that a decision on the matter need not be made prior to the attack. Such a decision could be made in accordance with how the situation unfolded. Hoepner wanted to avoid a small encirclement, as the forest region of Bogoroditskaya, roughly 45 kilometres in width and depth, would be in his path.[101] This would cause the temporary separation of the XXXX Panzer Corps from the XXXXVI Panzer Corps during their advance, and would therefore prevent them from being able to support one another. Hoepner was also concerned, not unjustly, that the formation on the left, the XXXXVI Panzer Corps, would become entangled in fighting with elements of the Russian reserves near Spas-Demensk too early on and that it might thereby be brought to a halt. Such a development had to be prevented so that the XXXX Panzer Corps would not be on its own as it approached Vyazma. If both panzer corps proceeded around the forest region, they could advance together along the Yukhnov–Roslavl road and then pivot to the north to drive towards the area near and to the south of Vyazma. After that, they would probably have enough time to fully establish a westward-facing front. There would be the constant danger that the left panzer corps would find itself tied down in fighting after it had advanced beyond the forest region and that the ability of both panzer corps to re-establish contact afterwards would consequently be delayed or prevented altogether. Hoepner regarded the demand for a

---

[101] The partly marshy forest region of Bogoroditskaya lay halfway between Spas-Demensk and Yukhnov, north of the Roslav–Yukhnov road.

small encirclement as an unwarranted intervention of the highest levels of command in the task he had been given. He thought that such intervention might cause the failure of the operation. It was his view that only the infantry elements of the panzer group should advance along the inner line of the envelopment. He wanted to commit the 252nd Infantry Division to that inner line, with the idea that it would maintain contact with the outer wing of the infantry front of the Fourth Army. But the only way in which the pocket could be sealed in the east was through the successful employment of the mobile formations. The LVII Panzer Corps would be kept in reserve at the outset so that it would be available to plug any gap that might arise in the ring of encirclement. It might also be needed to provide security further to the east.

(b) The Vyazma pocket

The beginning of the attack was earmarked for the end of September, but preparations took slightly longer than anticipated in the sector of Panzer Group 4 as well as on the southern wing of Army Group Centre. Only at 0530 hours on 2 October did the panzer group roll forward. It was a beautifully clear and sunny autumn day, with no sign of the bleak and rainy weather that had predominated in the lead-up to the attack. It was soon apparent that the enemy had been completely taken by surprise. Both pincers plunged into enemy territory more or less according to plan, although it cannot be claimed that enemy resistance was broken at once. The XXXX Panzer Corps, as hoped, made good progress. By the afternoon of 4 October, the 10th Panzer Division, on the right wing of the panzer corps, had covered more than 110 kilometres and had occupied Mosalsk. It took Yukhnov the following morning and pivoted to the north-west so as to approach Vyazma. Enemy resistance was also weak in front of the 2nd Panzer Division, the other formation of the same panzer corps. From 5 October, it too was well on its way towards the vicinity near and to the south of Vyazma. The commander of the panzer group had allocated SS Motorised Division Reich to the panzer corps on 3 October so that, depending on the development of the situation, it would be available for security measures in the east or reinforcement duties along the line of encirclement.

In the combat zone of the XXXXVI Panzer Corps, the advance proceeded more slowly. On the left wing of this panzer corps, the 5th Panzer Division fought fiercely against enemy reserve forces on the road to Yukhnov. It was still going slowly on 4 October. The formation on the right wing of the panzer corps, the 11th Panzer Division, took Spas-Demensk at 1730 hours, but more enemy forces continued to appear from the west. Unfortunately, the commander of the Fourth Army had already decided on the morning of 3 October that the XXXXVI Panzer Corps was to pivot to the north on the western side of the forest region of Bogoroditskaya. It thus looked as if we would only be aiming for a small encirclement. This would put the enemy forces to be encircled within striking range of our left flank and would create uncertainty with regard to where and when we would seal the pocket. We no longer knew if the XXXXVI Panzer Corps would be able to regain contact with the XXXX Panzer Corps. The intended meeting point for both panzer corps on the eastern side of the ring of encirclement was Andriany, which lay 20 kilometres to the south of Vyazma. The distance that the XXXXVI Panzer Corps would have to cover from Spas-Demensk to Andriany amounted to 75 kilometres. Combat conditions would be severe, and the state of the roads could be expected to deteriorate. The commander of the panzer group therefore had to be prepared to employ elements of his reserve formation, the LVII Panzer Corps, beside the XXXX Panzer Corps in the event that the XXXXVI Panzer Corps fell behind. But it was not yet clear whether this measure was necessary or whether it could even be carried out. Such a state of confusion prevailed on the one good road, Roslaval–Yukhnov, that Colonel-General Hoepner found it necessary to appoint the commander of the LVII Panzer Corps as traffic control commandant. His task would be to restore order on the road and ensure that the divisions under his command were brought forward as quickly as possible. SS Motorised Division Reich in particular had been significantly held up and now needed to advance swiftly.

The formation on the right, the XXXX Panzer Corps, continued to make good progress. The left column of the 10th Panzer Division reached the south-eastern outskirts of Vyazma at 0730 hours. The town was only weakly defended and was in our hands by 1030 hours. The right column of the panzer division had swept to the north. Once it arrived in the vicinity of the town, a firm defensive sector could be set up to its west. The enemy now began to reinforce his own defensive efforts. We had thus far encountered only scattered elements of Russian forces, but larger formations began to materialise from the west during the course of 7 October. However, by reaching Vyazma, we had successfully completed our envelopment manoeuvre. Now it was of the utmost importance that the ring of encirclement be drawn tighter! Our northern neighbour, Panzer Group 3, had also managed to envelop the enemy. On the morning of 7 October, the 7th Panzer Division (of the LVI Panzer Corps) stood to the north of Vyazma, on the Minsk–Moscow highway. It was there that it had established contact with our panzer group. By that evening, the XXXX Panzer Corps was holding the obstacle line that ran from the area west of Vyazma to that south-east of Andriany. There was a worrying wait for news at the headquarters of Panzer Group 4, but we finally received a report later that night that informed us that the left wing of the XXXX Panzer Corps had met with the right wing of the XXXXVI Panzer Corps near Andriany. This was according to plan. The 5th Panzer Division, on the left wing of the XXXXVI Panzer Corps, had been detained by enemy attacks from the north-west, but the 11th Panzer Division, on the right wing, had made better progress, albeit on roads that had been transformed into mud by the heavy rain of the previous day. These two panzer divisions had therefore become separated, but the XXXXVI Panzer Corps believed that it would possess sufficient strength to occupy its sector of the obstacle line. The 252nd Infantry Division was on its way. It was to reinforce the obstacle line and possibly relieve elements of the two panzer divisions. Meanwhile, the 258th Infantry Division had veered far out on the left wing of the XXXX Panzer Corps so that it could make use of the road to Yukhnov and advance more quickly. Its leading elements arrived in the area east of Yukhnov as early as 6 October to relieve the 10th Panzer Division, which had created a security line along the Ugra shortly beforehand. Fortunately, it turned out that the enemy forces facing this security line were not particularly strong. As far as we were aware, there were no concentrations of enemy troops anywhere to the east. It looked as if the advance on Moscow might have good prospects of success! But the pocket that had been formed needed to be dealt with first.

In the following days, the encircled enemy applied the greatest pressure against the southern wing of the XXXX Panzer Corps and against the entire front of the XXXXVI Panzer Corps. After his initial attempts to escape via Vyazma, the enemy had shifted his focus to the more easily defendable terrain in the southern part of the pocket. It was there that he tried to surge forward against the 11th Panzer Division, especially on the night of 10/11 October, but to no avail. From 12 October, his attempts to break out of the pocket subsided. At noon that day, the XXXXVI Panzer Corps, whilst holding on to its own sector, assumed responsibility for the sector of the encirclement front that had belonged to the XXXX Panzer Corps. The XXXX Panzer Corps itself withdrew from the line of encirclement and prepared for the drive along the highway towards Moscow. It was the desire of the headquarters of the panzer group that its mobile forces be ready as soon as possible for this decisive thrust. The ring of encirclement had become so tight by 13 October that the fighting there could be regarded as having reached a satisfactory conclusion. On 14 October, in the aftermath of the battle of encirclement, the panzer group was able to report that it had captured 140,000 prisoners, 154 tanks, and 933 guns.

There were still many enemy troops concealed in the forests. They needed to be mopped up, but that was a job for the infantry divisions. The panzer divisions had to push further to the east!

(c) The drive on Moscow

1. *Plans for the conduct of the operation*

On 7 October, with the drive on Moscow about to commence, there prevailed an atmosphere of boundless confidence at the headquarters of Army Group Centre and that of the OKH. The Vyazma operation had been a major undertaking that had required careful planning, and it had subsequently been executed relatively quickly and easily. At that stage, the pocket had yet to be eliminated, and the number of hostile troops that had been encircled was still unknown. Nonetheless, it was clear that a significant quantity of the enemy's forces had been or was soon to be destroyed. There was now a large gap in the main Russian front line, and it seemed as if the enemy lacked the reserves to close it immediately. The temporary weakness of the enemy had to be exploited! The army group order of 7 October therefore set highly ambitious tasks and objectives for the continuation of operations:

> On the southern wing, the *Second Panzer Army* shall advance on Tula (170 kilometres south of Moscow) as early as possible. From there, it will attack Moscow from the south.
>
> The *Second Army* will primarily be occupied with mopping-up operations around Bryansk and in the impenetrable forest region further east.
>
> Without delay, the *Fourth Army* is to advance:
>
> (a) with the recently subordinated XIII and XII Army Corps towards and over the Kaluga–Medyn line;
> (b) with the LVII Panzer Corps (19th Panzer Division, 20th Panzer Division, 3rd Motorised Infantry Division), initially under the direct command of the Fourth Army, towards the Protva crossings in Maloyaroslavets and Borovsk; and
> (c) with all available forces of Panzer Group 4 along the highway from Vyazma to Mozhaysk.
>
> In the combat zone of the *Ninth Army*, the initially available forces of Panzer Group 3 (XXXXI Panzer Corps) are to push to the line running from Gzhatsk to the area south of Sychevka. From there, they can intercept enemy reinforcements that might try to approach the Vyazma pocket from the north-east. As further elements of this panzer group become available, they will assemble along or behind this line so as to be ready to thrust in the direction of Kalinin or Rzhev in the near future.

It can be concluded from this assignment of objectives that the army group was of the view, more so than the OKH and Hitler, that the campaign in Russia had already been decided in our favour. It believed that what was to follow was simply a case of mopping up stragglers and making the most of our success. With this order, the army group had already laid out the manner in which the attack on Moscow was to be conducted. The Second Panzer Army, and later the Second Army, were to attack the city from the south and south-east. The Fourth Army was to approach from the west and Panzer Group 4

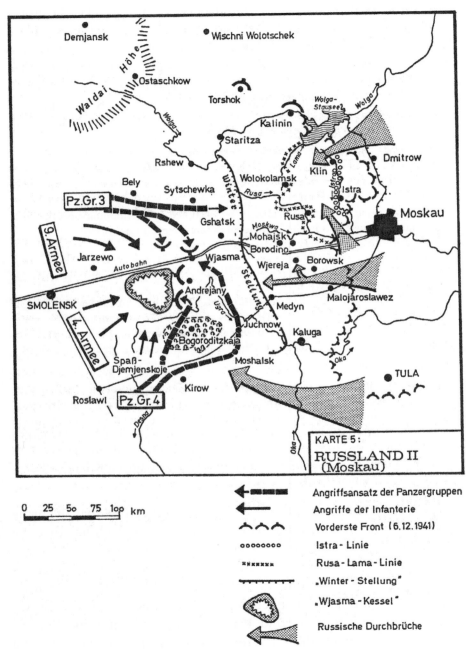

Demjansk
Wischni Wolotschek
Höhe
Ostaschkow
Waldai
Torshok
Volga-Stausee
Wolga
Wolga
Kalinin
Staritza
Dmitrow
Rshew
Klin
Istra
Bely
Sytschewka
Wolokolamsk
Rusa →
Pz.Gr.3
Gshatsk
Rusa
Moskau
9. Armee
Moskwa
Mohajsk
Borodino
Jarzewo
Autobahn
Wjasma
Wjereja
Borowsk
Andrejany
Medyn
Malojaroslawez
SMOLENSK
Ugra
4. Armee
Juchnow
Kaluga
Bogoroditzkaja
Spaß-
Djemjenskoje
Moshalsk
Oka
TULA
Pz.Gr.4
Kirow
Roslawl
Desna
Oka

KARTE 5:
RUSSLAND II
(Moskau)

Angriffsansatz der Panzergruppen

Angriffe der Infanterie

Vorderste Front (6.12.1941)

Istra - Linie

Rusa - Lama - Linie

„Winter - Stellung"

„Wjasma - Kessel"

Russische Durchbrüche

0   25   5o   75   1oo km

Map 5: Russia (Moscow)

was to do so from the north. According to the army group order, neither the Ninth Army nor Panzer Group 3 would be required for the assault on the city. It was foreseen that these formations would carry out a flank operation to the north, beyond the Kalinin–Torzhok line in the direction of Vyshny Volochyok. Not only was this plan confirmed by the higher levels of command on 14 October; the objectives it set were also expanded. Hitler was the driving force in this regard, but the OKH and the army group, both of which had assessed the outcome at Vyazma too optimistically, more or less went along with him, despite the fact that the mud season had set in on 13 October.

Colonel-General Hoepner was greatly disappointed when Field-Marshal von Kluge informed him of the new operational plan. The effects on the entire army group seemed to be bad enough, but what was demanded of Panzer Group 4 was dramatically different from what Hoepner had in mind. It was his opinion that the entire panzer arm needed to be concentrated for the final thrust on Moscow. The active involvement of the infantry was of the utmost importance, as was the participation of Panzer Group 3! Instead, Hoepner found that his reserve formation, the LVII Panzer Corps with its three mobile divisions, had been taken away. Hoepner himself was to be put in charge of the ring of encirclement near Vyazma. He was to be kept in the rear even though, as a panzer commander, he ought to be sent to the front. What use would SS Motorised Division Reich, at that time on its way from Yukhnov to Gzhatsk, be on the highway to Moscow if it were on its own to begin with? He tried to change Kluge's mind, but the die was cast. Kluge told him that the direct subordination of the LVII Panzer Corps to the Fourth Army would only be temporary and that it would be reallocated to Panzer Group 4 in due course, but Hoepner did not hold his breath. He could well imagine that the three mobile divisions of the panzer corps would soon be split up amongst the various infantry corps at the front. And this was precisely what ended up happening!

Hoepner was unable to comprehend why Panzer Group 3 was not to partake in the assault on Moscow. The northern formation of this panzer group, the XXXXI Panzer Corps, had not played a role in the encirclement at Vyazma. It stood to the north of the highway on 8 October and could have easily proceeded eastwards from there towards Moscow. If it had been reinforced with SS Motorised Division Reich, it could have conducted a powerful thrust along the 200-kilometre stretch of highway from Vyazma to Moscow. It would have most certainly overcome the little enemy resistance that existed at that time. Considering the fact that this panzer corps turned to the north and reached Kalinin, also 200 kilometres distant from Vyazma, as early as 13 October, there is no reason why it could not have taken Moscow by that date. There was no highway leading to Kalinin, so an advance on Moscow ought to have been comparatively straightforward. After 13 October, however, reaching Moscow would be much more difficult. The mud season had begun.

The stabbing operation to the north by Panzer Group 3 and the Ninth Army in the direction of Vyshny Volochyok, which the OKH hoped would not only relieve the pressure on Army Group North but also lead to a Russian retreat along the front as far as – if not beyond – the Valdai Hills, was something that greatly occupied the mind of Colonel-General Hoepner, even though he would not be directly involved in it. Given what he knew of the terrain in the vicinity of the Valdai Hills, he did not consider it a good idea to send mobile forces in that direction. It will be recalled that the County of Demyansk was characterised by unfriendly terrain and was operationally meaningless. Hoepner had regarded as futile the prior commitment of two panzer corps to that area. Like the terrain along the Volkhov and near Lake Ilmen, the area bordered to the south by Ostashkov and Vyshny Volochyok was impassable and could barely offer valuable opportunities to mobile forces. In such terrain, the Russian defender needed only the smallest number of forces to bring a German attack to a standstill. At the time that it had become clear that the advance on Leningrad had been brought to a halt and that it would no longer be possible to take the city, Hoepner had made the following comment to me: 'It's a good thing we're not required to launch an attack from Leningrad towards Moscow!' Hitler had imagined an advance directly from Leningrad to Moscow, but the bad terrain that lay between the two cities would have made progress quite slow and taken its toll on the panzer forces. It can therefore be understood why Hoepner was not in favour of the plan to send the Ninth Army and Panzer Group 3 to the north. In a report he wrote at a later stage, before the gates of Moscow, Hoepner made the following remark about the operational planning of the high command from 7–14 October: 'It seems to me that too many objectives were set and that they exceeded what the available forces could achieve.'

2.   *The advance is stopped by mud*

The commander of Panzer Group 4 had occupied himself very early on with the question as to how his panzer forces were to be released from the encirclement front so that they could quickly advance on Moscow. The temporary gap that had been created in the main enemy front could only be properly exploited with mobile forces, as the infantry would not be fast enough. Unfortunately, the elimination of the Vyazma pocket would still require some time, and it was against the panzer group that the bulk of the enemy forces in the pocket were applying pressure. This made impossible the early release of the panzer group. The only formation under its command that was therefore available for the push on Moscow was that which was in reserve, the LVII Panzer Corps. The leading division of this panzer corps, the 3rd Motorised Infantry Division, had reached the area south-west of Yukhnov on 7 October, while the other two divisions remained on the road that led to Moscow. So that perhaps one more mobile division could be made available, the XXXX Panzer Corps had been instructed on 6 October to commit only a few elements of SS Motorised Division Reich to the encirclement front and only if it was absolutely necessary. Otherwise, the SS division was to be sent to the north towards Gzhatsk. With these arrangements, the commander of the panzer group had seen to it that roughly half the mobile forces under his command were ready for the immediate continuation of the advance.

Yet he also prepared for the release of the entire panzer group from the encirclement front. The infantry needed to arrive as soon as possible to reinforce this front and relieve the mobile forces. Only the 252nd Infantry Division was available, for the 258th Infantry Division had been sent eastwards, and rightly too, by the XXXX

Panzer Corps towards Yukhnov so that it could relieve the 10th Panzer Division of responsibility for the security front there. The XXXXVI Panzer Corps was to insert the 252nd Infantry Division into the encirclement front without delay so that elements of the panzer divisions under its command could be released. This panzer corps would also work in close cooperation with its left-hand neighbour, the VII Army Corps, so that perhaps some parts of the 197th Infantry Division could be used to release additional panzer forces.[102] It was in this way that the commander of the panzer group hoped to make forces from his southern panzer corps available before the battle of encirclement reached its conclusion. However, the 252nd Infantry Division was delayed, as the commander of the Fourth Army wanted it to march to the east. Both the panzer group and the panzer corps strongly opposed this idea. Kluge gave in, but, by then, two days had gone by.

The headquarters of the panzer group had initially thought that the XXXXVI Panzer Corps would be released first, for the encircled enemy had fought most fiercely in the immediate vicinity of Vyazma to begin with. Yet the situation had developed quite differently. The enemy had shifted his efforts to the thickly forested southern part of the pocket, and it was against the sector of the 11th Panzer Division, especially at night, that he had applied his greatest efforts to break out. Fighting at night in impenetrable terrain had placed a considerable strain on the troops trying to hold the encirclement line! A handful of enemy units had almost escaped the pocket, but our tanks had destroyed them the following day. The delayed arrival of the 252nd Infantry Division on the southern wing of the XXXXVI Panzer Corps meant that the 5th Panzer Division was tied down in heavy fighting for much longer than desired. As soon as the leading elements of the 252nd Infantry Division arrived, they were committed to the encirclement front at once. But this did not lead to the immediate release of the 5th Panzer Division. It had to help the 197th Infantry Division, in whose sector the enemy had achieved local superiority.

---

[102] Not only the XXXXVI Panzer Corps but also Panzer Group 4 sought the cooperation of the VII Army Corps in this regard.

As the enemy's will to resist began to diminish from 12 October, it became clear that our northern panzer corps would be available before our southern one for the continuation of the advance along the highway. The XXXX Panzer Corps sent some units of the 10th Panzer Division eastwards that very day. From noon, the XXXXVI Panzer Corps had assumed responsibility for the entire stretch of the encirclement front that lay within the zone of the panzer group. From 13 October, the whole panzer group was available for the assault on Moscow, albeit in a severely weakened state.

It was now too late for a rapid advance on Moscow! The mud hindered our progress. A thrust towards the enemy capital would have had a reasonable chance of success if sufficient mobile forces had been committed to it before the change in weather of 13 October. The enemy was unprepared to defend the city at that time. As has been outlined, Panzer Group 3 could have reached Moscow if it had immediately advanced along the highway. Instead, on 13 October, Panzer Group 3 stood far to the north in the operationally unimportant region near Kalinin. The question to consider was whether the LVII Panzer Corps would have the same chance of success if it was now to be sent along the highway. The best answer we could come up with was 'maybe', but it was a plan that Hoepner wanted to pursue. Four mobile divisions, including SS Motorised Division Reich, probably would have managed to reach the city. However, it was doubtful whether the narrow spearhead would be strong enough on its own to resist the counter-attacks the enemy could be expected to launch against it. Yet it is worth bearing in mind that Colonel-General Hoepner was a highly capable military commander. He would have done everything in his power to bring the forces of his panzer group to the battlefield before Moscow and to concentrate them energetically against the decisive point. He certainly would have employed the LVII Panzer Corps to its maximum potential, but he was denied the opportunity to do so. It will be recalled that this panzer corps ended up being sent further to the south and that its three mobile divisions became no more than battering rams for isolated infantry attacks.

The value of the capability of the military commander in situations like this cannot be overestimated. While the time available for a task and the strength possessed by a formation may be limited, the problem-solving capacity of a good commander is not. Challenging situations require exceptional leadership. When it came to the question of how to lunge all the way to Moscow, only mobile forces would do. The two most important considerations were, first, to correctly exploit the units that were available and, second, to reinforce those units to the greatest extent possible. These forces needed to be led by a commander who knew how to use them. Colonel-General Hoepner was one of very few in the German Army to have proven himself as a panzer leader, and he was at that time available to lead the charge on Moscow. But he was instead held back to deal with the elimination of the Vyazma pocket. This ought to have been a task for the infantry. In the meantime, the advance on the enemy capital was being handled in a rather haphazard manner. Hoepner was not in the spot where the most decisive action was taking place. He was justifiably disappointed.

The measures taken on 7 October are an indication of the confidence of the German leadership. It already saw itself as the irrefutable victor on the battlefield. The Russian leadership supposedly had nothing left with which to fight. It is only this attitude that can explain the ambitious assignment of objectives and the lack of concern about the mud season. Rather than concentrating its forces against Moscow, the city that had been the ultimate operational objective from the very beginning of the campaign in Russia, the German leadership chose to set objectives that would take our formations far to the north, east, and south-east. The Second Army, for example, was given the task of driving towards Voronezh! The setting of such far-flung objectives originated with Hitler. Astonishingly, much of the post-war literature has credited Hitler with military ingenuity, even though this was something he never actually possessed or demonstrated. He had become a major political figure through his ability to act skilfully and ruthlessly, and his military decisions were often informed by political considerations and methods. Yet this was no match for military experience. In politics, success might be achieved through argument and bluff; on the battlefield, a decisive outcome depends on the ability to grasp the facts and perform well with the available forces. The most important fact at that time was that Moscow had to be taken. We therefore had to commit as much as possible in that direction. Our forces were limited. With too many objectives, our performance on any one front was bound to suffer. We had to be aware of what we could realistically achieve and what defensive measures the enemy had at his disposal. Another important fact was that the deterioration of the weather would have a negative impact on the conduct of field operations. Hoepner was by no means the only military commander with reservations. There were signs that the trust in the supreme command was beginning to fade.

What remained strong was our effort to reach the objective that we had been given. Nevertheless, the true victor was the weather. Although all mobile divisions were released and sent eastwards between 13 and 16 October, the constant rain meant that only the highway could be used by German traffic. Any attempt to approach Moscow by other means failed miserably. Our troops therefore had to proceed one behind the other, which of course slowed everything down. From Gzhatsk, the XXXXVI Panzer Corps attempted to make use of the old post road. We hoped that this would widen the front of Panzer Group 4 slightly and enable us to envelop any Russian troops we encountered. The enemy had not yet managed to close the gap that had been made in the front, but we were unable to exploit this. Only very slowly did we struggle forward. In the meantime, the enemy reinforced his front. He could do so easily, given that Moscow was his centre of communications. In the middle of October, the leading elements of the panzer group on the highway clashed with the first Russian division to have arrived from the Far East.[103] This was a new and well-equipped unit. It was nonetheless hurled back by the XXXX Panzer Corps. After that, the panzer corps penetrated the defensive line 20 kilometres west of Mozhaysk and pushed through the battlefield where Napoleon had won a bloody victory at the battle of Borodino in 1812. But more Russian forces from the Far East, approximately 20–30 combat-ready divisions, were

---

[103] This division was the Russian 32nd Rifle Division. According to prisoner statements on 11 September, this was the first formation of the Far East Military District to have been transported from Manchuria to the west. More divisions from the Far East appeared in the course of the next few weeks, primarily in the combat zone near Moscow.

on their way! We had no reserves whatsoever to draw on. So confident had our leadership been that some German troops had started to return to the Fatherland. The VIII Army Corps had been sent to the rear in the second half of October to be regrouped and refreshed. It had only just been subordinated to the panzer group, but was now replaced with the IX Army Corps.

The forward struggle lasted several days. The terrain hindered any meaningful progress. Even the highway became increasingly useless. Its condition deteriorated to such an extent that only tracked vehicles could move over it. A short time later, the highway had become impassable at one location between Vyazma and Gzhatsk and at another between Gzhatsk and Mozhaysk. Thousands of vehicles found themselves unable to move.[104] Our efforts to resolve the situation were considerable, but it was very much looking as if our advance had come to an end. The highway had to be closed off on 2 November. Yet how would our troops be able to fight? How would they be supplied? The unpredictability of the weather meant that supplies from the air would be unreliable. Now that we were bogged down, the enemy decided it was a good time to launch a heavy attack. He did so on the highway approximately 30 kilometres east of Mozhaysk, fully exploiting our immobility. It was a terribly demanding and nerve-wracking situation for the panzer group. Any reports or warnings that we sent to the higher levels of command were of no use. Perhaps their content was not conveyed clearly enough to Hitler? Or perhaps Hitler gave only his stereotypical reply: 'Nothing is impossible for the German soldier!' Hitler never stopped to consider that every German soldier, though highly capable, was just a human being. Colonel-General Hoepner frequently suggested that Hitler should see for himself the effects of the mud. Any military commander would have regarded it as his duty to do so. If Hitler had seen the state of the highway between Gzhatsk and Mozhaysk, he might very well have concluded that the continuation of the advance was hopeless! But Hitler did not visit the front.

---

[104] At the beginning of November, we estimated that there were between 2,000 and 3,000 vehicles that were unable to move on the stretch of highway between Gzhatsk and Mozhaysk.

A special supply column was created for the urgent delivery of ammunition to the VII Army Corps, which was struggling at the front on the highway. Only this supply column was permitted to use the closed highway. With considerable effort, it managed to reach and resupply the army corps. For most of our formations, though, supply and movement would be impossible until the frost. Finally, on 5 November, the frost arrived and conditions gradually improved.

German efforts to advance during the mud season had been in vain and had cost much blood and energy. The enemy had enjoyed all the advantages in this period.

3. The last effort

Although our troops were exhausted and poorly equipped for winter, Hitler insisted that the assault on Moscow be resumed as soon as possible. The mud season had drawn to a close, and the ambitious objectives that had been set remained unaltered. Yaroslavl, a large industrial city which lay on the Volga 250 kilometres to the north-east, was still one of those objectives when preparations were being made on 6 November for the renewal of the offensive. Nevertheless, the first concern was to top up supplies, especially fuel and ammunition. Our units had been living from hand to mouth for several weeks, and that was if the hand got anything at all. There had been some improvement in the flow of supplies from 27 October when the railway line to Gzhatsk was finally operational. The line was extended another 45 kilometres a short time later, so our trains could travel as far as Uvarovka, immediately to the west of Borodino.[105] According to the calculations of the quartermaster of the panzer group, the resupply of what was most needed would take at least six days. This meant that the middle of November was the earliest time the advance could resume. Colonel-General Hoepner advised against advancing further

---

[105] Translator's note: A major problem for German logistics on the Eastern Front was the need to relay the tracks in Russia, which were of a wider gauge than those in Central Europe. The ability of German rolling stock to be used for the delivery of supplies was dependent on the efficiency with which railway lines could be converted. Changing the gauge, if carried out thoroughly, was a time-consuming process.

and even recommended that a withdrawal be conducted instead. We could abandon the worthless terrain we were currently fighting for and establish a strong position a little further back. What use were our initial successes if we arrived outside Moscow drained and bled dry, unable to resist the enemy onslaught? In a well-prepared winter defensive position, we would probably be able to repel any attacks launched by the enemy. Hoepner's recommendation was rejected. The enemy was supposedly, as always, 'on his last legs'. Of course, this was nowhere near the truth. Additional Russian forces continued to arrive from the Far East, and we had no reserves to match them. But the order had been given for the renewal of the advance. There was a small ray of hope when the commander of the Fourth Army informed the commander of Panzer Group 4 on 11 November that the objective to be reached would be the Moskva–Volga Canal.[106] Moscow was finally the one objective of Army Group Centre. It was now imperative that all the forces that could be made available be committed to the assault on the city. Without delay, the Second Panzer Army had to attack from the south, the Fourth Army from the west, and Panzer Group 3 from the north. Colonel-General Hoepner emphasised to Field-Marshal von Kluge the urgency of carrying out this united attack. The troops of Panzer Group 4 had fought incredibly hard. We owed it to them to arrange the greatest possible support for them.

The necessity of attacking in unison must be emphasised, for it was at that moment a certain dishonesty in leadership took place for the first time. It may have been unintended, but it sheds light on the way in which the attack unfolded before Moscow. Panzer Groups 3 and 4 began to roll forward on the northern wing in the middle of November. Field-Marshal von Kluge had been in favour of this early start by the northern wing and had got his way, but Colonel-General Hoepner had not agreed with it and had made this clear to the field-marshal. If we wanted to attack and were convinced that we could do so, then all our formations ought to have attacked simultaneously. This would have denied the enemy the opportunity to shift his forces to any one

---

[106] The Moskva–Volga Canal flows northwards from Moscow, connecting the Moskva with the Volga.

defensive location. Once the moment arrived for the northern sector of the Fourth Army (Panzer Group 4) to advance, the southern sector (especially the combat zone of the XIII Army Corps) was heavily attacked by the enemy.[107] Kluge's response was to leave the four corps that were directly under his command in their initial positions on the southern side of the highway.[108] Both panzer groups were nevertheless to continue their advance, as was the Second Panzer Army from the south, in the vicinity of Tula. In between, on a front roughly 150 kilometres in width, no advance occurred. This provided the enemy with freedom of movement, and he fully exploited it.

Due to the fact that the Fourth Army had decided that its southern sector was to stay put, Panzer Group 4 discovered that it was in the unpleasant situation of having to attack whilst also maintaining contact with the XX Army Corps, which remained where it was to the south of the highway. The southern formation of the panzer group, the VII Army Corps, still had to cover 100 kilometres along the highway in order to reach Moscow. As the panzer group advanced towards the city, its southern flank would become ever more extended. Moreover, there would be no reinforcements to cover that flank. The VII Army Corps, and probably also the IX Army Corps, would have to devote more forces to the protection of the southern flank the further forward they advanced. Nonetheless, the flank would be so incredibly stretched that any security line established with the forces at the disposal of the panzer group would be lacking in strength. This would be a significant source of danger for the panzer group. Any military commander with a degree of common sense would not have considered such a risk to be worthwhile. It would come back to haunt us at a later stage! Colonel-General Hoepner constantly urged Field-Marshal von Kluge to order the advance of the southern sector of the Fourth Army. The

---

[107] Panzer Group 4, with five corps under its command, made up the northern sector of the Fourth Army. The southern sector consisted of four corps that were all directly subordinate to the Fourth Army.

[108] These four corps had been at the front for approximately one month. The front line had barely changed during that time. These formations (the XIII Army Corps, the XII Army Corps, the LVII Panzer Corps, and the XX Army Corps) therefore stood in reasonably well-developed positions, quite unlike Panzer Group 4!

field-marshal declared that he planned to conduct such an advance, but he repeatedly postponed it. Finally, after a delay of 14 days, the LVII Panzer Corps and the XX Army Corps commenced their advance on 1 December. The other two corps were engaged in fierce defensive fighting. After some initial success, the two attack corps had returned to their jump-off positions by noon on 3 December. They had only conducted a half-hearted advance. The commander of the panzer group told the commander of the Fourth Army in no uncertain terms that he felt as if he had been left in the lurch. If the performance of the Fourth Army in the second half of November and the first few days of December was a true indication of the striking power of the German Army, then Panzer Groups 3 and 4 should never have been ordered to attack in the first place.

Both panzer groups nevertheless made progress in their advance on Moscow from the north-west. The enemy resisted with the utmost tenacity. The panzer groups pushed him back, but at no point did they achieve a breakthrough. On 23 November, our forces crossed the Moscow–Leningrad road in two locations: Solnechnogorsk was occupied by the 2nd Panzer Division (of the V Army Corps of Panzer Group 4) and Klin by the 7th Panzer Division (of Panzer Group 3). The enemy was thereby denied the ability to use this road. The V Army Corps was now to proceed on either side of the road, while Panzer Group 3 was to push to the east towards the Moskva–Volga Canal. Reaching the canal at Dmitrov and Yakhroma, Panzer Group 3 was in a good position to cover the left flank of the thrust of Panzer Group 4. But only a few battle groups managed to press forward. They were the last forces that could be gathered in an attempt to extend our 100-kilometre lunge ever so slightly further. Meanwhile, new enemy forces continued to appear. The number of Russian tanks that stood in our path kept growing. The spearhead of the 2nd Panzer Division, approaching Moscow from the north, reached a point approximately 30 kilometres away from the Kremlin. It then came to a halt. At noon on 3 December, Hoepner reported to Kluge that the striking power of Panzer Group 4 had been depleted. The high command needed to decide whether a withdrawal was necessary. The panzer group was at that moment holding territory that protruded far to the east. It was a precarious position. Hoepner recommended that a retreat of 50 kilometres be carried out. He ordered his own troops that afternoon that they were to pause for three days. But he did not yet receive any corresponding order from his superiors confirming the cessation of the attack. Only on the morning of 6 December did the panzer group receive from the army group the order to retreat to a defensive position behind the Istra. Even the Second Panzer Army, approaching Moscow from the south, had overextended itself and had to stop its advance at roughly the same time as Panzer Group 4.

The assault on Moscow was over. The German forces had reached the end of their tether. We hoped that, as a result of the impossible situation, the necessary action would be taken by our military leadership. We could no longer fool or deceive ourselves. Our propaganda was nothing short of harmful in this regard. In his final appraisal of the situation outside Moscow on 5 December 1941, Colonel-General Hoepner made it clear to the Fourth Army why any continuation of the attack was impossible. He also criticised the constant underestimation of the enemy:

> Before the front of the panzer group are 17 rifle divisions, 2 rifle brigades, 4 cavalry divisions, and 12 tank brigades. Many of these units are weakened, but they are nonetheless numerically superior to what we have at our disposal.
> Our propaganda has portrayed the enemy as an already defeated force, worn out and unable to resist us. In reality, he continues to defend himself fiercely. It is obvious that he is ready for a winter campaign (fur hats, felt boots, padded trousers, and padded jackets), while our troops still have no protection from the cold. Cases of frostbite are increasing. This takes as much a toll on our men as does the enemy. Moreover, the Russians have well-prepared defensive positions to sit in. Our men are exposed to the harshness of the terrain!

That was the situation! The enemy had managed to bring us to a standstill, and we were compelled to retreat shortly afterwards. This had enough of a demoralising effect on our troops without the help of our propaganda. We had previously been in control of the situation, but now the enemy had taken the initiative. The disadvantageous psychological effect of the dramatic change in the situation was something that greatly occupied the mind of Colonel-General Hoepner. He did everything he could to bolster the spirits of the troops under his command. It was at least good for us that the decision to cease the attack, though made quite late, occurred before the enemy had a chance to overrun us. It was because of the threat of the growing numerical strength of the enemy that Hoepner had recommended a withdrawal. The overstretched panzer group would have been unable to defend itself effectively against an enemy counter-attack. Hoepner was particularly concerned about the weakness of the IX Army Corps. However, there were no reserves available to reinforce this army corps, let alone to help carry out a fighting withdrawal. The assault on Moscow had used up the last of our strength!

(d) The struggle to create a new front

The central sector of Panzer Group 4 stood far to the east and would need to conduct a retreat of 60 kilometres in order to reach the rear defensive line that had been recommended by Colonel-General Hoepner and approved by Army Group Centre. The southern wing of the panzer group, positioned on either side of the highway and along the Moskva with the VII Army Corps and elements of the IX Army Corps, would need to hold on to begin with. This southern wing was vulnerable. Its extension was a risk that might have barely been possible in attack, but it was a severe weakness in defence. The front curved quite sharply in the sector of the VII Army Corps, offering the enemy a good opportunity to execute a pincer attack against the German forces to the north of the Moskva (Panzer Groups 3 and 4). Hoepner therefore sought to reinforce this weak point of his front. He planned to do so with the 2nd Panzer Division, which was at that time fighting on the northern wing of Panzer Group 4. Once the northern wing commenced its withdrawal, the 2nd Panzer Division would become available.

The panzer group started its retreat on 6 December. Despite the attacking enemy and the unfriendly weather, the retreat was carried out more or less according to plan, with the panzer group reaching the Istra Line on the night of 11/12 December. The heavy casualties that ensued were inevitable, as our troops no longer enjoyed full mobility. Our artillery was especially handicapped. There were only enough tractors for half of our guns, and our draught horses were utterly exhausted and unable to make it far on the bad roads. We had to blow up some of our artillery pieces as well as several tanks that had run out of fuel. Fortunately, we were able to keep the enemy in check. In contrast to the situation on 6 December, that which came into being on 11/12 December offered slightly better security. The front line of the panzer group had been shortened by one-third and could be defended more easily, but it was not a proper defensive line. The lack of reserves meant that there were small gaps in the front that could not be filled. Nevertheless, Hoepner had seen to it that an orderly retreat had taken place. This helped to restore the confidence of the troops to some degree.

The commander of Panzer Group 4 could be content with the success of the withdrawal. However, he was unable to reposition the 2nd Panzer Division as intended. The situation had deteriorated considerably for Panzer Group 3. As early as 4 December, Russian counter-attacks had been launched against Panzer Group 3 not only from the east (over the Moskva–Volga Canal) but also from the north (from the area south of the Volga). Panzer Group 3 did not possess sufficient strength to hurl these counter-attacks back over the canal. By the time Panzer Group 4 commenced its withdrawal on 6 December, the enemy to the north had advanced so far westwards that the rear of the left wing of the panzer group was in danger. The enemy thrust was directed towards Klin. The town was an important junction through which all the divisions of Panzer Group 3 needed to conduct their withdrawal. There was no route available to the south of this town. The Russians reached the road to the north of Klin on 8 December and stood, as reported by Panzer Group 3, on the northern outskirts of the town on 9 December. Panzer Group 3 had been placed under the command of Colonel-General Hoepner the previous evening so that he could do everything possible to extricate it from the serious situation it faced. The enemy was threatening to cut off Panzer Group 3 from Army Group Centre. It was in the vicinity of Klin that the 2nd Panzer Division had to intervene. Subordinated to Panzer Group 3, this panzer division was no longer available for action on the right wing of Panzer Group 4, be it with the VII Army Corps or the IX Army Corps. It was not possible for Panzer Group 4 to create any other reserves whilst it carried out its withdrawal to the Istra Line. The fighting in the combat zone of Panzer Group 3 went back and forth for the next few days, and it was with great fortune that the German forces in Klin managed to evade encirclement. The retreat order issued by the army group on 6 December had been too late for Panzer Group 3. This experience ought to have taught the German leadership that a withdrawal needed to be ordered in a timely fashion.

While the envelopment of Panzer Group 3 from the north had been avoided, that of Panzer Group 4 from the south had yet to be. German forces along the highway and the Moskva were dangerously exposed. Beginning early on 11 December, the enemy launched an assault over the Moskva to the north and north-west, in the direction of Volokolamsk, which formed the southern arm of a pincer attack. This assault struck the left wing of the VII Army Corps, which we had been unable to reinforce. The overstretched units of the army corps on the north bank of the river were smashed into smaller pieces. They defended bravely, albeit without hope. The severe frost meant that the river was not at all an obstacle for the enemy. His tanks simply rolled across it! Furthermore, he was well-equipped for the winter. We were not. On 12 December, the enemy thrust cut through the sole supply road of the IX Army Corps at a point halfway between Zvenigorod and the town of Ruza. It seemed as if the enemy had achieved a great success. For the next two days, no word was received of the whereabouts of the three infantry divisions of the army corps. But then the first of their elements began to appear to the west of the Ruza River. More troops of the army corps continued to arrive, including horse-drawn artillery units. It was finally possible for the army corps to establish a new defensive line behind the river, with its strongest point concentrated in the vicinity of the town of Ruza. Even the shattered 267th Infantry Division, which had belonged to the VII Army Corps and which we had feared had been lost, arrived behind the new defensive line, although it was primarily just the infantry components that had survived. Its artillery units had fought courageously on the night of 11/12 December, but they were destroyed.

The southern arm of the Russian pincer attack had struck Panzer Group 4 at the very moment it was most vulnerable. The southern wing of the panzer group had been extremely weak and had been in urgent need of reinforcement. That had not been possible once the 2nd Panzer Division had been committed elsewhere. Only during the course of 12 December did the formations on the northern wing of the panzer group (the XXXXVI Panzer Corps, the XXXX Panzer Corps, and the V Army Corps) arrive behind the Istra Line. The northern sector of this line was possibly in danger due to the enemy breakthrough to the north of Klin, in the combat zone of Panzer Group 3. It was for this reason that Colonel-General Hoepner had proposed the withdrawal of the defensive front to a position behind the Ruza and the Lama. The VII Army Corps, on the southern wing of Panzer Group 4, would remain on the highway. The army group had approved this recommendation, so it was carried out on 13 December. The Lama was held by the V Army Corps to the north of Volokolamsk and the XXXXVI Panzer Corps to the south of the town, while the Ruza would be defended by the IX Army Corps. Meanwhile, the VII Army Corps held the sector bordered by the Moskva on the left (at roughly the point where the Ruza flowed into it) and the highway on the right. This sector remained the point of main effort of the enemy attack. The Fourth Army had made the 20th Panzer Division available for the support of Panzer Group 3. It was also considering making the 3rd Motorised Infantry Division available to Panzer Group 4 in response to the Russian attack over the Moskva. Both divisions had come from the LVII Panzer Corps, whose units had in the meantime been dispersed across the front of the Fourth Army. An indication of the degree of dispersal was the fact that the elements of the 20th Panzer Division were fighting on three different sectors of the front. One of these battle groups was composed entirely of foot soldiers, another was partially motorised, and the third remained fully motorised. It would take about three weeks for the entire panzer division to be reunited. But for now, the fully motorised battle group, on its way to Volokolamsk, went into action in the vicinity of the town of Ruza. It served as the covering force for the retreating IX Army Corps and later became the backbone of the defensive position there.

The combat strength of our units at that time was as low as 25 per cent. The maps at the OKW were probably marked with hundreds of divisional flags whose imaginary strength and mobility far exceeded what the real divisions possessed. Our performance in the snow and on the bad roads sometimes did not correspond to even 10 per cent of what was expected by the supreme command. If the German formations were to remain effective in the current circumstances that prevailed on the battlefield, all measures to be taken had to be ordered in advance. Our planning had to be conducted with as much foresight as possible. Any delay in issuing orders could be costly.

The rather fortunate development of the situation in the sector of the IX Army Corps was the result of the initiative shown by its various unit commanders. They were determined to bring their troops safely behind the Ruza. Any units that encountered the enemy had to fight their way through, be it by day or night. It became clear shortly afterwards that the army corps had retreated westwards through a predominantly northbound Russian attack. The German and Russian lines of movement had crossed one another. It was likely that both sides were primarily concerned with reaching their objectives, so the annihilation of one by the other was not strictly necessary. There had therefore been no need, as had at first been feared, to remove the IX Army Corps from our situation maps. Instead, after a few days had passed, the army corps had managed to secure itself behind the Ruza. With that, the southern wing of Panzer Group 4 (the VII Army Corps and the IX Army Corps) had withdrawn successfully to the new defensive position.

Also successful was the retreat of the northern wing of Panzer Group 4 and the whole of Panzer Group 3 to the Ruza–Lama Line. While enemy forces infiltrated the front here and there, they were unable to achieve a breakthrough and were intercepted. The towns of Istra and Klin, both of which had been sites of fierce fighting, had been relinquished according to plan on 14 December. After that, Panzer Group 3 had fought its way back to a position behind the Lama. There may have been initial doubts regarding whether the new defensive position could be held, but our confidence began to grow. Perhaps the enemy was not so overwhelmingly superior as we had thought! The German troops felt that they could fully trust their commanders, even in the most difficult situations. The enemy conducted a number of assaults against the entire front of Panzer Group 4 on 20 December, all of which were repelled. The most vulnerable point in the combat zone of the panzer group remained the highway. The fighting there was nonstop. But even Volokolamsk was in danger. This town was an important junction for German traffic. It was apparent that the enemy was increasingly directing his attacks towards objectives that would give him access to roads and rails. It was also apparent that we were increasingly having to react to such attacks. Panzer Group 4 had consolidated its front, but it had so far been unable to create the reserves that would have guaranteed greater security. Nevertheless, we were looking forward to the approaching Christmas season. Enemy disruptive action could be expected, but we also hoped that there might be periods of calm.

(e) Hitler's Halt Order

This part of the book, which deals with the measures taken by Hitler in the difficult days of December, begins with an overview of the situation that had developed up to the middle of the month in the combat zone of Army Group Centre. The assault on Moscow in October had brought the Ninth Army, on the left wing of Army Group Centre, into a northward-facing position whose left sector joined with the now stationary Army Group North in the vicinity of Ostashkov and whose right sector stood at the western end of the Upper Volga Region. With a width of 200 kilometres, the front of the Ninth Army was considerably overstretched. Its eastern wing was incapable of resisting strong enemy pressure and was compelled to give up Kalinin and Torzhok. The weak forces of the Ninth Army had been concentrated on that eastern wing, but to no avail. Along the eastward-facing Lama–Ruza Line were Panzer Groups 3 and 4. This front was in the process of being fortified. It extended over the highway to join the front of the Fourth Army, which, in the middle of December, was still in its old position. The Second Panzer Army, whose situation east and south-east of Tula had been fraught with danger, had withdrawn to the south-west. However, to the south-east of Kaluga, a gap had come into being between the Second Panzer Army and the Fourth Army. The enemy exploited this gap by pouring strong forces into it. This was to become a great source of danger for Army Group Centre from the middle of December. Further south was the Second Army, which was at that time to the east and south-east of Orel and was falling back in the face of a powerful enemy offensive. So that some control over the situation could be restored, the Second Army was placed under the command of its northern neighbour, the Second Panzer Army. This larger formation was designated Army Group Guderian.[109] Despite the fact that the retreat from Moscow since 6 December had proceeded smoothly, the crisis in the area of Army Group Centre was by no means at an end. Aside from the defensive fighting in the sector of Army Group Guderian and the ever-growing weakness that was the Kaluga gap, there were clear signs that the enemy was preparing to launch an envelopment attack from the vicinity of Ostashkov. This would be intended by the enemy to strike as far into our rear as possible and would probably be aiming towards Vyazma or perhaps even Smolensk.

When, at the beginning of December, Army Group Centre ceased its offensive and initiated its withdrawal, it did so on its own authority and without obtaining any written directive from Hitler. Even if the matter was discussed over the telephone, the decision to retreat was made on the battlefield. The remarkable development of the situation and the urgency with which a decision needed to be taken meant that there was no time to await an order from the supreme command. The commanders of Panzer Group 4 and the Second Panzer Army decided for themselves to halt the advance on 3 December. The commander of Army Group Centre approved this decision on 6 December, and Hitler finally did so on 8 December. Even though the enemy had yet to launch a full-scale counter-offensive, this initial retreat was regarded as a necessary measure by the army group. It was the intention of Field-Marshal von Bock to withdraw those of his formations that had advanced furthest to the east and were therefore most exposed.

---

[109] Translator's note: Army Group Guderian can be regarded as an enlarged army rather than as a full army group.

Panzer Group 4 was one of those formations, and it would be brought back to the Istra Line in the first instance. This would help to shorten the front line of the army group. After that, Bock planned a further withdrawal. For Panzer Group 4, this would be to the Ruza–Lama Line. This would further unite and solidify the front of the army group. Finally, the army group, as foreseen by Bock, would conduct one last retreat to a well-prepared defensive line for the winter. The shortage of forces and the lack of supplies limited the defensive possibilities of the army group to such an extent that the consolidation of its front was of the utmost importance. Multiple enemy attacks could be expected during the withdrawal, but only those which threatened its execution were to be repelled. Proper defensive fighting on the German side could only be conducted once our forces were in the right position. The front had to be shortened so that it could be more effectively defended with the available forces. The shortening of our supply lines would also be an advantage, although the quantity of supplies that could be brought to the front still needed to be increased. Overall, it was a challenging task to carry out this retreat. It was also a great responsibility that had been placed on the shoulders of the commander of the army group.

What was Hitler's attitude on the question of the retreat of Army Group Centre? This question could not have been easy for a man who did not think along military lines, who did not give consideration to the human factor, who had a romantic notion of sacrifice, who was prejudiced, who reacted emotionally, and who could not free himself of the desire for admiration. He did not order the cessation of the assault on Moscow, but he tacitly and belatedly approved the measures taken by his military commanders. He also reluctantly allowed the initial withdrawal, as he could not think of any reason to prevent it at first. Hitler was the sort of 'military leader' who was incapable of taking a decision at the decisive hour. He did not know what he wanted. But he resented the fact that such an important decision had been made without his involvement and that he had been unable to intervene. It was not long before his sense of humiliation got the better of him, and he began to feel a strong urge to countermand what had already been ordered in the time being.

To be examined first is Hitler's Directive No. 39 of 8 December. The halt had already taken place, and he had waited for quite a long time before issuing this directive. What he ordered seemed to correspond to what was necessary given the military situation, i.e. it appeared as if it would allow Field-Marshal von Bock to proceed with his withdrawal plan. The most important part of the directive is the following passage:

> The surprisingly early onset of winter in the east, its severity, and the consequent difficulties it will cause to the delivery of supplies, compels us to immediately cease all major offensive operations and to go over to the defensive.
>
> In detail, my orders are as follows:
>
> 1. The bulk of the German Army in the East will go over to the defensive as soon as possible along a front that can be defended with the available forces and whose position is to be determined by the commander-in-chief of the army. Our units, especially the panzer and motorised divisions, are then to be refreshed and refitted.
> 2. Where the front is to be brought back without any pressure from the enemy, a rear position must first be prepared that will offer our troops better living conditions and defensive possibilities than they have hitherto possessed.
> 3. The position of the front must enable the troops to be easily quartered and must be so placed that it can be defended with the minimal possible effort. It must also be capable of being supplied with the greatest possible ease, particularly during the thaw.

This order reveals that Hitler had recognised that we needed to establish a winter defensive position and that, quite rightly, the choice of its location should be left to the commander-in-chief of the German Army (paragraph 1). The order also made clear the purpose of establishing such a defensive line: it was to provide the troops with everything they needed to fight and was to enable the creation of reserves and even the refreshing of units (paragraphs 1 and 3). This last detail raised a few eyebrows. The directive made no mention of brand-new reserves of the kind that are necessary in critical situations. Instead, our reserves were to be drawn from the exhausted troops at the front. This small flaw in the directive need not have caused concern. The refreshment of our units was indeed of great urgency, but it was nonetheless a dream that could not be realised any time soon. As far as offering a long-term vision goes, this directive was of the sort that could be expected from a superior headquarters. But how was paragraph 2 to be interpreted? How was it supposed to harmonise with paragraphs 1 and 3? It placed a restriction on our forces that was incomprehensible from a military perspective. It stated that if any particular sector of the front was not under attack, that sector would not be allowed to be withdrawn until a well-constructed rear position was ready. Why? A rear position would typically be ordered, prepared, and manned as a precautionary measure in accordance with how a situation was expected to develop. It would have been impossible to arrange the retreat of just a few segments of the front of Army Group Centre. The whole front had to move back in unison. Otherwise, we would neither establish a linear defensive front nor manage to shorten the front line. Our defensive efforts would be in a state of chaos. What was it that paragraph 2 was supposed to achieve? It made no military sense.

At the OKW, Hitler's military headquarters, the man responsible for drafting directives, and later orders, was the chief of the operations staff, General of Artillery Alfred Jodl. Paragraph 1 almost certainly came from his pen and would have been sufficient as a directive on its own. The author of paragraph 3 is unclear, but that of paragraph 2 could only have been Hitler. It was from this time that Hitler began to exert more control over military operations. The impact on the defensive fighting in the winter of 1941–42 was considerable. Confusion reigned on the Eastern Front. Although Hitler initially left it up to the commander-in-chief of the army to conduct the withdrawal, he did so reluctantly and with reservations. He had therefore taken quite some time to issue his directive. It will be recalled that the withdrawal in the combat zone of Army Group Centre had been underway since 6 December, and even that date had been too late for Panzer Group 3. Hitler had simply been too slow with his order. If he wanted to oversee the conduct of operations himself, he ought to have announced his final decision on 2 December, or 3 December at the latest. But Hitler was unable to make a decision with an eye to how the situation might unfold. He disliked committing himself to what was for him an unappealing course of action. It was consequently unclear how the military leadership was supposed to function effectively if Hitler was going to direct operations himself in such an indecisive manner.

As a result of this delay, the commander of Army Group Centre could only issue his defence order on 9 December, although he had already given it much thought before that date. He ordered the preparation of the winter defensive position which, in the area of Army Group Centre, would follow the Oka and the Ugra (a left, northern tributary of the Oka); run past the western side of Medyn, the eastern side of Gzhatsk, and the eastern side of Rzhev; and follow the course of the upper Volga to the boundary with Army Group North. The front as it existed on 6 December was 1,100 kilometres in length. The new line would shorten it to 700 kilometres, i.e. by a good one-third. If our troops could reach this new line relatively unscathed, we might have a reasonable chance of being able to defend ourselves. But the winter defensive position still needed to be prepared. Colonel-General Hoepner took the view that this position did not yet offer sufficient security against the enemy. He recommended that the old Desna Line be used instead as our winter defensive position. This was the line from which the assault on Moscow had started at the beginning of October. It lay another 150 kilometres to the rear and was at least already partially prepared as a proper position. It would also deny the enemy the opportunity to conduct an envelopment. The position proposed by Army Group Centre would be vulnerable to an attack in the north, against the Ninth Army, and in the south, against the Fourth Army. Field-Marshal von Bock probably regarded the position he had recommended as one that gave up the maximum amount of territory that could be asked of Hitler at that time. He did not suggest any position further to the rear. Concerns over what Hitler wanted were already beginning to influence the details of operational planning. Bock knew that the position he proposed could not be held with certainty. It was too dependent on the conduct of the enemy. He also knew that the Desna Line would offer greater security during the spring mud season. If we evacuated the territory to the east of the Desna Line and destroyed everything of military value in that territory, we would be able to slow and then stop the enemy advance. However, Bock first needed to obtain greater freedom of action for his forces, as this was currently restricted by the enemy and, unfortunately, even by Hitler. To the north-west of Moscow, the enemy was still maintaining pressure against Panzer Groups 3 and 4, but this was not the most serious threat to the army group. The Ninth Army was weak and overextended in the north, as were the Fourth Army and the Second Panzer Army in the south. By 18–20 December, both panzer groups were in the process of consolidating their front lines, and it could even be said that their sectors had become more stable than the rest of the front of the army group.

On the afternoon of 18 December, the headquarters of Panzer Group 4 received the order from Hitler that has later become known as the Halt Order.[110] It arose from the unfounded assumption that the impact of the weather and the difficulties of supply would hinder a large-scale withdrawal. Hitler feared that such a withdrawal would lead to the loss of much weaponry and equipment. He continued:

> Commanding generals, commanders, and officers are to intervene personally to compel the troops to resist fanatically, even if the enemy has broken through the flanks and into the rear. This is the only way to gain the time necessary for reinforcements to arrive from the Fatherland and from the west, which I have already ordered. Only once our reserves have occupied rear positions can we think about a withdrawal to those positions.

The rest of the order foresaw relief measures and reinforcements for Army Group Centre, but these would not have an effect until the spring of 1942. There was no suggestion in the order as to how immediate assistance could be provided. Yet this was of the greatest urgency.

Hitler expanded on his Halt Order on 21 December. What he added was based on the thoughts he expressed during a conference on 20 December. A passage from paragraph 1 of this supplementary order is quoted here, as it reveals Hitler's mindset when it came to military leadership:

> The fanatical will to defend the ground on which we stand must be drummed into the troops with all the means at our disposal, no matter how severe.

---

[110] Translator's note: The Halt Order outside Moscow in 1941 should not be confused with the Halt Order outside Dunkirk in 1940.

When all the troops are animated by this same fanatical will, the attacks of the enemy, even if they infiltrate or penetrate the front in some locations, will be condemned to fail in the end. Wherever this will is at all lacking, the front will begin to teeter and will stand no chance of being brought into a prepared position. Every officer and man must understand that they will be exposed to the dangers of the Russian winter to a far greater degree if they were to retreat rather than put up resistance in their current, even if hastily established, position. Aside from that, a retreat will involve a considerable and unavoidable loss of matériel. The spectre of the Napoleonic retreat threatens to become reality.

Napoleon's disastrous withdrawal from Moscow in 1812 was often uppermost in Hitler's mind. Hitler believed that a retreat in the Russian winter would demoralise the German troops, for they would feel hopeless and defenceless in the vast snowscape. It was incredible that Hitler had only become concerned about the effects of the winter in the context of retreat. The troops had already been suffering in the winter for a whole month.

Colonel-General Hoepner probably best expressed our feelings towards the Halt Order in a report he wrote in the depths of winter on 24 December 1941:

It is not a question of fanatical will. The will is there. It is strength we lack. The forces we have are too few, and the area they must defend is too large. The enemy intends to break through into our rear and to cut off our supply lines. This would be decisive. The ability to hold out in any position is dependent on strength and supply. Nowhere have we established such a position this far into enemy territory. There has been no time to do so. There has also been a shortage of men and matériel. The frost makes it difficult to dig into the ground and to construct defensive installations. The quantity of supplies is never enough. The starved and frozen soldier can neither fight nor work. The soldier without ammunition can neither shoot nor put up resistance. If there is no fuel, we can neither move reserves nor deliver supplies. If new tanks and replacement parts cannot reach the front, the panzer arm will become inoperative. If our gun grease freezes up, our machine guns will be unable to shoot and the breechblocks of our artillery pieces will be unable to open.

We have also given considerable thought to our tactics and to the will to fight, but these cannot compensate for shortages in matériel and personnel. It will be a long time before we can establish positions of the kind that existed in the First World War. We have neither the time to build them nor the forces to occupy them. In contrast, the enemy has masses of men to draw on and is far better equipped for a winter campaign than we are. Given our experiences thus far, it is doubtful whether the enemy will ever bleed to death. We have become highly sceptical over the last four weeks about the assumption that he is using up his last available forces. I know that we must persevere and triumph despite all the odds. I know that we must maintain the will to fight and that we must remain strong. There is no need to demand of me my commitment along these lines. But I must be allowed a certain amount of freedom in the command of my forces. It is often necessary to act quickly in order to deal with a small setback or to prevent a larger one. I have a better view of the means at our disposal and of the possibilities of their use than does a headquarters sitting 1,000 kilometres behind the front.

These were the most important points of criticism. The Halt Order was unanimously opposed by the commanders at the front. How were we supposed to lead our troops effectively if, instead of acting immediately in accordance with what was dictated by the situation, we had to await the approval of Hitler? If such approval were at all forthcoming, it would likely be too late. Hitler was notoriously indecisive, especially if the question he had to address was something he preferred to avoid. But the enemy could not be expected to wait. He would continue to attack and would exploit any opportunities that presented themselves. Hitler failed to recognise that the enemy had seized the initiative. This enemy was far more powerful than us, and he was striving hard for victory. It was more important than ever that we exercise foresighted and skilful leadership and that we be able to act with agility and adaptability so that, until help arrived from the Fatherland, we could gradually compensate for our temporary weakness, exhausted troops, lack of reserves, and shortage of supplies.

How was the Halt Order supposed to improve the situation at the front? Did Hitler really believe that German posts standing in deep snow in temperatures 20–40 degrees below zero would be able to have much of an effect if they were to 'cling to the ground' with 'fanatical resistance' and 'fanatical will'? Such vocabulary was utterly meaningless on the battlefield. The implied threats in the order certainly would not help. Those who were anxious would only become more so; those who were brave did not need to be threatened. This goes to show that Hitler lacked any sort of bond with the German soldier. He lacked any appreciation of the plight of our troops. Fanaticism and duress cannot be helpful in solving problems at the front. Only by issuing clear orders and setting a good example can troops be inspired. Commanders must demonstrate foresight, care, fairness, and camaraderie if they are to gain and maintain the trust and confidence of their troops. Men fight gladly and willingly if they sense they are doing so for their comrades, their community, and their security.

This was the reality of the situation at the front before Moscow in the middle of December. The men were not driven by some fear of a Napoleonic retreat. Yet they were aware that their fate was very much in the hands of their leadership. Several gaps had come into being along the front, as the available forces were few and the area to be covered was large. Hitler did not recognise that the length of front to be defended ought not to exceed what our forces were capable of. The German soldier was indeed highly capable, but he could not just be ordered to redouble his efforts. Orders of this kind were worthless. It seemed as if it would require pointless sacrifice on a large scale to convince Hitler of this. The second half of December was the perfect time to withdraw to the winter defensive position. Our forces could be spared and refreshed. The Halt Order would not allow this.

An example of how Hitler responded to a request to retreat is recorded in the war diary of Army Group Centre on 30 December 1941 (Field-Marshal von Kluge had in the meantime, on 18 December, become the commander of the army group):

> On the renewed request of the commander to withdraw the Fourth Army, the Führer remarked that such requests were nonstop and that there was no end in sight. We might as well go back to the Dnieper or the Polish border. He does not understand why the whole front must be brought back if it is not being attacked everywhere along its length. He said that he had to be the voice of cold reason in the face of the feelings of those at the front. Any advantage of the shorter line to be brought about by a withdrawal would be greatly offset by the loss of matériel. He sees no alternative to the current position if we do not want the front to collapse. The Führer finally asked whether the pressure applied by the enemy was in the form of strong artillery barrage fire. Field-Marshal von Kluge answered no. The Führer said that he was obviously behind the times, as he had often been under 10-day drumfire during World War I. Nevertheless,

the troops would have to hold their positions, even if their inventory level was down to 10 percent.

This excerpt demonstrates clearly how Hitler would reject any request for a retreat. He would blow everything out of proportion in order to say no. There was no question of the Fourth Army withdrawing to the Dnieper or the Polish border. It was rather a question of establishing the winter position that he had ordered. He apparently could not understand why all sectors of the front had to be withdrawn if only some of those sectors were under attack. An entire front must be withdrawn simultaneously and linearly; otherwise, the sectors that remain further forward will be enveloped and cut off by the enemy. Hitler's 'cold reason' amounted to suicide.

The advantage of shortening the front line was to create a defensive position that could be held with the available forces. Hitler himself had ordered this in his Directive No. 39, but he now claimed that the matériel loss that would ensue would be too great. This was not true. If we disengaged at the right time, there need not be any loss of matériel at all. Yet the second paragraph of the directive also reared its head! There was technically no 'rear position' of the sort it described.

Hitler's comments regarding his experiences in World War I demonstrate his complete lack of understanding of the combat conditions on the Eastern Front in World War II. The nature of warfare in Russia in 1941 was quite different to that in France in 1917 and 1918. Hitler had experienced static warfare, but we were now dealing with mobile warfare. A defensive position in World War I was characterised by multiple lines of long and deep trenches standing behind wire entanglements and minefields. To the rear of this first position would be another, almost identical second position of multiple lines. However, on the front before Moscow, such elaborately developed lines did not exist. There were no wire entanglements and few trenches. Thousands of rounds of artillery drumfire directed against a narrow sector was impossible on the Eastern Front. There was not enough ammunition. Our batteries had on average barely half the number of guns that those of World War I had possessed. Half of the army artillery units of Panzer Group

4 were *without* guns in December 1941! Their personnel were being used to construct installations for the winter position in the vicinity east of Gzhatsk.

Hitler's ignorance of conditions at the front was alarming. How could he lead as a military commander if he did not understand how the individual elements functioned and worked together? Field-Marshal von Kluge may have been astonished by what he heard from Hitler. Kluge told Hitler that the course of events might overtake any orders he (Hitler) gave. The war diary of Army Group Centre describes Hitler's annoyance with this. 'Borovsk must be held!' he insisted. His irritation increased when Kluge explained that doing so might be impossible. 'We shall wait and see!' concluded Hitler. Once more, although it was clear that a withdrawal was necessary, he postponed a decision on the matter.

An entry in the war diary of Army Group Centre on 31 December 1941 provides an example of Hitler's inconsistency. When Kluge made a repeated request for the withdrawal of the Ninth Army to the winter defensive position, Hitler replied: 'The tragedy here is that the troops know they have a prepared position to the rear. They are therefore less motivated to fight hard.' Yet Hitler had specified in his directive that the troops could retreat if a rear position had been prepared. Such inconsistency is unacceptable in the command of military forces. Orders must be followed resolutely, but the orders themselves must be resolute. Orders might be modified depending on changes in a situation, but they should not be influenced by shifting ideas of what is meant by certain terms, in this case the 'rear position'. Hitler was a master at manipulating words in the field of politics, but this was dangerous if applied to military orders. The meaning of what is stated in an order must be crystal clear. It would be no exaggeration to say that the results could be deadly if the wording of an order was vague or disingenuous.

Colonel-General Hoepner had formed a negative opinion of Hitler at an early stage, and it set the tone for the conduct of Panzer Group 4. When we learnt of the Halt Order, we considered it not only to be incorrect but also dangerous. It would paralyse and probably even disrupt the command of our units. The panzer group would lose mobility and would be unable to do anything. We had thus far been superior to the enemy in terms of command and mobility, but these qualities were in danger of being taken away. Our inferiority in numbers had always been offset by the skilful concentration of forces. Now, our men were bound to be worn down as they tried to hold on to ground against an overwhelmingly large number of well-equipped Russian troops. Hoepner was not the only one to revolt against such foolishness. And he would do so in word and deed.

All the army commanders at the front in those winter days voiced their opposition against the Halt Order, and there was no lack of criticism over Hitler's leadership at that time. A unit that is required to hold a position 'to the last man' cannot be used effectively in the further conduct of operations, especially if that unit is destroyed. The result is that a gap arises in the front at the location where the position was supposed to be held.[111] We had no reserves that could intervene or fill such gaps. There was nothing with which to prevent the enemy from surging forward.

The Halt Order was nonsensical. The paralysis it would cause might usher in defeat. All levels of command had to be free to act in accordance with the constantly changing situation. The commanders of our units, be they battalions or larger formations, were carefully chosen and highly capable men. Functionaries could have been put in charge of our units under the conditions that would be created by the Halt Order. Hoepner commented that a lance corporal could have taken his place. The doctrine of the German Army was highly developed. We knew how to lead, how to interpret the conditions on the battlefield, and how to inspire all the men and their commanders to do their duty. This doctrine was universally applicable and clearly laid out in the authoritative service manual *Truppenführung*. It did not need to be modified. The poorly formulated Halt Order was disruptive, did not correspond to the method of command that had been established, and was not what we soldiers were used to. In fact, it was a thoroughly bad example of how to practise military leadership. It could not work on

---

[111] From Hoepner's comments on the Halt Order to the army group on 18 December 1941.

the ever-evolving Eastern Front. What we needed were clear orders that conformed to the developments.

Was the Halt Order even necessary at that time? It has already been proven that it would be difficult to obey, but was there any justification for issuing such an order? Our retreat in the middle of December was under control and therefore did not require Hitler's intervention. Rather, his involvement hindered and endangered our efforts. It is true that the enemy had infiltrated the front in some locations and that a few gaps had arisen which were difficult to plug. A systematic withdrawal to the winter defensive position would shorten the front line and therefore remove these dangers. It was still possible, and indeed an urgent necessity, to carry out this withdrawal. The danger in the north against the Ninth Army was growing. The enemy seemed to be preparing for an attack there that would be the northern arm of a large-scale envelopment. This would be deadly for Army Group Centre if its front line was embroiled in fighting too far to the east. There was on top of that the already existing threat of a southern envelopment from the Kaluga gap. Hitler's intervention thus caused much damage. We lost a lot of time and even more blood.

The propaganda at that time painted a picture of a front and a military leadership that had been so impressed, fanaticised, and emboldened by the Führer's words that any Russian attacks against German forces were dashed to pieces. This was far from the truth. Standing in the snow and frost in the vast expanse of Russia, the inadequately supplied and barely reinforced German troops were not particularly receptive to Hitler's fervent yet impractical statements. But this propaganda achieved its intended effect in the Fatherland, for it managed to repair Hitler's damaged reputation. Who there was still able to discern what was real under the torrent of distorted representations of the glorious Führer, his steadfast personality, and his unshakeable will? The propaganda coup at home did not inspire anyone at the front. For Hitler, one particular success brought about by the Halt Order was the request made by the commander-in-chief of the army, Field-Marshal Walther von Brauchitsch, on 18 December to be relieved of his command. Hitler granted this request and took over as commander-in-chief himself. This had probably been his plan all along. He was now able to solidify his control over the army and directly influence the conduct of operations on the Eastern Front.

It could not realistically be expected that the Halt Order would have a positive effect at the front. Any men who were anxious in nature would only become more so. They would therefore become more careful and less inclined to act. Hitler's intervention was pointless. The withdrawal of the German front was under control. The shift from offence to defence can be psychologically dangerous, but the German military leadership had handled this successfully. Yet Hitler imagined that our competent soldiers, who had come so close to Moscow and were aware of their superior fighting qualities, would suddenly despair and flee in confusion. Thus far, none of the Russian attacks had led to a decisive success. It is regrettable that some of the post-war literature has bestowed positive significance on the Halt Order, depicting it, rather as did the wartime propaganda, as a decisive act on Hitler's part that stabilised the situation at the front.[112] The true effect was quite the opposite. The Halt Order contained unreasonable demands and suggestions of cowardice. Rather than offering help, it caused much resentment.

All the army commanders protested. Many refused to pass on such an order. The situation was too serious. It needed to be handled with action, not words. Few of the men at the front heard the precise wording of the order. Hitler had not intended the order for the individual soldier anyway. He had intended it for the field commanders, who were supposed to 'compel the troops' to fight in the snow for every inch of ground to the last. Hitler demanded the fighter and was indifferent towards the human being. He did not care, gave no consideration, and never expressed his thanks. He can by no means be regarded as the saviour of the front.

---

[112] The book by Kurt von Tippelskirch, *Geschichte des zweiten Weltkriegs* (Bonn: Athenäum, 1951), 242–44, is without basis on this matter. Alfred Philippi and Ferdinand Heim – *Der Feldzug gegen Sowjetrußland 1941 bis 1945* (Stuttgart: Kohlhammer, 1962), 100–01 – believe, without going into detail, that Hitler was able to 'shock the troops and their commanders' through 'brute force and evocative power'.

Unfortunately, the Halt Order had come into being and had begun to have an effect. Colonel-General Hoepner had immediately recognised the damage it could cause and had opposed it. This order occupied his mind for several days. Even though the situation in the combat zone of Panzer Group 4 was under control and therefore did not require him at any point in the near future to seek permission from Hitler for a withdrawal, it was the violation of a tried and tested principle that he feared. He was fully prepared to act in accordance with what he believed.

(f) The dismissal of Colonel-General Hoepner

The slow and complicated system of obtaining Hitler's approval for any withdrawal was in force from 18 December. This meant that any request to retreat, even from a lower-level headquarters, had to be passed up the chain of command until it reached Hitler. Such a request, if not rejected at some point on its way up, had to be checked and modified each time before it took the next step on its way to Hitler. If a panzer division wanted to retreat, its request would have taken five steps by the time it arrived at the OKH! It was required that the commander at each level, or in exceptional cases his chief of staff, check the withdrawal request himself before he passed it upwards. Yet the main responsibility of a commander was to lead the troops at the front. He could not always be at his headquarters, but this would become the case under the new system. Under the command of Panzer Group 4, for example, were 17 divisions and seven corps, and Colonel-General Hoepner was also responsible for Panzer Group 3 at that time. The conditions of the Halt Order would have made it necessary for him to spend his entire time at his headquarters. He would have barely had a chance to visit the front. The commander of a formation in the field needed to be able to intervene at the front at any moment. Every situation had to be evaluated on its own terms. Factors that he had to consider included the activity of the enemy, the strength of the available forces, and the flow of supplies. These factors changed from one situation to the next. A poorly supplied unit could not be given the same task as a fully supplied one. A commander considered such factors in relation to the units directly under his command. This was not the responsibility of a superior headquarters. Hitler seemed to remain oblivious to the disruptive impact of his interference. It would take at least 24 hours for a decision to be made – if one was made at all. This gave rise to confusion and delay. Any calculation of the ammunition level of a unit was thrown into disarray if it had to hold on for another 24 hours after it had provided its assessment of the situation. Only a unit with ammunition at its disposal could put up resistance to an enemy attack. If it ran out of ammunition in the meantime, an order by Hitler that this unit should stay put would be disastrous. The situation at the front was delicate enough without Hitler's intervention, but it now seemed as if his active involvement in the conduct of operations had to be accepted. This was costly for our troops and handed the advantage to the enemy.

For Panzer Group 4, the impact of the Halt Order was that it set the Ruza–Lama Line as the position from which any withdrawal required permission. The situation was reasonably stable on the front of the panzer group. It was quiet during the Christmas season, but then Russian attacks against the highway and in the vicinity of Volokolamsk intensified towards the end of the year. Volokolamsk in particular became the focal point of the fighting towards the middle of January 1942. When the town itself was lost, the fighting in its vicinity degenerated into a battle of attrition. There were a number of violent clashes, and our troops were put under a great deal of stress, but the enemy did not manage to achieve the breakthrough he was aiming for. The front held on until it was ordered to retreat in the second half of January.

This retreat to the winter defensive position, planned in detail, was automatically inhibited by the Halt Order. Even the construction of the defensive position had been forbidden by Hitler after it had been ordered by the army group. He had thought that a position to the rear would make the troops more inclined to retreat and less inclined to fight hard. The commanders at the front increasingly disregarded Hitler's views. Construction forces were already at work and, without weapons, were unable to be employed in combat. Hitler officially permitted the construction of the winter defensive position to resume on 29 December. In those sectors of the front where construction had already been carried out, the result proved to be advantageous for our defence.

The situation deteriorated for the formations to the north and south of Panzer Group 4, which, on 1 January 1942, was redesignated the Fourth Panzer Army. It was the situation to the south, in the sector of the Fourth Army, which first began to have an impact on the panzer army. The enemy had applied considerable pressure against the LVII Panzer Corps, had broken through the front between Maloyaroslavets and Borovsk, and, by the end of December, sent forces through the new gap towards the west and north. The severely weakened XX Army Corps had been pushed back to the north, so Field-Marshal von Kluge decided on 3 January that it should be placed under the command of the panzer army. It was a side effect of the Halt Order that the army group would allocate the forces of a unit that had been pushed back to a neighbouring unit that had not yet been pushed back, thereby making the neighbouring unit responsible for a gap that had come into existence through no fault of its own. The Russian breakthrough demonstrated that the forces at the disposal of the Fourth Army were lacking in strength and ought to have been withdrawn to the winter defensive position beforehand. Now it was the task of the panzer army not only to ensure the safety of the XX Army Corps but also to plug the gap that had been punched through the front of the Fourth Army. This gap grew from day to day. Only by violating two principles of the command of military forces could the demands of the Halt Order continue to be fulfilled.

The first principle is that the wings on either side of a gap in the front need to be united under the same command. These wings can then coordinate their counter-measures in the most effective way possible, preventing the widening of the gap. However, the gap that had arisen in the front of the Fourth Army could not be closed. The wings on either side, lacking unity in their efforts, had fallen back in the face of enemy pressure.

The second principle that the Halt Order violated was the ability to relocate our forces to create a point of main effort. The few reserves that had been created by the Fourth Panzer Army were taken away and squandered to the west of Vereya in an attack to the south that was supposed to re-establish contact with the Fourth Army. These reserve forces were insufficient to carry out such a task. The only result was the weakening of the front of the panzer army. In the meantime, the extensive front of the XX Army Corps, not at that moment under attack, was supposed to stand idly by, its forces unable to be withdrawn and employed more usefully elsewhere. The army corps could have quite easily evacuated its pointlessly held front so as to reinforce the attack to the south, which would have then had a good chance of reaching the northern wing of the Fourth Army. The gap would have thereby been closed. The enemy was not necessarily that much stronger, but he was permitted to concentrate his forces against a point of main effort. We, on the other hand, were no longer allowed to move our forces to where they were most urgently needed.

Field-Marshal von Kluge became too concerned with sticking to the requirements of the Halt Order. He gave the panzer army the task of closing the gap that the enemy had prised open, even though he was not convinced that this was the solution to the problem. It was a stopgap solution, but not a militarily sound one. Developing here was one of the most harmful consequences of the Halt Order. The commander of the army group was sacrificing his military convictions for the sake of this order. He was faced with the dilemma of having to obey Hitler's amateurish Halt Order on the one hand and of needing to restore the situation at the front on the other. Perhaps he hoped to be able to do both, but he must have been aware that what he was demanding of the formations at the front was unreasonable. We really needed to be focusing on our defence rather than throwing our exhausted troops into poorly prepared attacks. Defence was the responsible course of action! An appropriate balance certainly had to be struck at that time between obedience, responsibility, and conscience.

The beginning of January was when Field-Marshal von Kluge entrusted the Fourth Panzer Army with the task of looking after the XX Army Corps and closing the gap that had arisen in the front of the Fourth Army. It was only a short time before that point, at the end of 1941, that the commander of the army group had been confronted with the alarming result of the first two weeks of the Halt Order. The fighting had been fierce along the entire length of the front. A proper front line could hardly be spoken of. It was more serpentine in nature, with many indentations and islands of resistance. The Kaluga gap offered the enemy the chance to advance far to the west against almost no resistance. However, the enemy now seemed to be applying the greatest pressure towards the north-west in the direction of Yukhnov and Vyazma. The 19th Panzer Division fought to defend Yukhnov. The sole supply road of the Fourth Army ran through the town from Roslavl. If this supply line were to be disrupted, which was what ended up happening, any defensive efforts further to the east would be hopeless. To the north, in the combat zone of the Ninth Army, the main Russian thrust aimed to go over the Volga near and to the west of Rzhev so as to strike deep into our flank and rear. The forces of the Ninth Army were so weak that even the penetration of the winter defensive position in its zone seemed to be a real possibility. The commander of the Ninth Army urgently requested on 31 December that he be allowed to retreat. Kluge rejected this, although it is hard to believe that he would have felt comfortable in so doing. His actions were overseen by Hitler. A double envelopment of the bulk of Army Group Centre threatened to become a reality within the next few weeks. Kluge could see this, so he must have had mixed feelings about obeying Hitler at that time. While he constantly emphasised the requirement to conform to the Halt Order, he also discussed with his army commanders the details of the so urgently needed withdrawal to the winter defensive position. Unfortunately, this position had already been partially penetrated in the sector of the Fourth Army. Colonel-General Hoepner firmly believed that a retreat to the winter defensive position would have to be carried out soon, although he had yet to grapple with the army group over the matter. All preparations for the withdrawal had already been made. The lines to which we would withdraw had been determined, as had the locations of the boundaries between the formations of the panzer army. Why wait if the enemy was on the verge of a breakthrough anyway? What were we hoping to achieve in our current positions? These questions were asked more insistently as time went by. The Halt Order had no purpose.

Given the circumstances, it can be understood why Field-Marshal von Kluge wanted to assign the Fourth Panzer Army such a burdensome task. It was by no means a good solution, but Kluge had found himself confronted by an emergency. The gap near Borovsk was still much smaller than that near Kaluga, so the latter required more attention. He handled the means he was entrusted with like a broker, selling off the most valuable shares of his business during a slump in the desperate hope that it would provide temporary relief. The client, Hitler, could find no solution for the calamity he had caused other than to underline his Halt Order with a new order on 31 December 1941:

> Every inch of ground is to be defended to the last. Only then will bloody losses be inflicted on the enemy, his morale weakened, and the superiority of the German soldier brought to bear.

Hitler, Kluge, and Hoepner each had strong and differing views on the conduct of operations. The situation was bound to come to a head. As has been described, the XX Army Corps had become separated from the Fourth Army and, on 3 January 1942, had been placed under the command of the Fourth Panzer Army in what was an utterly hopeless situation. The forces that had been thrown into the attack, whose goal was to close the gap, were the remaining elements of the 10th Panzer Division, the 3rd Motorised Infantry Division, and the 267th Infantry Division. Despite making some headway to begin with, they could not prevent the further advance of the numerically superior Russian forces. Borovsk, which Hitler had emphasised as the cornerstone for all counter-measures, had already been lost. In the following days, the enemy pushed northwards towards Vereya, the traffic and supply centre of the XX Army Corps. The forces he sent westwards through the gap were not quite as strong. The 267th Infantry Division fought there and found itself separated from the corps to which it belonged, the main group of which remained further to the east. The enemy pressed ever closer to Vereya. The four infantry divisions of the XX Army Corps did their best to defend an overextended front, the so-called balcony to the east and south-east of Vereya which stretched across 60 kilometres as far as Borovsk. The enemy did not conduct any attack there. He was seeking to pin down our forces instead. The situation continued to escalate, with the army corps in serious danger of being cut off in its worthless balcony. We wanted to bring the army corps back to a position closer to Vereya and had already been requesting permission from the army group to do this for several days! Two of the divisions of the army corps were eventually allowed to retreat, thereby freeing up some of the panzer forces that had arrived for use elsewhere (e.g. closing the gap). Nevertheless, Hitler continued to insist in most cases that German forces hold their current positions.

The prospects of the XX Army Corps as we at the headquarters of the Fourth Panzer Army saw them are best outlined in an excerpt from a report I completed on the morning of the decisive day of 8 January:

> The unfortunate situation that we have warned the army group about on a number of occasions has now arisen. The XX Army Corps is being withdrawn too late. It has been repeatedly emphasised that the enemy is pushing his forces towards the west. It has also previously been brought to the attention of the army group that the enemy is attempting to outflank us. With the seizure of Vyshegorod on 7 January, the enemy is only 11 kilometres away from Vereya. The road along the Protva Valley is now at his disposal. Most of the forces of the XX Army Corps are still standing 35 kilometres to the east of Vereya without any good connection via road to the west. It is clear that an orderly retreat of all forces will no longer be possible. It is also clear, regrettably, that if the XX Army Corps is pushed back to the north, the gap between it and the Fourth Army will become larger.
>
> There can be no doubt that the order for the retreat of the XX Army Corps and also of the VII Army Corps must be given at once. If we do not do so, the XX Army Corps will most certainly be annihilated. This will make necessary the retreat of the entire front of the panzer army to the Gzhatsk position, which is a part of the planned winter defensive position. It might perhaps be possible to create reserves as a result of the shorter front. We can no longer be certain whether such a withdrawal will succeed. The headquarters of the panzer army had recommended at the beginning of the month that it be carried out on 5 or 6 January.

The attempt to close the gap to the Fourth Army had failed. Our forces were too weak, whilst those of the enemy were too strong. The Russian advance to the north in the direction of Vereya was threatening to cut off any route of retreat for the XX Army Corps. As Colonel-General Hoepner saw it, the last moment had arrived for a decision to be made regarding the southern wing of his panzer army. The worthless halt tactic had to be given up and the XX Army Corps withdrawn via Vereya to the south-west. This was the only way that forces could be made available quickly enough to hold up the northward push of the enemy on Vereya, re-establish contact with our forces further west (the 267th Infantry Division), and aggressively extend our front to the south. It must be remembered that the XX Army Corps was 35 kilometres to the east and south-east of Vereya at that time, holding an eastward-facing front 30 kilometres in width as well as a southward-facing front of approximately the same width. The focal point of the fighting was still in the vicinity of Borovsk, which had by this time fallen into the hands of the enemy. While he was able to make use of the accommodation in the town, our troops were compelled to place themselves immediately to the north in the open countryside. They stood in the snowscape rather than in a well-prepared position. There was no reason to hold on to this piece of land. We were probably so doing because Hitler could see on his map that it was close to Borovsk, which he had previously insisted ought not to be relinquished. Borovsk lay 25 kilometres to the south-east of Vereya, and the enemy, approaching from the south, had already come to within 11 kilometres of the latter the previous evening. Yet the 15th and 183rd Infantry Divisions, as well as the few forces of the 10th Panzer Division, had to remain on standby for no reason at all. They were not allowed to partake in the decisive battle further to the west.

No, that just would not do!

There was no longer any guarantee that the XX Army Corps could be safely withdrawn to the west. The area it occupied was becoming ever more cramped, and the distance it would have to cover to complete its withdrawal was considerable. Under such circumstances, this withdrawal would last a week and could only be executed if the individual units of the army corps disengaged one after the other. If the enemy took Vereya in the meantime, an eventuality we wanted to prevent, the army corps would be pushed back in the wrong direction (to the north). The gap to the west would become ever larger and would be able to be exploited by the enemy. This was precisely how the situation in the Kaluga gap had unfolded. It should have served as a warning for Field-Marshal von Kluge as the present commander of the army group.

However, it seemed as if military thought and action had been lost once the Halt Order had come into force. This order was effectively the imposition of an arbitrary wish on the part of Hitler without any regard as to whether it could actually be carried out. And he continued to make unreasonable demands. He decided that he wanted the 5th Panzer Division, the only panzer formation remaining on the northern wing of the panzer army, to intervene immediately in the fighting to the south of Vereya. After consulting with the commanders of the 5th Panzer Division and the XXXXVI Panzer Corps, Colonel-General Hoepner rejected Hitler's request, even though it put a strain on his relationship with his superiors. This shift of the panzer division could not be carried out. Movement from north to south in the combat zone of the panzer army was difficult. The only available road that crossed the highway in the direction of Vereya went via Mozhaysk. This road was restricted to one lane due to the snow and was already overburdened with the supply traffic of the XX Army Corps.

Moreover, the 5th Panzer Division formed the backbone of the front of the XXXXVI Panzer Corps. The tanks of the panzer division were in action in the sectors of the panzer corps and the V Army Corps, and were thus unavailable to be sent elsewhere. The release of the panzer division would only be possible if freedom of action could be obtained in the vicinity of Volokolamsk. In other words, a withdrawal would need to be conducted. Yet it could not be expected that Hitler would approve such a measure.

The proposed 150-kilometre shift of the panzer division would also consume a great deal of fuel. This fuel was not available and would therefore need to be delivered first.

It was mainly the traffic conditions that prevented any consideration of the shift of the panzer division at that moment. The Volokolamsk–Mozhaysk road was the only supply route of the V Army Corps, the XXXXVI Panzer Corps, the IX Army Corps, and the VII Army Corps. Traffic was always flowing in both directions along this road. The stretch between Mozhaysk and Vereya was, as mentioned, restricted to one lane. Any traffic coming from Vereya was therefore diverted to the north-east, reaching the highway near the front and then heading west along that highway. This detour increased the travel distance from Vereya to Mozhaysk from 17 kilometres to 47 kilometres. The point where traffic joined the highway near the front lay only 3 kilometres from the forwardmost line, well within the effective range of enemy artillery. It is an indication of how precarious the supply conditions had become between Mozhaysk and Vereya that, despite the shortage of fuel and the risk of casualties from artillery fire, a route that was 30 kilometres longer had to be chosen.

In a nutshell, there were too many obstacles preventing the transfer of the 5th Panzer Division. It would have barely been of use to the XX Army Corps in any case, for the journey would have taken too much time. The army corps needed immediate assistance. It could not afford to wait. If it were permitted to abandon its balcony, it could shorten its front line and thereby make forces available from what was already under its command. Instead, Hitler renewed his demand for the transfer of the panzer division. Field-Marshal von Kluge asked of Colonel-General Hoepner if he could not just carry out the transfer as a favour. This was out of the question. Hoepner refused to transfer the panzer division, and even his successor would reject the idea most energetically. The relationship between Hoepner and Kluge was more strained than ever. The fact that the panzer division remained on the northern wing of the panzer army was something that Hitler took as a personal affront. If Hitler had chosen to visit the front of the panzer army at that time, he could have seen for himself how impossible the situation was. But Hitler never visited the front. It became ever more difficult for the military leadership to deal with such lack of understanding.

Further developments brought about what the Halt Order had been bound to give rise to sooner or later. On 8 January, towards 0930 hours, Colonel-General Hoepner reported to the army group the situation of the XX Army Corps and described in detail what his intentions were. He emphasised that the front had to be altered not only in the combat zone of the army corps but also across the entire area of the panzer army. Field-Marshal von Kluge agreed with Hoepner's appraisal of the situation and told him that he wanted to speak with Colonel-General Halder about it. He phoned back towards noon not to approve Hoepner's request but rather to check once more whether the Fourth Panzer Army would be able to help resolve in our favour the volatile situation faced by the Fourth Army. He could not have been under any illusions that this would be possible! It was an astonishingly pointless telephone call in which he recognised neither the limitations of the panzer army nor the desperate situation of the XX Army Corps. Hoepner took the opportunity to enquire whether a decision had been made regarding his request for the withdrawal of the panzer army. Kluge answered this question in the negative, but he added: 'Halder is on his way to the Führer. This decision is important and will be made quickly. You should prepare to withdraw at short notice.'[113] Hoepner and his chief of staff, who overhead the conversation, had gained the distinct impression from what Kluge had to say that the retreat was going to be approved at any moment. Hoepner attempted to telephone Halder himself, but only got as far as Halder's orderly officer. Halder did not call back. The day of 8 January was too fraught with tension. The XX Army Corps could not be kept waiting in its perilous position.

At 1245 hours, with no word from his superiors, Colonel-General Hoepner decided – in accordance with his convictions, his responsibility, and his conscience – to order the withdrawal of the XX Army Corps. There was nothing else that could be done! The army corps was to conduct its withdrawal at the latest moment, after nightfall if possible. Beyond that, there could be no further delay. Hoepner accepted the responsibility that came with his decision, even if it might end up being interpreted as disobedience. He knew that Kluge objectively agreed with his appraisal of the situation. However, it seemed as if objectivity was no longer the primary consideration in the conduct of operations. The Halt Order took precedence.

Only towards 1900 hours did Kluge telephone Hoepner and reproach him for the withdrawal he had ordered: 'I cannot approve your order. You know exactly what the Führer demands. At any rate, you should have reported your intentions to withdraw beforehand.'[114] Yet he did not countermand Hoepner's order. He might have been able to do so

---

[113] From my notes on 9 January 1942 regarding the developments of 8 January.
[114] Kluge's words over the telephone to Hoepner on 8 January 1942 at 1855 hours.

given that there were still rearguard units occupying the current line, but he probably realised that the withdrawal was not so inconvenient. The contravention of the Halt Order in this situation was justifiable. Not convincing is Kluge's remark that Hoepner should have given prior warning of his intention to withdraw. Hoepner had requested several times that the panzer army be allowed to retreat, and he was told on each occasion to await authorisation from the Führer. Such waiting was precisely what Hoepner wanted to avoid. For the sake of his troops and his conscience, it was something he had to avoid. His troops would have been no better off if he had merely protested and was ignored by Hitler. Unfortunately, Kluge could not handle the fact that Hoepner had taken matters into his own hands. When the field-marshal phoned Hitler to inform him of the commencement of the withdrawal on the southern wing of the Fourth Panzer Army, he did so without any delicacy. 'Hoepner has retreated!' he announced.[115] It was not Hoepner's recalcitrance that necessarily bothered Kluge; rather, the field-marshal probably felt humiliated by the fact that a subordinate had found the courage that he himself had been unable to summon up. The confidence he had placed in Hitler was taking its toll, for it increasingly required that he act in a manner contrary to his military and soldierly convictions.[116]

Late on the evening of 8 January, towards 2330 hours, Field-Marshal von Kluge informed Colonel-General Hoepner over the phone that he had been relieved by Hitler of his command of the Fourth Panzer Army, and that he was to report to the headquarters of Army Group Centre on the morning of 9 January. A short time later, the colonel-general entered the office of his chief of staff, a large classroom in the school in

---

[115] This is according to the account of the man who was at that time the first general staff officer of Army Group Centre, Lieutenant-Colonel Henning von Tresckow, and who was later, in 1943, a regimental commander under my 168th Infantry Division. Tresckow was present when Kluge phoned Hitler and blurted out these words. He formed the opinion that Kluge had done so in the heat of the moment. Kluge would subsequently put in a good word for Hoepner, but Hitler's anger had already been aroused.

[116] Even the chief of staff of the army group, Major-General Hans von Greiffenberg, told me over the telephone on 8 January 1942 that he disagreed with the conduct of the field-marshal.

Gzhatsk. The gleam of light of an old kerosene lamp barely illuminated the solitary desk and two chairs that stood in the room. Remaining by the door, Hoepner said calmly: 'Well, Beaulieu, the time has come!' I had been prepared for such news all day and had heard the approach of my commander's footsteps, perhaps slightly heavier or slower than usual. I met him by the door and shook his hand warmly. I admired him greatly, as did so many others. 'There was nothing else you could have done,' I said. 'The men of the XX Army Corps will forever be grateful to you, just as everyone here is.' The counter-pressure he provided as we shook hands indicated how he felt. He made no remark against Hitler; none against Kluge. This exemplary officer kept his thoughts to himself. 'Ruoff will be my successor,' he said, 'so I am happy for you. But now I will have to pack.'[117] With a goodnight salute, he took his leave.

I remained behind and could not help brooding over the events of the day. It did not come as a surprise that Colonel-General Hoepner had been relieved of his command. His dissatisfaction with the impact of the Halt Order had been growing from day to day since 3 January. The measures of the army group were quack remedies lacking in any conviction. Any discussions with Field-Marshal von Kluge were increasingly unproductive. He never visited our headquarters after Hoepner had told him in November that the field-marshal had left Panzer Group 4 in the lurch. 'The halt must always remain the basic principle!' was what Kluge would say to us. Hoepner understood that Kluge was in a difficult position, but did this justify the abandonment of our military principles? No! That was a boundary that could not be crossed. From an objective point of view, the balcony should have been evacuated a long time ago. Yet Hoepner was somehow supposed to demand of the XX Army Corps that it maintain its position, even though this would severely weaken the front of the panzer army. It was impossible! The army corps probably ought to have been withdrawn on 6 January at the

---

[117] General of Infantry Richard Ruoff was the commander of the V Army Corps, which was fighting on the northern wing of the panzer army. Hoepner held Ruoff in high regard.

latest. Hoepner had returned from Vereya that day and had written right at the beginning of his report:

> Do you know, it is terrible to see a commanding general crying before you out of utter despair at the senselessness of what is being demanded of him. His army corps must naturally be rescued from this situation. I have assured him of this. The feeling of responsibility of a reliable and capable soldier is being trampled on for the sake of that fellow.[118] No, this will not do!

Hoepner had already decided that a withdrawal would have to be carried out. He eventually gave the order on 8 January without having obtained the approval of his superiors. However, he had done all he could that morning to encourage Kluge to support his decision. Could Kluge have been persuaded? He was just as aware as we were of the desperate situation at the front! His bond to Hitler and to the Halt Order was the factor of uncertainty. Hoepner never believed in this order, so he chose to be disobedient. Hitler's reaction could be foreseen, but did Hoepner hope to be able to sweep Kluge along with him just as he had hoped to be able to do so with Field-Marshal von Leeb before Leningrad? Did Hoepner hope that a withdrawal in one sector would set the wheels in motion for the entire, well-prepared retreat plan? He had made some remarks along these lines, and he had also expressed his concern that all our preparations to fall back might end up being in vain. Such a concern was justified given the way in which the situation unfolded in the combat zones of the Fourth and Ninth Armies. Despite the risk, Hoepner wanted to initiate the withdrawal. He had already been disappointed by Kluge's conduct, but if there was even a small chance that the field-marshal might support his decision, it was a risk worth taking. However, Kluge provided no such support, and Hoepner became his sacrifice to Hitler.

The field-marshal had promised a final decision by noon. The panzer army had therefore prepared to fall back. A deadline of 1300 hours had been agreed with both the XX Army Corps and the VII Army Corps before the withdrawal would commence. Without any word from Kluge, Hoepner ordered the withdrawal at 1245 hours. He was the one man

---

[118] The reader can decide for himself who is meant here.

who assumed responsibility for doing what needed to be done. Sadly, he was the one man who was relieved of his command.

The officers and civilian officials of the headquarters of the panzer army organised a short farewell the following morning for their highly esteemed commander. Colonel-General Hoepner's parting words deserve to be recorded here:

> I have been relieved of my command of the Fourth Panzer Army for not following an order of the Führer. I have been bound to the army since my youth. My commitment is to the German soldier. I have always been aware of the enormous responsibility that comes with the decisions I make.
>
> The actions I have taken are ones I would take again. I know that this means the end of my military career, but I am also confident that I have fulfilled my duty to my army and to my people. It is my hope that every man here will be able to say the same at the end of his career.

Short and crisp, as always. But we knew what he thought and what he wanted. He made no further mention of Hitler beyond the fact that he had disobeyed the Halt Order.

All the more outraged were we at the panzer army when we learnt of the manner in which Colonel-General Hoepner was discharged. As Hoepner reported to the headquarters of the army group, Field-Marshal von Kluge revealed to him the orders of the Führer:

1. Colonel-General Hoepner endangered my authority as the commander in chief of the Wehrmacht and as the head of state of the Greater German Reich.
2. Colonel-General Hoepner will be expelled from the Wehrmacht and will suffer the consequences arising therefrom.

This was typically Hitler. However, the settlement of the 'Hoepner case' as Hitler wanted was legally inadmissible. Hitler, as the supreme commander of the Wehrmacht, may have been able to relieve an army commander of his post and even take measures to ensure a settlement was reached that was objective and free from external influence. Any investigation and judgement would have been subject to a court martial, as would have been the case for any other soldier. Colonel-General Hoepner himself sought a court martial after his dismissal. The result would surely have been in his favour. The unsoldierly Hitler did not oblige. No sentence took place in that year of 1942. Despite what has been written in some post-war publications, Hoepner was never demoted. He retained his dignities and rights as a discharged officer, living in his old home in Grunewald in Berlin until a bomb landed on it. The matter regarding Hoepner's dismissal was tacitly sorted out by the then deputy chief of the Army Personnel Office and chief military adjutant to Hitler, Major-General Rudolf Schmundt. The adjutant of the Fourth Panzer Army, Colonel von der Schulenburg, was accompanying Hoepner to the Fatherland and took the opportunity to pay Schmundt a visit. Schmundt declared that he had unfortunately been absent when Hitler had decided to dismiss Hoepner. Had he been present, he said, he thought that he probably would have been able to convince Hitler not to direct his anger at Hoepner. When Schmundt had spoken with Hitler afterwards, Hitler had stated: 'I had to make an example out of Hoepner, but his family should still be provided for.' Schmundt finally requested that Hoepner leave to him all further arrangements. The Führer, he said, had had his tantrum and had now fallen silent.[119] The tacit arrangement was agreed to, and Colonel-General Hoepner was officially discharged from the army at the end of June 1942. Hitler probably realised that he had gone too far.

★

When I returned to my desk after bidding the commander of the Fourth Panzer Army farewell on the morning of 9 January, I found there a copy of the retreat order of the Fourth Army, our southern neighbour, that had been issued the day before:

> In order to prevent a double envelopment by the enemy and to reduce the gaps to the neighbouring formations, the Fourth Army will withdraw its front sector by sector. This process will commence on 8 January at 2300 hours and will continue into the early hours of 9 January.[120]

---

[119] According to the notes of Colonel von der Schulenburg.

[120] Telex message sent by the Fourth Army at 2125 hours on 8 January and received by the Fourth Panzer Army at 1040 hours on 9 January.

As chaotic as the events of 8 January had been, this clarified what had happened to some degree. Field-Marshal von Kluge had fought bitterly for a withdrawal of the entire front, even for the Ninth Army. This was why he had told Colonel-General Hoepner to prepare to withdraw. The debate with Hitler had gone to and fro the whole day. Hitler had finally approved the retreat of the Fourth Army, as even he was unable to deny the hopelessness of its situation. But this was all he had approved. Military leadership had been reduced to horse trading. The Fourth Army fell back so as to close the gaps to its neighbours, yet the Fourth Panzer Army was somehow supposed to remain where it was! The gap between these two armies would have only become wider. Even today, Hitler's art of military leadership remains incomprehensible. Field-Marshal von Kluge had not pushed further after that. At least the desperate situation of his old Fourth Army had been alleviated somewhat.

Thanks to the decision that had been taken by Colonel-General Hoepner, it was not long before the retreat of the entire front of Army Group Centre to the winter defensive position got under way. After the withdrawal of a few isolated sectors, the entire front commenced its retreat on 15 January and completed it on 24 January. The dismissal of the commander of the Fourth Panzer Army had not been entirely for nothing.

Conclusion

The panzer arm had Erich Hoepner to thank for its successes. He had been committed to its establishment at an early stage, and he had demonstrated to the world its operational capability by carrying out a rapid thrust on Warsaw in September 1939. He was proud of the fact that he had been able to lead the spearhead of this important operation. In fact, he saw in the panzer troops the continuation of the traditions of the old heavy cavalry, whose actions had often decided the outcome of a battle.

At the beginning of the 1920s, Hoepner the cavalryman had already been thinking about the resurgence of the cavalry in a more powerful form. This resurgent arm would need to employ armour and take advantage of the motor, for the horse had become too slow and too vulnerable. The three cavalry divisions allowed by the Treaty of Versailles needed to be modernised. Their striking power had to be as great as possible. The ratio of cavalry to infantry in the German Army was relatively high at that time, as there were three cavalry divisions and seven infantry divisions. A way had to be found to maximise mobility and firepower. Hoepner's efforts during his time as a general staff officer in the Inspectorate of Cavalry Troops in the Reichswehr Ministry in 1921 and 1922 were unsuccessful. Some poorly equipped motorised test groups were established later on for a short period, but they were soon dissolved due to the inability of many of their participants to comprehend the purpose of their task. It is worth noting that another general staff officer in the Reichswehr Ministry, Captain Heinz Guderian, began to deal with the question of the panzer arm at roughly the same time as Hoepner and met with more success.

Hoepner did not give up. By the autumn of 1937, he became the commander of the 1st Light Division, the creation and organisation of which he had played a substantial role in. He saw the light division as a modern replacement for the cavalry division. This new formation was, so to speak, a light panzer division. The panzer division itself was created on Guderian's initiative. The differences between the light division and the panzer division had come about as a result of the different starting points of their respective creators. The organisation and intended use of these new formations were also slightly different. Nevertheless, Hoepner and Guderian agreed on the most important point, and that was the need for independent motorised combat units. The infantry was still the main arm of the service, but it was planned that the motorised units would be able to decisively determine the outcome of a battle. The OKH took the view in 1939 that any differences in the organisation of the panzer and light divisions could be corrected at a later stage. It would depend on what we learnt from our experiences. After the campaign in Poland, it was decided that panzer and light divisions would be organised in the same way and that they would henceforth be known as panzer divisions. General Hoepner greatly welcomed this, for it was in the interests of the united development of the panzer arm. The organisation, training, and supply of its units could be standardised.

A panzer commander was in the making. Hoepner was filled with enthusiasm and loved his profession as an officer. In November 1938, he was appointed commanding general of the XVI Panzer Corps. This put him in charge of the panzer divisions of the army, and he put a great deal of effort into their perfection. It was under his leadership in March 1939 that the first large mobile formation moved into Czechoslovakia. Hoepner did his utmost to reach the capital of the country as quickly as possible so as to bring the campaign to an end and minimise bloodshed. The German–Czechoslovak frontier was crossed on 15 March at 0500 hours. As early as 0900 hours, Hoepner stood with the spearhead of his formation on the grounds of Prague Castle! The advance had been a complete success. Hoepner had been convinced that a rapid thrust could form the basis of a decisive outcome. By taking the enemy by surprise, the panzer troops would have a good chance of victory.

The advance of Hoepner's formation into Poland in September 1939 demonstrated most convincingly what a panzer corps could achieve when employed correctly and skilfully. Within eight days, the XVI Panzer Corps had covered a distance of 250 kilometres and stood just outside Warsaw. It was therefore in the right place to partake in the decisive fighting near the Bzura. Amidst the confusion regarding the whereabouts of the enemy, Hoepner's qualities as a panzer commander came to the fore. While his superiors were inconsistent in their planning and their orders, Hoepner himself did not waver. He adhered to his task with tenacity and confidence. His decisions were based on accurate assessments and on a clear focus on the operational objective. His good sense of the intentions of the enemy and what was and was not possible stood him in good stead. These qualities shone again and again.

Hoepner always strove towards his objective, so long as it could still be reached and despite the obstacles that were put in his path. This was the case during the campaign in France, during the 800-kilometre advance on Leningrad (probably the most instructive example of a resolute and long-range thrust of a large panzer formation), and during the assault on Moscow. He possessed greater confidence than his superiors. He believed it possible not only to reach but also to take Leningrad with the forces at his disposal. His superiors feared that his forces would be in too much danger. Yet it should be emphasised that Hoepner was not careless. He remained fully aware of his responsibility to take care of the forces under his command. Nevertheless, he was bold and probably would have seized Leningrad.

Moscow was a different situation! Hoepner was of the view that the final thrust launched in the middle of November 1941 ought not to have been undertaken. He had advised against it. What use would it be to bleed ourselves to death before Moscow? Even if we entered the city, how would we hold on to it in our weakened state? He had a clear view of the limitations of what was possible and rejected the idea that the advance should be attempted for the sake of Hitler's strategy. Nonetheless, the renewal of the advance was ordered, so Hoepner did everything he could to push forward at the decisive point until he could go no further. He decided to bring his forces to a stop even though he knew that his superiors would not be happy about it. He remained steadfast in his belief that he had done the right thing, without any concern for what the personal consequences might be.

The decision of 8 January 1942 crowned Hoepner's achievements as a military commander and as a human being. The decision itself was by no means difficult. The Fourth Panzer Army needed to make forces available as soon as possible to close the gap to the Fourth Army. At the same time, the XX Army Corps was in great danger of being cut off in the balcony it occupied. Nothing would have been simpler and more natural than to solve both problems by withdrawing the army corps. The military decision in this situation could be regarded as a matter of course. The obstacle that was the Halt Order had to be swept aside, even if the penalties for disobedience could be most severe. Nobody could accuse Hoepner of cowardice. If they had done so, it would not have affected him, as he was very much the opposite. In any case, not even Hitler made such an accusation. What displeased Hitler was the feeling that his authority had been violated. It would, however, have been cowardly to do nothing or to evade responsibility for making the right decision. There was no chance of that with a man like Hoepner. He would not accept useless and hopeless sacrifice. He chose to be disobedient and to bear the consequences. He did so without hesitation, even though it meant the end of a career that he very much loved. In his last letter to his wife before being executed on 8 August 1944 in Plötzensee Prison in Berlin, Hoepner wrote: 'I die with soldiers by my side and remain myself a soldier until the last moment.' Only 10 years later did this letter reach her.

Hoepner's aversion to National Socialism developed at an early stage. During his time as the chief of the general staff of the military district in East Prussia between 1933 and 1936, he encountered a number of reprehensible governmental functionaries. The most notorious of these was Erich Koch, the head of the administrative district in East Prussia. Hoepner did not shy away from the thankless task of opposing the excesses of the regime, and he naturally belonged to the small number of those high-ranking officers who, in support of Walther von Brauchitsch and Franz Halder, were ready to lead their troops to remove Hitler from power. Unfortunately, this plan was rendered useless when the Munich Agreement was concluded in the autumn of 1938. The Army leadership had not expected that the Western Powers would allow the German annexation of the Sudetenland in western Czechoslovakia. Hitler's threats alone had once more led to victory. Would he now show moderation? Hoepner doubted this and eventually joined the resistance. He did not take part in the preparations for the plot of 20 July 1944 and was brought in too late to help carry it out. Although he had made himself unreservedly available to the conspirators, they did not make full use of his abilities prior to going ahead with their poorly prepared assassination attempt. Nevertheless, his valiant support of the resistance ended with his execution.[121]

In a letter to me on 4 May 1960, Halder wrote: 'You probably knew my old friend Hoepner far better than I did. He and I met one another during our younger years in the general staff, and we later had several discussions on matters relating to the resistance. He was firm in his opinions, demonstrated great initiative and decisiveness, and tended, as hard as it was to do then, to follow his heart rather than his mind.'

Hoepner was indeed driven strongly, perhaps even entirely at first, by his heart. This was always revealed to those who knew him well. He exercised greater reserve and self-control as he matured, yet forever maintained a sense of justice. He was the ideal superior officer. He filled his men with enthusiasm and would provide as much assistance as possible without being disruptive. He was equally a commander, a comrade, a teacher, and a human being. All these qualities were united so harmoniously and imperceptibly in the one man. He led with brilliance whilst remaining modest and enjoying life. As he wrote to his son in his will: 'We must learn from our great field commanders, win victories, and remain modest!' He concluded with

---

[121] See the *Kaltenbrunner Report*, especially volume I of 24 July 1944, 7.

the words of Field-Marshal Helmuth von Moltke the Elder: 'The value of one's life will not be determined by the splendour of success but rather, even in the event of failure, by the upholding of duty and integrity.'

This was how Erich Hoepner lived. He was the quintessential military commander and human being.

Index